CONTROLLING LAWN & GARDEN INSECTS

Created and designed by
the editorial staff of ORTHO BOOKS

PROJECT EDITOR
Susan A. Roth

WRITER
L. Patricia Kite

ARTIST
Amy Bartlett Wright

PHOTOGRAPHERS
Saxon Holt
Ron West

ASSOCIATE AND PHOTO EDITOR
Pamela Peirce

GRAPHIC DESIGN
Finger Vesik Smith

Ortho Books

Publisher
Robert J. Dolezal

Production Director
Ernie S. Tasaki

Managing Editors
Michael D. Smith
Sally W. Smith

System Manager
Leonard D. Grotta

National Sales Manager
Charles H. Aydelotte

Marketing Specialist
Susan B. Boyle

Operations Coordinator
Georgiann Wright

Administrative Assistant
Deborah Tibbetts

Senior Technical Analyst
J. A. Crozier, Jr.

Chevron Chemical Company
575 Market Street, San Francisco, CA 94105

Acknowledgments

Art Director
Craig Bergquist

Copy Chief
Melinda Levine

Copyeditor
Rebecca Pepper

Editorial Coordinator
Kate Rider

Layout & Pagination by
Linda M. Bouchard

Editorial Assistant
Andrea Y. Connolly

Proofreader
Leslie Tilley

Composition by
Bob Miller

Production Artist
Lezlly Freier

Indexer
Frances Bowles

Color Separations by
Creative Color

Lithographed in USA by
Webcrafters, Inc.

Consultants

Dr. John Davidson
  Dept. of Entomology
  University of Maryland
Dr. Wayne Moore
  Berkeley, Calif.
Dr. Harry Niemczyk
  Dept. of Entomology
  Ohio State University

Photographers

Ralph Adkins: 55L, 67L
Max Badgley: 10L, 48, 49, 54L, 60L, 62, 68L, 74L, 85L, 85C, 87L, 92R
Allen Boger: 23L
Kristie Callan: 82L
Sharon J. Collman: 89
David J. Cross: 74R
James F. Dill: 24, 45T, 47R, 52L, 60R, 63, 68R, 69R, 75R, 81R, 84R, 94L
Gwen Fidler: 6T
Charles Marden Fitch: Front cover C, Front cover RC, Front cover LC, 6BL, 28, 32, 76L, 87R, Back cover LL
Saxon Holt: 12, 14L, 14R, 15, 16TL, 16TC, 16TR, 16BL, 16BR, 17BL, 17TR, 19, 21, Back cover TL, LR
Angus J. Howitt: 57L, 57R
Keith Kennedy: 37R, 44L, 54R, 58R, 64, 77L, 77R, 81C, 84L
Ray R. Kriner: 1, 43, 45B, 61L, 69L, 71L
Dwight Kuhn: Front cover LL, Front cover LR
Fred Lyon: 22
Ernest Manewall/Shostal Assoc.: Front cover TR
Charles McClurg: 52R
Michael McKinley: 10R
Wayne Moore: 53R, 83L, 83R, 85R, 86L, 92L
Jean R. Natter: 4
Ortho Photo Library: 11, Back cover TR
Cecil Quirino: Front cover TL, 51
Rutgers University, Department of Soils and Crops: 31
Anita Sabarese: 59R, 61R, 72
Michael D. Smith: 90L
Avril L. Stark: 81L
Ron West: 6BR, 8T, 8C, 8B, 9, 26 (all), 27, 29, 34L, 34R, 35, 36, 37L, 38L, 38R, 39L, 39C, 39R, 40, 41, 42L, 42C, 42R, 44R, 46, 47L, 50L, 50R, 53L, 55R, 56L, 56R, 58L, 59L, 65L, 65R, 66, 67R, 70L, 70C, 70R, 71R, 73L, 73R, 75L, 76R, 78, 79L, 79R, 80, 82R, 86C, 86R, 88L, 88R, 90R, 91L, 91R, 93L, 93R, 94R

Special Thanks

CoClico & Co., Inc., Interior and Exterior Landscape Design, San Francisco, Calif.; Wade Fujino; Mary Gilley; Mantis Manufacturing Co., Huntingdon Valley, Penn.; Simons Nursery, San Jose, Calif.; Strybing Arboretum, San Francisco, Calif.

Front cover
Top left: Spotted cucumber beetle on corn.
Top right: Scarab beetle on zinnia.
Lower left: Slug eating strawberry.
Center: Leaf miner damage on columbine.
Lower center: Gypsy moth larvae on oak leaves.
Right center: Parsleyworm on parsley.
Lower right: Colorado potato beetle larva, eggs, and adult.

Title page
The fall webworm may look pretty, but it makes ugly webs in which it defoliates tree branches.

Back cover
Top left: A hose-end sprayer turns your garden hose into an insecticide applicator.
Top right: Closely examining your plants is often the best first defense against pests.
Lower left: Introducing purchased ladybugs to your garden may aid an insect-control program.
Lower right: A squeeze-canister duster provides an effective and convenient way of applying insecticidal dusts.

CONTROLLING LAWN & GARDEN INSECTS

INSECTS IN YOUR GARDEN

Japanese beetle

Insects, both good and bad, abound in your garden. The bad insects—the pests that feed on live plants—often devour a considerable portion of backyard food crops and disfigure or kill lawns and expensive ornamental plantings. Anyone who has lost a rugged elm tree and the welcome shade it casts to elm leaf beetle attack or who has had a green bean crop devoured by marauding Mexican bean beetles knows the destruction insects can wreak. Some gardeners seem to wage a losing battle against these unwanted garden inhabitants, but you can successfully control them if you know the most effective methods. This book provides all the information you need to prevent insects from damaging your lawn and garden.

The first step in effective control is to understand your enemy. That is why this first chapter provides a short lesson on insect development and life cycles. The last chapter of this book is an extensive insect pest encyclopedia that describes the appearance and living habits of the most common garden pests. This encyclopedia will enable you to identify and eliminate any pests that threaten the health and productivity of your garden.

The second step in controlling pests is to develop a sound battle plan and a powerful arsenal. To this end, the second chapter, "Using Insecticides Safely and Effectively," discusses the use of various control methods. Do not skip this important chapter! In it you will learn how to select, from among the numerous offerings at your garden center, the best insecticide to control a particular pest. In addition you will find out how to apply it

Many insects live in your garden. These harlequin bugs are among the many that damage garden plants.

Understanding insects is the first step in protecting your garden from pests. How do insects find your garden? How do they damage plants? Where do they live in the winter? Here are some answers.

safely without harming yourself, your plants, or the environment. Not all sprayers are suited to every task; this second chapter describes the different types of equipment available to the home gardener and tells how to take care of these tools so that they serve you well for years.

The third chapter, "Additional Methods of Pest Control," discusses natural pest control methods that many gardeners use in addition to insecticides. You will learn how to trap insects and take advantage of natural predators and parasites that help control pests. Good garden housekeeping also goes a long way toward insect control, and this chapter describes how simple practices such as cleaning up fallen fruit, raking up leaves, and tilling the soil can help keep pest populations under control.

Identifying the Pest

Gardeners waging war on insect pests often mistakenly accuse the bugs they easily see of causing all the mischief in the vegetable patch or flower bed. Slugs and snails get heaped with most of the blame, with earwigs and pillbugs not far behind. Meanwhile, the true culprit, perhaps so small you can't see it without a magnifying glass, feeds away voraciously deep within a bud, tunnels inside a twig, or buries itself 3 inches underground.

Many barely visible insect pests are difficult to recognize: Thrips and mites are so tiny they resemble specks of dirt. Others, although big and colorful enough to be noticed, develop protective strategies: Scale insects often look like a part of the bark; fall webworms feed within silken nests; leafrollers curl leaves around themselves and feed from the inside out; leafminers tunnel in the narrow space between upper and lower leaf surfaces.

Destructive insects can establish their headquarters on any part of a plant, from treetops to roots, and symptoms do not always coincide with pest location. Insects feeding on roots cause aboveground parts to wilt. Borers in stems kill branch tips. Leafhoppers inject toxins into leaves that turn the entire plant brown.

Each pest has its own modus operandi. It is important not to jump to conclusions when you see problems in your garden. Look the plant over carefully, checking for obvious and not-so-obvious insects. Observe the symptoms carefully, and then check in the pest encyclopedia to see whether you can identify the pest from its photo and description. If the pest description and plant symptoms do not seem to jibe, check out the plant again. You can also get excellent help in insect identification from a reputable local nursery or from your county agricultural cooperative extension service. Remember, identifying the pest is the first step in control; understanding its habits is the second step.

WHAT MAKES AN INSECT AN INSECT?

An insect is an *invertebrate,* an animal without a spine or backbone, that has three distinct body regions or segments: *head, thorax,* and *abdomen.* Its shell-like skeleton, called an exoskeleton, is external, providing both support and protection. Internally secreted substances, primarily chitin and proteins, make up the shell.

Most insects have three pairs of legs that are attached to the thorax, giving them excellent balance and mobility. Al-

though some insects are wingless during brief periods of their lives, most adults have one or two pairs of wings that are connected by muscles to the thorax. Insect blood is a thick, clear or yellowish green liquid that carries nutrients and waste products but not oxygen and carbon dioxide as mammal blood does.

An insect's main sensory organs—mouth, two compound eyes, and two antennae—are on its head. The abdomen contains most of the digestive and reproductive organs as well as breathing holes. Taste organs usually exist on the lips and on feelerlike organs behind jaws, antennae, and feet. Sensory hairs all over an insect's body are connected to nerve endings and tell the insect where it is, what position it is in, the direction in which air is moving, and even how to fold its wings. Insect eyes, although capable of detecting the slightest movement, actually focus poorly, so they do not see clear pictures. Instead, they see pattern and color, being so sensitive to the latter that some bees pollinate only red flowers whereas other insects prefer blue. Still others, such as beetles, are not fussy about color as long as the plant looks or smells edible.

Noninsect Pests

Scientists classify insects as animals belonging to the class Insecta in the phylum Arthropoda. Sometimes pillbugs, sowbugs, snails, slugs, spiders, daddy longlegs, mites, ticks, centipedes, and millipedes are brought up in conversations about insects. Yet these common garden pests are not really insects. Most are insect relatives, belonging to the same phylum but to a different class; others are not related to insects at all but belong to an entirely different phylum, which is the largest classification group.

Regardless of how scientists classify mites, slugs, and other garden inhabitants, gardeners often call them all insects or bugs, because once they are in your garden, they behave much like insects. Since the same insecticide and cultural methods often control both true insects and insect relatives, this book crosses scientific boundaries and includes noninsects in the pest encyclopedia.

INSECT GROWTH AND DEVELOPMENT

When you understand insect development and growth stages, your attempts at insect control are likely to be more successful. This is because you will be able to time control methods to coincide with susceptible insect stages. Knowledge of insect life cycles is therefore crucial. Once you recognize the different forms an insect pest takes during its life span, you will be able to spot a pest invasion before it ruins your crops. You will also know when a particular insect is most vulnerable to control methods and when it is least susceptible.

Insects grow and change from the time they hatch from the egg until they reach reproductive maturity. This change

Top: A grasshopper exhibits classic insect form. You can easily see its three-segmented body (head, thorax, and abdomen), six legs, wings, two compound eyes, and two antennae. A shell-like skeleton covers its body.
Left: Although a butterfly's appearance is very different from that of a grasshopper's, its body has the same basic insect structure. This black swallowtail butterfly has three body segments and six legs.
Right: Examine your garden for insect inhabitants in various life stages. These striking striped eggs will hatch into harlequin bug nymphs.

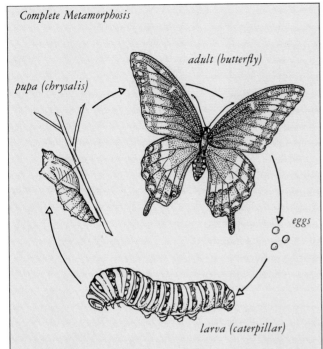

Complete Metamorphosis

pupa (chrysalis)

adult (butterfly)

eggs

larva (caterpillar)

In species that undergo complete metamorphosis, the immature and mature insects look very different. The parsleyworm caterpillar is one such species. The egg hatches into a larva (caterpillar), which rests as a pupa and then emerges as an adult butterfly. The adult parsleyworm is a black swallowtail butterfly.

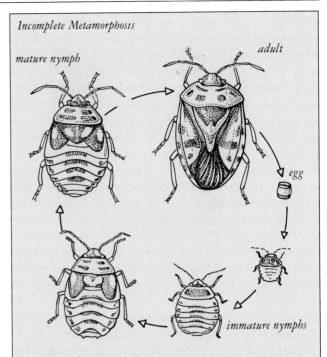

Incomplete Metamorphosis

mature nymph

adult

egg

immature nymphs

In species that undergo incomplete metamorphosis, the immature insects resemble mature ones. The harlequin bug has such a life cycle. An egg hatches into a wingless nymph, which grows and molts, shedding its skin several times. A winged adult emerges after the last molt.

in form is called metamorphosis. Most insects follow one of two major patterns: complete metamorphosis or incomplete metamorphosis, sometimes called *gradual metamorphosis*.

Whether its metamorphosis is complete or incomplete, as any insect grows larger, it begins to outgrow its relatively rigid exoskeleton, which does not expand. The shell grows tighter and tighter, becoming like a too-small coat, until eventually it splits open to reveal a new developing shell beneath. This shedding of skin is called *molting*. The forms between molts are called *instars*. Most insects undergo from three to eight instars, but, depending on temperature, food supply, and species, there may be as many as 20 instars before the insect reaches full sexual maturity.

Complete metamorphosis involves major changes in body shape as a young insect changes to an adult. The same insect exists in four very different forms: egg, larva, pupa, and adult. The egg hatches into a wormlike larva. When fully grown, the larva stops feeding and pupates, often spinning a protective silken cocoon or forming a capsulelike puparium. A butterfly's pupa is called a *chrysalis*. Here the insect rests, briefly in some species, over the winter in others. Legs, wings, antennae, and reproductive

organs form. When the pupal wrapping finally splits, a soft-bodied, pale, relatively small but fully formed adult wriggles out. After a few hours the new exoskeleton hardens and darkens and the insect is ready to fly, crawl, or hop away.

Insects that undergo complete metamorphosis include beetles, whose larvae are often called *grubs*; flies, whose larvae are called *maggots*; and moths and butterflies, whose larvae are called *caterpillars* or *worms*.

Incomplete metamorphosis involves a gradual change from young to adult. The eggs hatch into young called *nymphs*, which are miniature versions of the adults, except that they may be wingless or have short wings. As the nymphs grow, they molt several times before reaching reproductive size and maturity. Insects undergoing incomplete metamorphosis include grasshoppers, earwigs, whiteflies, and aphids.

Larvae and nymphs usually feed heavily and can damage plants severely. Adults may or may not feed. Often their only goal is to mate and lay eggs. With some insects, such as the parsleyworm, the larval stage destroys foliage, but the adult form, in this case the black swallowtail butterfly, feeds harmlessly on flower nectar. The adult gypsy moth does not feed at all, and the female does not even fly. However, both the larval

and adult forms of the Mexican bean beetle feed voraciously on foliage. In egg form, insects will not directly harm your plants. But because eggs often turn into destructive larvae or adults, you should know when they will hatch and where they are located in order to apply controls properly. For example, cankerworms lay eggs on branches, lace bugs on leaf undersides and within bark cracks, spittlebugs inside stems or between leaf blades, thrips inside plant tissue, June beetles several inches deep in the soil, and bagworms in protective silken bags that dangle from tree branches.

Once you understand insect habits, you realize that control measures work best when applied at the proper time and place. For example, you are wasting your time and insecticide if you spray a tree for tent caterpillars once it has been defoliated. By that time the caterpillars are done feeding and have turned their attention to pupating and becoming egg-laying moths. Once maggots have infested apples, there is no insecticide you can use to prevent them from eating out the cores. The time to spray is when the overwintering adult flies are traveling about laying their eggs and before you see any damaged fruit.

HOW INSECTS DAMAGE PLANTS

Your garden offers quite a menu to insect pests. They dine on leaves, flowers, roots, stems, and trunks by sucking, chewing, mining, and even sponging. By feeding on leaves, pests rob plants of their essential food-manufacturing apparatus, thus slowing or stunting growth. Root injury slows water and nutrient absorption, causing the plant above to wilt and die off. When sucking out a plant's sap, insects siphon off nutrients necessary for plant growth. Some sucking insects inject toxic saliva that causes more damage to the plant than the loss of sap does. Although the results of sap sucking do not show as clearly as those of leaf chewing, the infested plant often sickens, wilts, turns yellow or brown, and sometimes dies.

A sucking pest feeds with hollow, needlelike stylets that form its beak. Piercing leaves, flowers, or other plant parts, the insect sucks up sap as if through a straw. Several kinds of sap-sucking insects slurp sap so quickly that they can't digest it all—the excess just comes out the other end. This sticky, sugary excrement, called honeydew, accumulates on foliage or stems. At first it is shiny and sticky, but later it turns black from sooty mold fungus, which grows on the honeydew. Although the fungus does not directly harm a plant, it shades the foliage, reducing the sunlight needed for plant growth.

Common sap-sucking insects include aphids, squash bugs, leafhoppers, mealybugs, chinch bugs, spider mites, harlequin bugs, whiteflies, and scales. Symptoms of sap-sucker attack include stunted foliage and blossoms; yellow, pale, or spotted leaves; and a general decrease in plant vigor.

Chewing insects attack plants more forcefully. Their teeth can mash and tear as well as chew, and they go after everything from nuts to cabbage. Symptoms

Above: Aphids sucked sap from this passion vine leaf as it emerged from the bud, causing the distorted appearance.
Center: Imported cabbageworms are among the insects that chew holes in garden plants.
Below: Damage from rasping thrips appears as brown scars on this lettuce leaf.

of chewing insects are rather obvious holes in foliage or flowers or tunnels in stems and trunks. Some chewing insects leave characteristic marks. For instance, weevils munch notches around leaf edges, creating ragged-looking foliage. Other chewers, such as elm leaf beetles, skeletonize leaves, eating everything but the veins. Some bugs eat only leaf undersides, others the top sides of leaves, and still others leaf insides. And some, such as cutworms, sever stems or eat entire seedlings.

Several large chewing insects, such as cicadas, crickets, and grasshoppers, may be familiar by sound as well as by sight. Others are equally large but are quiet. You have to poke around a bit to find armyworms, corn earworms, or even huge tomato hornworms, which often hide under leaves and can be traced via their obvious piles of droppings, which are called *frass*.

Some chewing insects are small and have hiding places you might not have thought possible. For example, a 1/10-inch-long leafminer lives comfortably in the narrow space between leaf top and bottom. Here it "mines" away with shearing mouthparts, creating straight, circular, or S-shaped tunnels as it proceeds.

Blister beetles, spotted cucumber beetles, bronze birch borers, cabbage loopers, root weevils, and wireworms are just a few examples of the many chewing insects that attack your garden.

The thrips seems to be the only insect that feeds by rasping. It scrapes leaf or petal surfaces with its filelike mouthparts, wounding the plant tissue and then sucking up the sap. In addition to roses, the thrips feeds on citrus, peach, grape, onion, gladiolus, chrysanthemum, daisy, daffodil, and many other garden and greenhouse plants.

Adult flies get by without sucking, chewing, or rasping; instead, they sponge up food. If the food is not liquefied enough for sponging, some flies spit digestive saliva on their targeted meal to predigest it, making it easier to sop up. Although some fly species, such as robber, tachinid, and hoverflies, can be beneficial to the gardener, others can damage garden plants. Fly larvae chew their way through fruits, nuts, and foliage.

Disease Vectors

One would think that the damage caused by feeding would be enough garden havoc for one pest to wreak. But many insect pests also transmit serious diseases to plants. Acting as *vectors,* aphids, mealybugs, leafhoppers, and mites, among others, transmit virus diseases from one plant to another. As it sucks sap from a plant, the insect can also ingest virus particles. These are carried along through the pest's digestive system, where they often multiply, and may be injected into other plants.

Insect-transmitted viruses can bring quick death or can slowly stunt a plant. Some plants do not show obvious symptoms but just do poorly. Mosaic viruses produce mottled foliage and stunted, ill-formed growth. Ring spot viruses cause pale rings on leaves as well as reduced productivity, and stunt virus infections stifle plant growth, often creating malformed flowers and bunched-up, deformed foliage. Aphids, whiteflies, and leafhoppers are the most serious virus vectors. A single aphid species can transmit over 50 different viruses. Aphids transmit the viruses that cause potato leaf roll, bean yellow mosaic, and corn leaf

fleck, among many other plant diseases. Whiteflies transmit geranium crinkle, and leafhoppers transmit peach yellows and a multitude of other viral diseases.

Insects also carry bacterial and fungal diseases from plant to plant. The elm bark beetle, which feeds beneath tree bark, picks up fungal spores of Dutch elm disease from infected trees. The pest then transmits the deadly fungus, which has wiped out most of the elegant American elms that once graced our towns and cities, to neighboring trees.

Bacterial wilt diseases infecting fruit and vegetable crops are carried from plant to plant in a similar manner. The bacterial diseases transmitted by insects include cucumber wilt and corn wilt, which clog the tissues that conduct water and nutrients in a plant. Fire blight, deadly to fruit trees, can be carried about by bees, who pick up the bacteria by walking over the sticky ooze on infected tree branches.

Other pests strike twice by injecting toxic poisons into plants. Hopperburn, a condition in which foliage looks scorched as if by fire, is caused by leafhoppers when they feed. Toxins injected by squash bugs cause wilted, browned foliage.

HOW INSECTS FIND YOUR GARDEN

You have to wonder just how a bug knows that there is good eating in your garden. When you plant squash for the very first time in your vegetable patch, why does it immediately become infested with squash bugs? And why do rose chafers zero in on your roses amidst all the other equally delicious flowers?

Insects have keen sensory perception. They tell one plant from another in the same way we do: by the color and fragrance of flowers and the shape, pattern, and texture of leaves. But their specific senses are more highly developed—some insects have sensory organs all over their bodies, including on their feet and antennae. Insects sense aromas from far greater distances than people can. Scientists studying swallowtail butterflies have determined that the butterflies learn to recognize the leaf shape of their host plants. Once they land on a correctly shaped leaf, the butterflies taste it with sensory organs on their feet to double-check their selection before laying eggs. Many moths travel at night, so they will

So far quarantine and blanket spraying have kept the Mediterranean fruit fly out of the continental U.S.

Plants from the nursery can sometimes bring pests to your garden. Examine them carefully before you buy.

home in on white or very light-colored flowers or be drawn by scent alone. Those night-blooming flowers that you planted for their marvelous perfume act as open invitations to moth pilgrims and their homesteading offspring.

Although insects see only shape and color, rather than a clear picture, they also have powers of perception that people lack; they can see and sense things we don't. For instance, bees see ultraviolet light waves and colors in flowers that the human eye does not perceive. These patterns act like traffic signs to pollinating or marauding insects, beckoning them to land in the right spot to assure pollination.

Many insects reach your garden by flying. Japanese beetles can fly as far as five miles in search of favorite host plants. Grasshoppers fly 50 miles per hour and have been blown as far as 1,200 miles out to sea with the help of a strong wind. Common milkweed butterflies, also known as monarch butterflies, migrate by the thousands to southern areas during the fall, and their offspring return north in the spring.

Other pests are so light and tiny that they can be carried miles by the wind without the effort of flight. Young gypsy moth caterpillars enhance wind travel with air pockets in their body hairs, which make them almost as light as air; when there is a strong wind they can soar as far as five miles in a day. Young spiders and some small caterpillars spin silk strands and use these to swing from high to low places. Spiders and mites also spin silk strands that act like parachutes when caught by air currents.

Many pests find your garden accidentally. Adult gypsy moths glue their egg masses to just about anything solid, including the undersides of trucks and cars, unintentionally assuring long-distance travel. Mites can hitch a ride on your gardening slacks; nematodes may be introduced to your garden soil by an already-infested nursery plant. A cutting or transplant from your neighbor's garden may contain overwintering scale eggs. Even ants help move insects about. They sometimes become so enthused about eating mealybug honeydew that they take a few mealybugs home as family providers. The queen ants of some species carry a fertilized female mealybug with them as a new nest dowry, assuring starter honeydew production. The travel possibilities are endless, and so are the possible pests.

Imported Pests

More than a third of the insect pests that trouble gardens and crops in North America did not originate here. They were imported from Europe, Asia, or South America in soil or on nursery plants or produce. These pests often cause only minor damage in their native habitat but, set free where there is no natural control from predators, parasites, or pathogens or where no other pest competes for their food, foreign pests can be devastating. Japanese beetles, gypsy moths, imported cabbageworms, Mexican bean beetles, cottonycushion scales, Mediterranean fruit flies, and brown garden snails are just a few of these imported pests.

The U.S. Department of Agriculture (USDA) has placed strict controls on the plants and produce that can be brought into the United States and into prime agricultural areas or across some state lines. Strict adherence to these rules and prompt full-scale eradication measures in case of outbreaks ensures that no more imported pests get a foothold in this country.

NOT ALL INSECTS ARE PESTS

Not every insect you see in your garden is going to make a mess of your plants. Some of the ugliest bugs, such as ground beetles, help you out every way they can by destroying snails, slugs, cankerworms, tent caterpillars, armyworms, cutworms, and moths. These creatures may be ferocious looking, but their ferociousness is limited to the destruction of hundreds of caterpillars and other harmful insects. Insects that eat other insects are called *predators.* They are your garden's friends.

Scavenger insects, such as certain scarab beetles, crane fly larvae, and soldier flies, are also garden friends. They feed on organic matter, such as fallen leaves and overripe fruit, with some species preferring animal excrement or carrion. Without scavenger insects, rotting plants and other organic refuse would pile up instead of being transformed, via the scavenger's digestive process, into good soil.

Insects that live part of their lives on other insects are called *parasitic* insects. These too are your friends. A commonly seen garden parasite is the braconid wasp, whose larvae feed on hornworms, eating them from the inside out and then pupating in tiny cocoons on the caterpillar's back.

It is sometimes hard to know whether a bug is good or bad. Some very-much-admired insects, such as certain exquisite butterflies, visit flower after flower harmlessly sipping nectar, but then their destructive foliage-eating larvae appear! The parsleyworm, the larva of the black swallowtail, is one such garden pest. Things become even more confusing when an insect has a beneficial stage and a harmful stage. The adult margined blister beetle feeds on fruit and foliage, but its larvae devour grasshopper eggs. Yellowjackets occasionally sting people but also act as valuable pollinators and pest insect destroyers. And if you think that aphids haven't a single point in their favor, then consider that they provide food for ladybugs and some predatory wasps, both of which eliminate many other annoying pests about your yard.

BASIC PRINCIPLES OF PEST CONTROL

To control garden insect pests effectively, you must:
• Detect an infestation early.
• Identify the insect correctly.
• Choose the best control methods.

Be on the Alert should be your motto. If you take a few moments once or twice a week to stroll around your property, observing the shrubs, trees, and lawn and closely inspecting flowers and edible plants, chances are you will notice any harmful pest before its damage gets out of control. Become knowledgeable about the plants in your garden, and know what pests and symptoms to look for during which seasons. When you see wilted, mottled, nibbled, severed, or otherwise unhealthy-appearing plants, suspect an insect infestation.

Closely inspect the plants. To help make your diagnosis, notice exactly where damage appears, such as between leaf veins or on leaf edges. These are clues that identify particular pests. If no pests make themselves known, consider leaf-, bud-, and flower-chewing caterpillars; beetles; weevils; slugs; and cutworms as your possible destructive visitors. Many hide in soil, debris, or other protective locations during the day. Night is the time to take a flashlight out and see if you can find them at work.

To research a bug, it helps to know its size, body shape, and color; whether it stays on the ground or flies; what plant part it infests; what damage and symptoms it seems to be causing; and the time of year you first noticed the problem. Check the photos and descriptions in this book to identify any possible insect pest.

If you cannot find your target pest in this book, or if you are not certain you have picked out the right one, call your county agricultural cooperative extension office. A home horticulturist or entomologist should be aware of what is in town, when and why it appears, and what to do about it. If a phone call does not produce a diagnosis, you can also bring or mail in a bug sample.

Keep in mind that not every bad bug needs to be eliminated. Decide whether the infestation warrants control. Do the insects threaten the health or life of the plant? Some infestations cause only limited damage; others kill valuable plants.

Often the first step in pest control is observation; learn to notice a pest's initial invasion before it gets out of control.

Will a little feeding damage on an azalea go unnoticed? Will your roses be too chewed up to be displayed on the dining table? Will your apple crop yield be decimated? Do you already have a freezer full of zucchini? Keep a close watch on any pests you decide not to control. Small infestations can limit themselves or can blow up into a population explosion. Insects have an enormous reproductive capacity, often increasing their number by a hundredfold in one generation.

In choosing control measures for your pest problem, be sure you know what bug you are after. Different insecticides work on different pests. If you apply the wrong control, you are wasting your time and insecticide, as well as doing nothing to alleviate the garden problem. You also want to be sure that the bug you are controlling is causing the damage.

You want to choose the most appropriate pest control method for your problem. See the next chapter for explicit directions on how to read insecticide container labels, select equipment, and use your insecticide purchase wisely. The entries in the pest encyclopedia recommend the most effective insecticides for each pest and tell you when and how to apply them.

Once you have wiped out an initial pest invasion, you can't be certain that it will not reappear later in the season or the following year. To prevent a return visit, certain cultural practices help your garden stay healthy. Keeping your garden clean should be a high priority—debris pileup, whether construction materials, autumn leaves, leftover plant tops, or rotting fruits and vegetables, acts as an insect haven and attractant. You want to eliminate bothersome bugs, not offer them food and lodging.

Healthy plants are pest resistant because they can often recover from insect attack by quickly replacing any damaged growth. By fertilizing and watering your garden as needed and locating particular plants where soil and sun exposure suit them, you are helping to combat pests. You can also grow pest-resistant plants, rotate crops, and encourage beneficial predators and parasites. The third chapter discusses these natural control methods.

Defending your garden territory against insect invasion becomes easy when you follow the basic principles of pest control. Be alert to the first signs of damage. Correctly identify the pest, and don't put off applying insecticide if necessary. Read the product label, and apply the insecticide at the proper time and exactly according to instructions. A spray or dust in time gives you beautiful, healthy, and productive plants all year.

USING INSECTICIDES SAFELY AND EFFECTIVELY

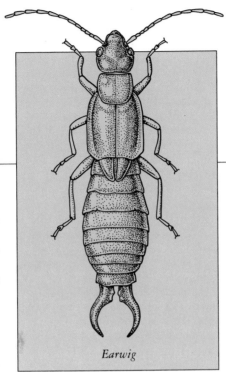

Earwig

Insect pests have been around for a long time, and so have attempts to eradicate them. The Roman scholar and natural history writer Pliny the Elder (A.D. 23–79) recommended using green lizard gall to prevent apple worms. Even earlier, in 1000 B.C., the Greek poet Homer wrote of burning "pest-averting sulfur," which both the Greeks and Romans used to eliminate annoying or destructive insects. During the ninth century, Chinese gardeners and farmers brushed the deadly poison arsenic on plants to control insects.

Insecticides and application equipment have come a long way since ancient times. They are effective against pest insects, have minimal, if any, odor, are safe for people, plants, wildlife, and pets when used properly, and increase both plant beauty and crop yield. And, unlike green lizard gall, these products come safely packaged and labeled with detailed printed instructions.

The first insecticides and fungicides were inorganic compounds, such as sulfur, arsenic, mercury, and copper. These controlled pests but often injured plants and could be deadly to people. The botanical organic compounds, plant-derived poisons such as rotenone and pyrethrins, were discovered in the early nineteenth century.

A kerosene emulsion became a popular insecticide in the late nineteenth century until mineral oil, still used today, gained appreciation for its insect-controlling properties. Farmers sprayed compounds such as Paris green, a mixture of copper and arsenic, on crops to control insect pests up until the 1940s, when scien-

Insecticides, used correctly, help you achieve your goal of a beautiful and healthy garden.

The guidelines in this chapter will help you to select the right insecticides and to mix, apply, and store them safely. You will also learn how to choose and maintain sprayers, dusters, and spreaders.

tists introduced modern-day synthetic organic insecticides to agriculture.

The first of these compounds were chemicals—such as DDT—which are classified as chlorinated hydrocarbons. In the 1950s scientific advances introduced the organophosphates, derivatives of phosphoric acid that break down into harmless compounds more quickly than do chlorinated hydrocarbons. These were followed in the late 1950s by the carbamates, derivatives of carbamic acid that also do not persist long. More recently scientists have created synthetic

pyrethrins, called pyrethroids, which are somewhat more effective and longer lasting than is the botanical form. Today most garden insecticides are organophosphates and carbamates.

EPA APPROVAL

All pesticides now marketed in the United States must pass stringent tests for effectiveness and safety before the Environmental Protection Agency (EPA) approves them for sale. Today, the EPA bans dangerous heavy metals such as arsenic and mercury in pesticides. Chemical companies the world over continually carry out research to test for new methods of pest control. When a promising compound is discovered, stringent testing begins. Testing a new pesticide takes 7 to 10 years and costs millions of dollars. The tests performed include:

• *Performance tests* to determine the product's effectiveness on every insect and plant to be listed on the pesticide's label

• *Toxicological tests* to determine how hazardous the compound is to people, animals, and the environment

• *Degradation tests* to determine how long the compound takes to break down to a harmless substance

• *Soil tests* to study how far the substance moves in the soil and how long it remains active

• *Residue tests* to determine how long the compound remains on plants and when crops are safe to eat

• *Phytotoxicity tests* to test which plants tolerate the pesticide and to determine application rates and intervals harmless to approved plants

• *Packaging and stability tests* to determine the best packaging and application method for each product and its shelf life under normal storage conditions

INSECTICIDES

All insecticides are poisons designed to kill insects and related pests. Like all household chemicals, such as dishwasher detergent, bleach, nail polish remover, gasoline, and paint thinner, to name a few, insecticides can be dangerous to people if used unwisely. Many people mistakenly assume that the botanical insecticides, such as rotenone, pyrethrins, and nicotine sulfate, pose less of a hazard just because they come from natural sources. Botanical compounds can be just as toxic as synthetic ones.

Rotenone, derived from the roots of South American members of the bean family, kills fish if it gets into a stream or pond. Pyrethrins, derived from the flowers of pyrethrum, a member of the chrysanthemum family, carry the reputation of being some of the least hazardous insecticides. Although not poisonous to warm-blooded animals, they may cause allergic reactions in people who suffer from hay fever. Pyrethrins lose their pest control powers in less than three hours.

The third common botanical insecticide, nicotine sulfate, comes from tobacco extracts. It is a deadly nerve poison if swallowed or if sufficient quantities are absorbed by the skin or inhaled. Homemade nicotine extract can transmit tobacco mosaic virus, which infects many kinds of garden plants.

Any insecticide can be harmful if used incorrectly, regardless of whether it comes from plants or from a laboratory. The wise gardener always reads every word on a product label when making a purchase, before preparing equipment, and immediately before insecticide use. Follow directions carefully, and reread the label each time you use the product (see page 20).

How Insecticides Work

Insecticides usually work as either a stomach poison, a contact poison, or both. Some work by smothering the insects. Contact insecticides go to work when a bug crawls over the sprayed or dusted area. Plant protection can persist for weeks or merely days, depending on the insecticide you choose. Stomach poisons must be eaten before any toxic action takes place. This usually means that the pests must eat some of the treated plant to receive its toxic meal, but some pests ingest insecticides when they lick their appendages during grooming.

Some pesticides are systemics. When applied to foliage or soil, a plant absorbs the insecticide, carrying it throughout its leaves, roots, wood, and flowers and delivering it as a stomach poison to feeding pests. Systemic poisons find primary use against sap-sucking insects feeding on foliage. Once absorbed, a systemic will not be washed off by rain or garden watering. Plant protection can last six weeks or longer, depending on the insecticide chosen. Because they are so long lasting and cannot be washed off, care must be taken in using systemics on food crops. Follow label directions.

Horticultural oils, applied as a dormant oil or summer oil (growing season) spray, work by smothering the eggs or larvae of insect and mite pests.

Broad-Spectrum Versus Specific Insecticides

Most insecticides, whether contact, systemic, stomach poison, or smothering oil, work on a broad spectrum. They destroy many pests in many situations. Diazinon is one such broad-spectrum insecticide, eliminating over 100 different pests, including aphids, mealybugs, mites, and flea beetles.

In contrast to broad-spectrum insecticides, some are specific, designed to control only one or two particular types of insect. For example, dicofol was designed to kill only mites and will not affect other pests.

INSECTICIDE FORMULATIONS

Insecticides are highly complex products manufactured to meet strict quality-control standards. This typically means that the active ingredients must be mixed during manufacture with a solvent or carrying agent so that they can be accurately diluted and applied. Only a small percentage of even a concentrated insecticide product is actually active ingredients—these are often measured in parts per million. The rest is inert.

The inert ingredients may simply be carrying agents, or they may be important ingredients such as emulsifiers designed to keep the pesticide in solution. A spreader-sticker prevents spray droplets from beading on waxy leaves and helps the pesticide to spread out evenly over leaf surfaces and adhere to the leaves. It also helps the spray penetrate wax-covered insects, such as mealybugs and scales. Gardeners once had to add a spreader-sticker to many insecticidal sprays and wettable powders, but most modern high-quality insecticides include them in the concentrate. However, if a pesticide label advises you to add one, it's a good idea. You can purchase spreader-sticker at your garden center.

Garden insecticides are sold in various forms; they may be oil-based or water-based liquid concentrates (also called emulsifiable concentrates) that need to be diluted with water, or they may be prediluted in ready-to-use aerosol cans or trigger sprayers. The pesticide may be mixed with an inert powder designed to be applied as a dust or as a wettable powder meant to be mixed into a suspension with water. Some are sold as baits that attract pests to taste them and then deliver poison along with the food.

In contrast to liquid concentrates, some wettable-powder insecticides require repeated agitation while in your

Before you purchase a pesticide, read the label carefully. Be sure it mentions the plant and the pest on which you plan to use it. If you are unsure as to which product to use, ask nursery employees for help. They can interpret the label and help you choose the right quantity for your needs.

sprayer, or their finely ground clay or talc ingredients will settle to the bottom. An emulsifier helps keep the powder in suspension, but without agitation settling occurs. Home gardeners usually prefer liquid concentrates, but some insecticides can only be formulated as wettable powders.

Making the Best Choice

Your garden center offers an array of insecticide choices available in aerosol, spray, dust, granule, or bait form. The proper choice may seem confusing. The best insecticide formula for you depends on the size of your garden, the extent and type of pest problem, and the kind of pesticide equipment you have.

Premixed pesticides in ready-to-use containers offer the greatest convenience but are the most expensive. They are perfect for small problems but uneconomical for large ones. For a limited infestation of aphids on a couple of rosebushes, an aerosol rose spray is a perfect choice. You don't have to mix anything, and it is right at hand whenever you notice a return invasion. But if your rose garden consists of a dozen prize bushes, you will find that using a liquid concentrate and a good sprayer is more practical in the long run.

Many gardeners like dust insecticides because the powder is readily visible—a useful harvest-time reminder in the vegetable garden. Dusts are easy to use because they don't need diluting. Some dusts even come in handy, inexpensive squeeze bottles, which offer convenience and good foliage coverage. For large gardens, purchase an economical sack of dust and apply it with a duster.

Although it is convenient, dust has certain limitations. On windy or breezy days, you can't apply a dust—it blows where you don't want it, such as on you, plants not listed on the container's label, or your neighbor's property. Dusts also do not adhere well to foliage during dry seasons. Apply them after a rain, after watering, or early in the morning while dew remains on foliage.

If you already have a fertilizer drop spreader for your lawn, you will probably appreciate a granular insecticide for lawn treatment. You will find granules handy for controlling soil insects in vegetable gardens or in shrub and flower beds where foliage is thick.

CHOOSING THE RIGHT EQUIPMENT

To do the best job of pest control possible, you need the best possible pest control equipment. This does not necessarily mean that the equipment should be expensive or elaborate, but it does mean that it should equal the job. The simplest equipment is no equipment at all—you can purchase ready-to-use sprays in aerosol cans or trigger sprayers, and dusts often come in squeeze canisters. These are convenient for small problems.

For larger problems or extensive plantings, you should have your own sprayer and duster. Choose a quality sprayer that meets your garden's needs.

Hose-End Sprayers

Many homeowners rely on a hose-end sprayer for most of their pest control problems. The sprayer consists of a glass or plastic jar and a nozzle that screws onto your garden hose. You put a water-and-insecticide mixture in the jar, and the nozzle further dilutes the mixture with water as you spray. Most hose-end sprayers have a fixed mixing ratio built into the nozzle. This ratio can vary from 24:1 (meaning that the nozzle mixes 24 parts of water into every 1 part of concentrate) for a foliar sprayer to 60:1 for a lawn sprayer.

Hose-end sprayers are easy to use. The product label tells you how much concentrate to add per gallon of spray. You measure in the correct amount and add enough water to fill the container to the mark on the side of the jar corresponding to the number of gallons of spray you are mixing. When you turn on the hose, the nozzle siphons the insecticide, further diluting it to the correct ratio.

Some hose-end sprayers come with a dial on top so that you can adjust the ratio. With these, you use undiluted concentrate in the container, and the nozzle does all the diluting.

When choosing a hose-end sprayer, select one with a versatile nozzle. You will want one that can vary from a fine mist to a long stream. That way you can use the same sprayer for different garden plants. Choose the mist selection for flowers, vegetables, and seedlings, where a forceful spray might disrupt blossoms or even tear out young plants. An elongated nozzle shaft is particularly good for spraying inside shrubs and hedges or reaching treetops. A rotating nozzle provides precise up, down, and jet spray patterns ideal for reaching leaf undersides. Choose a fan- or cone-shaped nozzle for

Hose-end sprayers are inexpensive and versatile. The one shown here has a choice of four spray patterns.

lawns, where a uniform spray pattern eliminates skips in coverage, and use a jet stream for reaching the tops of trees.

Some special features to look for when buying a hose-end sprayer include a control valve with an instant-on and instant-off feature. That, combined with a thumb-touch valve easily operated by both right- and left-handed people and a thumb slide that locks the sprayer in the on position, allows continuous spraying under your direct control. Your hose-end connector should always have an antisiphon device to prevent any spray material from being sucked back down the hose and into the water line should water pressure drop.

Hose-end sprayers are inexpensive and work well for a variety of garden spray jobs, from lawns to trees. Their major disadvantage is that you are limited by the length and flexibility of your garden hose. And if you don't have much water pressure, you may not be able to reach treetops. You might find the hose difficult to maneuver around intricate garden beds or rows of fruit trees, especially in cool weather when the hose may be less flexible.

Handheld Sprayers

A useful and inexpensive sprayer for delicate plants is the handheld trigger sprayer—the type often used for misting houseplants. (You can often purchase ready-to-use insecticide in similar containers.) A large sprayer holds about a quart of liquid; you have to dilute the insecticide properly, but then all you need to do is point the nozzle at the bugs and squeeze the trigger. Buy a trigger

Above left: Many insecticides are available premixed in convenient handheld sprayers.
Above center: When choosing a compression sprayer, look for one with a wide mouth for safe and easy filling.
Above right: For big jobs where hoses won't reach, a wheeled tank sprayer lets you do the work without carrying anything.
Left: fine spray. Right: coarse spray. All good-quality sprayers have adjustable nozzles that offer a range of spray types, from a fine mist to a coarse spray or far-reaching jet. The one you use depends on the type of plant and pest you are spraying.

sprayer with an adjustable nozzle, so that you can vary spray patterns from a fine mist to a farther-reaching stream.

Trigger sprayers are best for treating single plants, because your hand becomes fatigued if a lot of foliage must be covered. Also, if the bugs live on leaf undersides and you turn this sprayer upside down, you may end up giving your unwelcome guests a blast of air instead of pesticide. The spray from these sprayers does not reach very far, but you will probably use it only for close-at-hand pest problems.

Tank-Type Sprayers

Available for home use in sizes from 1 to 3 gallons, tank-type compression sprayers pick up where the small fry leave off. They are versatile and portable and require little pumping action on your part. You initially pump air into the container to build up the pressure, but to apply the spray, you need only squeeze the trigger.

Tanks are made of chemical-resistant plastic or metal and have the wide mouths necessary for easy and safe filling. At the end of a flexible hose is a trigger attached to a long wand. The wand

allows you to aim insecticide beneath leaves and low-growing plants or overhead with little reaching on your part. You can usually adjust the nozzle at the tip of the wand to deliver a fine mist for dense, low-growing plants or a strong stream for reaching tall plants. Larger models have 15- to 30-foot streams for reaching treetops.

Following the directions on the insecticide label, mix the proper proportions of insecticide and water directly in the tank of the compression sprayer. Secure the top tightly, and then pump air into the tank until pressure builds up and pumping becomes difficult. To apply the spray, just aim the wand and press the trigger. A valve inside the nozzle opens, and compressed air forces the liquid out through the nozzle. You may have to pump it again halfway through the spray job to restore the pressure.

If you have a home orchard or an extensive garden, you might be tempted to purchase a large compression sprayer so that you won't have to refill while treating your plants. The sprayers come with carrying handles, and larger ones also have shoulder straps. But keep in mind that the large models can become quite heavy. Water weighs in at 8 pounds per gallon, so a 3-gallon tank holds 24 pounds of solution. Add to this the weight of an empty sprayer and you may find that you prefer the smaller 2-gallon

size, even if you must refill it once or twice for big jobs.

You work a pump sprayer by continually pumping a displacement lever with one hand and aiming the wand and spray with the other. Nozzles adjust from a fine mist to a 30- to 40-foot-high jet spray that reaches treetops. Pump sprayers come in convenient 1-gallon sizes or larger versions.

If you have to treat a large garden or an orchard, your best choice may be a 5-gallon backpack pump sprayer. Although it is heavier than a large compression sprayer, a backpack sprayer rides on your back, not your shoulder, so you can usually carry the evenly distributed weight with less difficulty. The backpack sprayer handles enough insecticide solution to allow you to walk extensively without returning for additional supplies.

On the luxurious end of the sprayer scale is a battery-powered, wheeled pump sprayer, which you can effortlessly push around your property.

The main disadvantage of pump sprayers is that you must continually operate the pump by hand to keep the pressure built up in the tank. The electric pump sprayer eliminates this work, but for a price.

The trombone pump sprayer works on the same push-pull motion as a musical trombone, except that in lieu of music, a pulsating or surging spray emerges. The fineness of the spray depends on your nozzle adjustment. It produces one of the most far-reaching streams of any type of sprayer, extending 30 to 40 vertical feet, so some gardeners prefer the trombone sprayer for treating tall trees.

The sprayer itself is lightweight and less expensive than tank sprayers because it does not include a tank. You place diluted insecticide in a bucket, which you must carry with you and set on the ground while you are spraying. The weighted end of the 6-foot-long trombone's hose goes into the solution. The main disadvantage of this type of sprayer is that you must keep up a steady back-and-forth action with your hand to activate the pump.

When using a trombone sprayer, be extra cautious that you do not kick over the bucket while spraying. Also be sure to label the bucket "for pesticide use only," and don't use it for anything else!

Dusters

Good dusters emit a fine cloud of dust with each stroke of the pump. Ones with nozzles that adjust up or down offer you the most control and deliver dust to leaf undersides. When you select a duster of any kind, for safety reasons, always check that its construction permits dust release only when the handle is turned.

For small jobs, such as spot applications here and there in your yard, a ready-to-use dust in a squeeze container works effectively. Or try a plunger duster holding about one pint of dust. These also come in larger sizes. To dispense the

dust, you hold the container in one hand and draw the pump back and forth with the other. By adding an extension wand, you can keep the dust away from yourself and take better aim at the pests and leaf undersides. You can operate a pistol-grip duster with one hand.

Rotary hand dusters, sometimes called crank dusters, produce a steady stream of dust when you turn the crank. These require one hand to hold the container and the other to turn the handle. Rotary dusters provide excellent coverage on large areas, including vegetables, flowers, roses, shrubs, and small trees. You can use them for fungicidal dusts as well as insecticides.

One variety of rotary hand duster consists of a polypropylene hopper, a crank handle, a blower, and extension tubes. The nonrusting, noncorroding hopper holds up to 8 ounces of dust, and the tube end deflectors direct the material, avoiding dust clouds. Tube deflectors also enable you to dust leaf undersides and reach in and around shrubs.

A hand-operated bellows duster, available in sizes that hold from 1 teaspoon to as much as 8 pounds of dust, gives you a great deal of short- and long-range

A Whirlybird® Spreader gives a broad, steady coverage of pesticide granules with each turn of the handle.

flexibility. The knapsack duster, similar to this, has a backpack design due to its larger size.

Spreaders

Lawn treatments can often be applied with a spreader—the same one you use for fertilizer applications. A drop spreader provides the greatest control for applying insecticides because the granules drop straight down from the spreader's bottom. Adjustments on the bottom of the hopper calibrate the amount of insecticide that falls to the lawn while you walk at a steady pace.

Wheeled broadcast spreaders have a rotating wheel that throws the hopper contents outward in an 8- to 12-foot arc, but more material falls in the middle of the arc than at the edge—proper overlap of arcs is essential for even distribution. These spreaders work well on expansive lawns but may throw granules in too wide a pattern for small areas.

You can also apply granules in small areas with a handheld broadcast spreader, which you operate by turning a crank to disperse the contents. You can reduce the width of the arc by rotating the crank in the reverse direction.

Many insecticide dusts come in ready-to-use squeeze containers. You just pull the plug and squeeze out a fine cloud of dust.

MAINTAINING EQUIPMENT

Do not neglect your equipment if you want it to last for years. Although it may be sturdily built, a sprayer or duster performs optimally only when cared for properly. Your sprayer or duster comes with a label or instruction booklet detailing its proper use and care. Read it carefully; then hang the instructions on a wall or shelf near where you plan to store the sprayer. They will then be handy whenever you need to refresh your memory.

Most sprayer problems start when foreign material clogs a nozzle. Begin taking care of your equipment by cleaning your sprayer—even a brand-new one—before each use. The manufacturing process may have left behind metallic chips and debris, which can clog a wand or nozzle and cause parts to wear, or bits of rust and dirt may have gotten in during storage. Flush the sprayer with fresh water; make sure screens and nozzles are clean.

While using the sprayer, check every so often to see whether any dirt, sand, or grass has clogged the nozzle. If so, you will waste the water pressure trying to force spray past the foreign material and, instead of a far-reaching and effective mist, out will come short-distance droplets. Never attempt to clean a nozzle by poking anything other than the cleaning pin that may have come with the sprayer into the nozzle's opening. You will only end up widening the nozzle and ruining your spray pattern.

If a nozzle seems plugged, back-flush it with air or water. A hot-water soak can dissolve some stubborn deposits. Do not, under any circumstances, put the nozzle

in your mouth and blow through it. Insecticides are poisonous and can cling to a nozzle in small amounts despite washing.

Your sprayer also has screens that need regular cleaning. In general, a coarse screen protects the suction hose, a medium-mesh screen resides between the hose and sprayer apparatus, and a fine screen filters the nozzle. Keep these screens in place, and clean them with a soft brush dipped in water or detergent solution.

Pumps wear even with normal use, as does any piece of machinery, but wear accelerates with misuse. To avoid abrasive and clogging particles, dilute the insecticide with clean water, and keep your plunger cylinder off of bare ground, where it can pick up dirt, dust, sand, and other damaging substances.

Each time you finish using the sprayer, you must wash it inside and out to prevent corrosion and pesticide accumulation. Without thorough washing, some pesticide residue persists for months or even years, and if the pesticide is specific to one crop or plant, it might damage another the next time you use the sprayer.

Thoroughly flush the sprayer with water three times. Empty the wash water on an out-of-the-way section of yard or in a weed- or gravel-covered patch where it cannot run off into a ditch or pond. Be certain that any pesticide residue is not accessible to children, pets, livestock, or wildlife. During the last rinsing, put the top back on the sprayer and spray the water onto the ground to flush out the nozzle and hoses.

When you are not using the sprayer, hang it upside down or set it upside down on a shelf with a wedge beneath the canister so that it can drain and dry completely. Upside-down storage also keeps dust from settling inside.

You may need to oil moving parts of sprayers occasionally. Gaskets and pumps made of neoprene rubber or leather also require oiling.

You will find your duster easy to maintain. While dusting, occasionally tap the deflector at the tube end to prevent dust buildup, which might impair mechanical performance. Keep the duster clean by tapping out accumulated dust. Lubricate all moving parts with graphite, not oil. Insecticide dusts stick to oil and will clog the apparatus; graphite provides lubrication without causing dust to stick.

The hopper of your spreader requires cleaning after every use. When exposed to air, fertilizer or insecticide residues left inside can cake, becoming cementlike and difficult to remove. Hose out the inside of the hopper after use, and leave it in the sun to dry before putting it away. Keep moving parts lubricated with oil.

APPLYING INSECTICIDES PROPERLY

Labels on insecticides sold for home garden use include clear instructions about how to apply them. Insecticides needing dilution provide directions for mixing the product. Because some insects are more difficult to kill than others, the dilution rate may differ depending on the insect you wish to control. Pay close attention to mixing instructions; too little pesticide may not knock out the pests, and a double dose will not kill them twice! If you use too strong a mixture, you can injure the plants you are trying to rescue.

With most insecticide sprays, the label instructs you to spray the plant until it is "wet thoroughly" or to "spray to drip point." This means to spray until the mixture begins dripping off the plant. Unless you let the spray dry and then spray again, you usually won't apply too much. To get thorough coverage, spray the foliage from two or three directions

Store your pump sprayer upside down, either hanging or tipped with a wedge so the inside can dry. Hang the pump beside it, and provide a hook for the wand to promote drainage.

and from above and underneath. When the excess spray begins dripping onto the ground, stop spraying.

If the label says to spray leaf undersides, do so. Many insects feed, lay eggs, or crawl on the undersides of leaves. If your spray or dust reaches only the upper leaf surfaces, the pests beneath may escape. To be sure you reach the undersides of leaves, rotate the nozzle of your sprayer or duster upward and hold the wand low while you treat the plant.

Spraying Trees

You need the proper equipment to spray a large tree, or you will not be able to penetrate thick foliage or reach the top. A trombone sprayer, powerful backpack sprayer, or hose-end sprayer used with high water pressure can usually do the job. For trees over 40 feet tall, you may need to call in a professional. Before you try to spray a tree, test your equipment with plain water to be sure that it's powerful enough to propel insecticide to the top, or the spray may fall back on you as you aim upward.

Do not stand close to or beneath the tree; stand far enough away so that the spray drift settles on the ground, not on you. When you spray trees near a house or wall, you take the risk that the spray will bounce back, so aim the stream away from large, solid obstacles. Controlling drift when spraying trees can be difficult; do not spray unless the air is completely still (see page 21).

Adjust the sprayer nozzle so that it tilts upward to reach leaf undersides; runoff will wet the upper leaf surfaces. Start spraying at the top of the tree and work downward, zigzagging from side to side as you walk in a circle around the tree. Use as much pressure as possible; this displaces the foliage, allowing you to cover the trunk and branches at the interior of the tree.

Using Oil Sprays

Horticultural oils—very pure petroleum or mineral oil—control pests that overwinter on the buds, twigs, and bark of trees and shrubs. Dormant oils, so called because you apply them during a plant's dormant season, work best when applied in late winter or early spring, just before buds open. Most labels recommend only one application per season.

On certain plants, you can apply a more dilute oil spray during late spring and summer, when leaves are mature or almost full grown. If used too early in the season, oil can burn new growth. The

label may provide directions for mixing in other pesticides, such as malathion, for even-more-effective growing-season control.

Spray summer oil until the oil completely wets the plant and spray runs off onto the ground. It is important to cover both upper and lower leaf surfaces as well as to reach the trunk and small branches. You cannot overapply oil unless you repeat a spraying after the first spray dries. Do not apply oil when the temperature is lower than 40° F or higher than 85° F or if the humidity exceeds 90 percent, because these factors affect the oil's evaporation and plants can be injured.

If you have good water pressure, a hose-end sprayer should give good coverage for most landscape trees. Be sure the day is not a windy one, and stand far enough back so that no spray mist falls on you.

The oil film evaporates slowly, so do not respray or apply any other oil-based pesticide for about two weeks. Nor should you spray with oil 30 days before or after applying any type of sulfur spray or certain fungicides. (Read label directions.) A few plants are very sensitive to oil sprays, so double-check your container label before applying oil.

SAFETY MEASURES

Insecticides, like medicines, work safely and effectively when used properly but can be dangerous if misused. We tend to forget just how dangerous many of the products and items we use on a daily basis really can be. Serious accidents happen every day with automobiles, medicines, and household chemicals such as paint thinner and charcoal lighter. Most of these accidents are the result of carelessness. Such is the case with pesticides. Although they perform safely if used with the proper caution, an accident could happen if you are careless.

Insecticides may cause illness if absorbed through the skin, inhaled, or ingested. By pretending that the insecticide you are handling poses more danger than it does, chances are you will be properly cautious when preparing and applying it.

Read the Label

Your first safety step should be to read and understand the product label. That label may be the most expensive reading material in the world—millions of dollars went into testing the product to assure its safety and effectiveness when used as directed. So read those directions, and follow them exactly. You should read the label five separate times: before purchasing the product, before mixing it, before applying it, before storing it, and finally before disposing of any excess or the empty container.

It may seem a nuisance to stop to read the fine print when you are in a hurry to get rid of those bugs before they eat any more of your prize petunias, but do not skip steps. Take a few minutes to study the instructions each time you use an insecticide. Your safety and the safety of your garden could depend on it.

The EPA requires certain signal words to appear in large type on every pesticide label. These indicate the product's potential hazard. You will see one of the following three words on every label: *Caution, Warning,* or *Danger.* All insecticides are potentially dangerous, but "danger" on the label indicates the greatest hazard; "warning" means a moderate hazard, and "caution" means slightly hazardous.

Most insecticides for home use rate a caution or warning. The rating can depend upon the product's concentration; for instance, a 5-percent liquid concentrate may rate a caution, but a 10-percent solution may rate a warning. It is best to choose the least hazardous insecticide that will do the job.

The pesticide label offers instructions under several headings, often "Precautionary Statements," "For Insects Listed Below," "For Use On," "Do Not Apply To," "Directions for Use," and "Product Disposal."

The advice under "Precautionary Statements" includes information about possible toxicity to domestic animals, fish, wildlife, or beneficial insects such as bees. There you will also find information on the action to take in the event of accidental poisoning.

Check under "For Insects Listed Below" to see if the insect pest you want to control appears on the list, and read the "For Use On" list to see whether it includes the plant you are intending to treat. If a particular insect is infesting several different kinds of plants, recheck the list. Are all of your affected plants mentioned? If not, you may want to choose another insecticide.

Before you assume that what is good for one tree will be good for another, scan the "Do Not Apply To" section. Some pesticides injure certain plants, and this will be noted here. You may need another insecticide to take care of the plants mentioned. Extensive testing went into compiling the list of pests and plants on which the product can be used, so respect its advice. Do not use it on plants that are not listed, or injury may occur.

Be especially cautious about applying pesticides to food crops. The label tells you whether fruits and vegetables may be safely treated. It also tells you how long you must wait between spraying and harvesting. This waiting period varies according to the time it takes the product to degrade. If a label states "do not eat food crops for 10 days after spraying," figure on that when applying the insecticide. Always wash fruits and vegetables thoroughly when you bring them in from the garden, sprayed or unsprayed, in case there is any drift from neighboring property.

When you are certain that the product is designed to treat the pests and plants you have in mind, read "Directions for Use." These tell you what part of the

Study insecticide labels and follow the instructions exactly. This sample label shows how typical information is arranged under several headings to help you locate the details you need.

PRECAUTIONARY STATEMENTS

READ ENTIRE LABEL
USE STRICTLY IN ACCORDANCE WITH
LABEL CAUTIONS AND DIRECTIONS.

CAUTION

Hazards

Statement of Practical Treatment

Note to Physicians :

DIRECTIONS FOR USE

How to Use

Plants	Insects	Dosage	Comments

NOTE

Storage and Disposal

Notice:
Chevron Chemical Co © 1987
EPA Registration Number   09876 54321

Chevron
ORTHO

Insect Spray

Makes Up
to 8 Gallons
Spray

CONTROLS:

ACTIVE INGREDIENTS

INERT INGREDIENTS

Keep out of Reach of Children

CAUTION

NET CONTENTS 8 FL. OZ.

plant to treat, when and how often to spray, and how to mix the insecticide. Instructions may differ for each insect or plant type, so read this part carefully.

If you suspect that someone has been made ill by the insecticide, the label will be the most important immediate information you have. The "Statement of Practical Treatment" gives poisoning symptoms, emergency first-aid measures, and a note to the physician, which should include a telephone number to call for further information. If you work around your home with many household or garden chemicals, you may want to keep the telephone number of the local poison control center hotline near your phone.

Mixing Precautions

When diluting a liquid concentrate or wettable powder with water, avoid getting any of the powerful concentrated insecticide on your skin. It is best to start out wearing gloves. Unlined rubber or neoprene gloves work best, as long as you are not tempted to wear them later when washing the dishes. Never wear leather or cotton gloves when handling pesticides, because they could absorb the chemicals and become a constant source of exposure.

To prevent spills or splashes, handle containers slowly and carefully, placing the container on a solid surface at all times. Because you must measure concentrated insecticides precisely if you want the best results, do not assume that a pinch equals a teaspoon. Purchase a separate set of measuring spoons or cups for pesticide use, and mark them "for pesticide use only" in a bright permanent color. Never use utensils that you intend to use when cooking or that have been previously used for cooking (to avoid someone accidentally reusing them for food after they have been used for pesticides). Because young children enjoy playing with kitchen and measuring utensils and might be tempted to taste the contents, be certain these are kept out of sight and reach.

Measure all pesticides outdoors on the ground or on a low wall or step, not on your picnic table, standing upwind of the mixing container. Take inside all pet food and water bowls, as well as children's toys. Rinse off measuring spoons and utensils with your garden hose in an out-of-the-way corner, never in your kitchen sink.

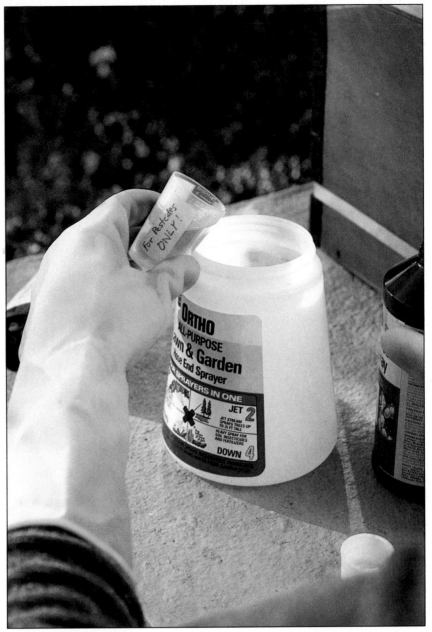

Application Precautions

When applying spray or dust, along with unlined rubber gloves you might want to wear a long-sleeved shirt, long pants, socks, rubber boots or shoes, and a brimmed, nonabsorbent hat. Check the product label to see whether these or other protective garments are recommended. Never smoke when handling or applying pesticides. Plan on setting your work clothes aside to be laundered after you finish applying the insecticide. (Do not wash them with other garments.) Then shower or wash exposed skin with soap and hot water as soon as possible, and certainly before smoking or eating.

Keep everyone, including pets, away from newly treated areas until insecticide sprays dry. This may take just a few hours or as long as 24 hours, especially with lawns. After dusting, wait several

When mixing insecticides, be sure to use a clearly labeled measuring cup or spoon; protect your hands with nonabsorbent rubber or neoprene gloves.

hours to be certain that airborne dust particles have settled. Do not let babies crawl on insecticide-treated areas.

Controlling Spray Drift

You must be cautious that spray or dust does not drift where it isn't wanted. This becomes a problem on breezy days. It is best to work when the air is calm, as is often the case in early morning or at dusk. Never spray or dust when there is wind. If there is a slight breeze, stand with the wind at your back to avoid spray mist or dust blowing onto your skin.

Pay attention to even slight breezes when you are spraying a pesticide, because the spray could drift back in your face.

Be careful to keep your face protected from downward-drifting spray. You might not think about this when spraying horizontally or down onto low-growing plants, but if you bend down to reach the undersides of lower leaves or aim upward to reach the top of a tall shrub, spray can drift downward toward your face. When spraying overhead, use as powerful a mist or stream as possible. This allows you to stand back from the plant and spray at a reduced angle, preventing downward-drifting spray from falling on you.

You can control spray drift due to air currents somewhat by varying the water pressure of the sprayer. The lower the pressure, the larger and heavier the droplets and the shorter the distance they will travel. Unfortunately, larger droplets cover foliage less thoroughly than a fine mist, but they also evaporate more slowly in hot weather.

In Case of Accident

If any insecticide accidentally splashes on your skin, wash it off right away with detergent and water. If insecticide splashes into your eyes, flush them immediately with running water while someone calls your doctor or emergency room. Continue cleansing eyes for 15 minutes, then seek medical treatment if you are advised to do so. Should insecticide spill on clothing, change it as soon as possible, and wash it before you wear it again. Do not keep or wash contaminated clothing with any other garments.

Pesticide poisoning can result from skin exposure, inhalation, or ingestion. Such exposure usually results from careless handling. Symptoms usually appear within two hours of exposure and include muscle twitches, headache, blurred vision, weakness, vomiting, dizziness, and chest discomfort. Although these symptoms can also be due to other illnesses, such as the flu, do not take chances; seek medical assistance immediately if you become ill soon after using a pesticide.

In the rare instance that someone using a pesticide must go to a hospital emergency room, bring the pesticide and its label along. The information and phone number it contains may be invaluable in assuring correct and prompt treatment.

If you spill a pesticide, ventilate the area with an exhaust fan. Then, wearing protective clothing, absorb the spill with cat litter or old rags, and discard these in a sealed plastic bag in the garbage. Scrub floors with strong detergent. Never smoke or strike a match around spills, because the fumes may catch fire.

Avoiding Plant Injury

You must also be concerned with plant safety when using insecticides. Plant injury, called *phytotoxicity*, can occur with overdose, when an insecticide is applied during extremely hot weather, or merely because a spray aimed at one plant drifts onto a nontargeted plant. The container label lists the plants that can be treated safely—do not use it on unlisted plants or you risk injuring them. If tests show that a plant is particularly sensitive to a pesticide, the label indicates this. If you must spray near a sensitive plant, design some type of screen to block drift.

Plant injury can result from pesticide that has been diluted incorrectly. If the label calls for 1 tablespoon of concentrate per gallon of water, doubling the concentrate won't kill the insect twice, but it may harm the plant. Mix carefully according to label instructions, and do not reapply sooner than the label directs.

The weather conditions can also affect plant sensitivity. When air temperatures are above 85° F, insecticides evaporate too quickly, possibly resulting in foliage burn and poor insect control. Injured foliage develops brown edges and tips soon after spraying.

When using oil sprays, do not work when the humidity exceeds or is expected to exceed 90 percent. High humidity slows oil evaporation, and leaf damage results when oil evaporates too slowly.

During warm, but not hot, weather, spray during the coolest part of the day, usually morning or late afternoon. Wind lessens at these times as well, and so spray or dust is less apt to drift. During hot weather, temperature inversions may occur; these prevent small spray droplets from settling on foliage and allow them to drift instead. The spray may land on nontargeted plants, resulting in damage.

Follow label directions! Diluting pesticides improperly, or using them on unlisted plants or under the wrong temperature and humidity conditions, can damage plants. These grape leaves show insecticide injury.

Do not treat wilted, dry, or otherwise stressed plants. Insecticide used under these conditions can be phytotoxic and cause foliage burn. If infested plants seem wilted, water them well and apply insecticide the next day.

Herbicides (weed killers) can harm ornamental plants as well as weeds. If you use your sprayer for applying herbicide to weedy patches or to your lawn, the residue left in the sprayer can injure plants the next time you spray them with insecticide. It is often better to use separate equipment for herbicides and mark them accordingly.

Safe Storage

Store pesticides (and measuring equipment) out of direct sunlight in a dry, well-ventilated place where temperatures will not exceed 110° F or drop below freezing. All shelves that hold insecticides should be sturdy and at an easy height for adult access, although out of a curious child's reach. A locked cabinet is ideal if you have young children. Keep all insecticide containers well away from pilot lights and other open flames or sparks because the fumes can be flammable. Be absolutely certain that no food, beverage, or eating utensils, whether your family's or your pet's, are stored with the pesticides. Check containers regularly for corrosion and leaks.

Pesticides and measuring equipment are best stored out of reach of children in a sturdy, locked cabinet. Never store them with any food that you or your pets will eat.

Never store undiluted insecticide in any container but the one it came in. Pesticides stored in food containers, especially soft drink bottles, tempt children to taste them. Nor should you remove any label or place anything over existing labels. When storing insecticides on a shelf, keep the labels plainly visible, and make certain the container cap is tight.

Safe Disposal

Try to mix only the amount of insecticide you need for each application. If you mix up too much spray solution, do not try to save it. During storage the diluted pesticide breaks down into an ineffective product or evaporates and becomes more concentrated. The pesticide also can corrode metal sprayers. The safest way to use extra solution is to apply it to other infested plants listed on the label. Never pour diluted or undiluted insecticides down the drain or sewer. These products can interfere with natural organisms in cesspools and sewage-treatment plants.

When you have used up a bottle or container of insecticide, check the label for disposal instructions. In general, it is all right to dispose of the container in the garbage if you follow a few precautions. When all undiluted pesticide appears to be gone, hold the empty container upside down for as long as 30 seconds over an out-of-the-way weed patch or other site away from desirable plants. Rinse the container by filling it one fourth full with water, putting on the cap tightly, and then shaking. Empty it by holding the bottle upside down for another 30 seconds. Repeat this procedure a second time. Then wrap the container in several layers of newspaper, and discard it in a covered garbage can. Never reuse a pesticide container.

It is best to purchase only the amount of insecticide you will use in one season. At season's end you can store excess insecticide if you keep it under the conditions described above. Most insecticides can be stored for three years at proper temperatures without the contents being affected. After this, both the container and the insecticide it contains must be discarded.

If you want to dispose of undiluted pesticide remaining in its original container, it is best to mix it up and spray it on listed plants or on gravel or weeds in an out-of-the-way place. If you do not want to spray it, check the disposal instructions on the label. EPA standards state that up to 1 gallon of liquid pesticide and 10 pounds of dry formula may be securely wrapped in newspaper and placed in your trash can. Check with your county dump if you have larger amounts.

Insect pests needn't ruin the beauty or productivity of your garden. You can control them safely and effectively by choosing the proper insecticide and application equipment. The key to success comes from reading, understanding, and following label directions.

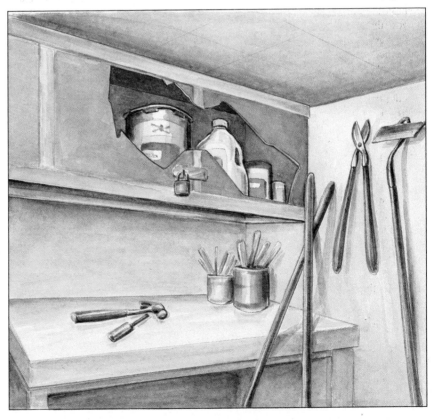

ADDITIONAL METHODS OF PEST CONTROL

Insecticides play a major role in effective pest control, but the minor-league players should not be overlooked. Beneficial insects keep pest populations in check during most years. You can also trap some pest insects or keep them off your plants with barriers. Good garden housekeeping discourages pests, and good cultural practices result in vigorous, more pest-resistant plants. When you combine these methods of discouraging pests with the judicious use of insecticides, you are using all the resources at hand to ensure that your garden flourishes free of pest invaders.

BENEFICIAL INSECTS

Not all insects harm your garden. In fact, many of them benefit it. Bees, of course, are well known for their pollination activity—without them your apple tree would never bear a crop. Other helpful insects, such as ladybugs and trichogramma wasps, kill insects by acting as either predators or parasites. Many of these probably already reside in your garden.

Predators and parasites help you with garden pest control, probably without your realizing it. Some of them are large, such as the praying mantid, and others are quite tiny, such as the trichogramma wasp. Look for the good guys in your garden wherever you see pest insects (see the photographs on page 26). Although beneficial insects often keep pests in check, if they and the pests get out of

Braconid wasps parasitize hornworms, helping to control them. Here, their cocoons line the sides of an infested pest. Leave parasitized hornworms in your garden so that the emerging wasps can attack other pests.

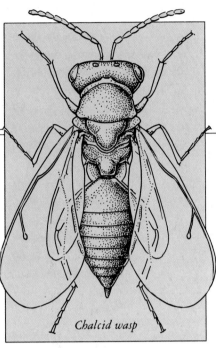

Chalcid wasp

Learn to encourage beneficial insects, select resistant plants, and use cultural control methods. Used together with insecticides, these methods provide you with a full array of pest-stopping weapons.

natural balance, as can happen during adverse weather conditions, there may be a pest explosion.

Because helpful insects usually multiply at about the same time as harmful ones, insecticides may kill them too. To avoid killing too many beneficial insects, it's best to use insecticides only when pests get out of control and then only on infested plants. By spraying only infested plants, where pests are concentrated, you spare the beneficial insects on other plants, and they can quickly replace those you have eliminated.

In most cases, rather than spraying plants routinely to prevent infestations, you should spray only when problems become evident. Exceptions to this rule are fruit trees and certain vegetables such as squash and corn, where certain pests cannot be controlled once they begin their damage. You may also want to consider preventive spraying on prized ornamental plants, such as roses, where even minor insect feeding can seriously damage the beauty of the plant.

Predators

Predators are meat-eating insects that devour other insects. They are usually equipped with strong jaws and chew or rip their prey apart. Their larvae also feed voraciously on small insects.

Antlions are fat little backward-walking larvae sometimes called doodlebugs. They partially bury themselves in tiny sand pits and wait for ants to fall in. Adult antlions do not look anything like their offspring but instead look like large, dark brown lacewings. The females place eggs in sand or sandy soil, and if the larvae hatch before spring, they remain in the ground until warm weather, emerging as adults during the summer months.

Dragonflies can whiz by at 60 miles per hour, each collecting as many as 100 mosquitoes in its mouth every day. They are also keen on beetles, moths, garden flies, termites, and other pest insects, catching them all on the wing. Dragonflies lay eggs in the fall on water plants or on the water's surface, and the young swim underwater, catching tadpoles, minnows, mosquito larvae, and whatever else seems edible. They overwinter as nymphs, sometimes taking two years to reach full wing-shimmering maturity.

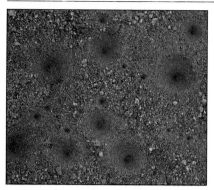

Antlions get their name because they hide at the bottom of sand pits and ambush unwary ants.

Snail-eating ground beetles have long, narrow heads that make perfect tools for probing under snail shells.

Praying mantids lay straw-colored egg cases in the fall. You can purchase these cases to assure spring hatchlings.

Dragonflies soar on iridescent wings, catching flying pests in midair. Shown here is a red-skimmer dragonfly.

Adult hoverflies pollinate while they feed on nectar; their larvae devour aphids, mealybugs, and leafhoppers.

Although yellowjackets can be pesky at a picnic, they also kill pests and eat dead insects, such as this grasshopper.

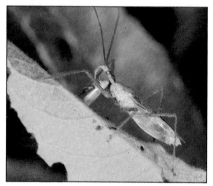

Assassin bugs, true to their name, make short work of leafhoppers, Japanese beetles, and caterpillars.

Both lacewing larvae and the winged adults eat large numbers of aphids, mealybugs, cottonycushion scales, and other insect pests.

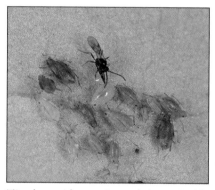

Tiny braconid wasps insert their eggs inside aphids. The hatched larvae kill the aphids as they feed.

Watch for the larvae of ladybugs—they eat even more aphids and other pests than the adults do.

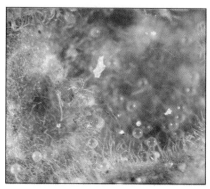

Predatory mites eat pest mites and the eggs of various other pest insects. Here two predatory mites attack one pest mite.

Plant shallow-throated flowers, such as daisies, to attract adult tachinid flies, which lay their eggs in pest insects.

Damselflies look and act almost like dragonflies, except that they are a little smaller, fly much more slowly, and hold their wings upward when resting instead of straight out to the side.

Predaceous bugs, such as assassin bugs, damsel bugs, and pirate bugs, feed on the body fluids of weevil larvae, midges, aphids, scales, red spider mites, chinch bugs, and thrips. Both the non-winged nymphs and winged adults pierce their prey with specially adapted beaks and then inject digestive enzymes that liquefy the food. Pirate bugs and damsel bugs can destroy 50 spider mites a day and can eat as many as 600 aphids in their lifetime. You will find them over-wintering under bark and leaves; they emerge in spring along with their prey.

The ladybug, also known as a lady beetle, was originally called Our Lady's beetle because of its tremendous value in crop pest control. Both the easily recognized adult and the seldom recognized larva destroy aphids, mites, mealybugs, and scales as well as other small garden pests. In spring, the adult emerges from its hibernation site under garden litter, or it hatches from a pupa hidden on a tree branch or leaf. In 5 to 13 days, each female ladybug glues as many as 1,500 orange eggs onto garden leaves. Those not eaten by predators reach adulthood in two to three weeks, so many beneficial ladybug generations occur in your garden between spring and fall.

Predaceous ground beetles run quickly this way and that as soon as you turn over a rock, log, or compost pile. They are not keen on light and come out only at night to snare tasty items such as snails, slugs, tent caterpillars, cutworms, cankerworms, and gypsy moth caterpillars. Different species may be colored dark brown, green, or black and grow to be over an inch long. Ground beetle larvae are light brown, have short legs, and look like flattened spirals with jaws. They usually remain in the soil, eating. Only one generation of ground beetles hatches each year.

You might mistake a hoverfly for a bee when you see it hovering over a flower, pollenating it while feeding on nectar. If you are uncertain, count its wings. The hoverfly has two compared to a bee's four. The hoverfly also does not sting. Sometimes known as a syrphid or flower fly, it is an insect killer only in its larval stage. A single hoverfly larva destroys an aphid a minute and also preys on mealybugs and leafhoppers.

Hoverflies begin life literally in the middle of their prey, because adult females often place their eggs in the midst of aphid clusters, where the hatching young will be sure to find food. The emerging larvae look like slimy green or tan ½-inch-long maggots with pointed mouthparts, which they use to puncture prey coverings. When they finish, only the covering remains.

Lacewing larvae, nicknamed aphid lions, suck body fluids from red spider mites, citrus mealybugs, thrips, leafhoppers, and aphids. Each can eat as many as 40 garden pests per hour. The fragile-appearing ½-inch-long green or brown adults feed primarily on aphids and mealybugs. Females lay about 500 eggs apiece, placing these on leaf undersides. The larvae are hungry as soon as they hatch, and they scatter throughout the garden searching for food, sometimes piling victim remains on their backs. Several generations may occur each year. Lacewings overwinter as pupae.

Mites can be pest or beneficial insects, depending on the species. Good mites will be predaceous, going after pest mites and pest insect eggs. Predaceous mites destroy bark beetles, Douglas fir beetles, purple scales, and cyclamen mites, which damage strawberries. Some mites eat so many pests that they expand, like tiny balloons, to 50 times their normal size.

Praying mantids hold up two spiny forelegs while waiting for a meal, as if saying a prayer before dinner. Mantids primarily destroy harmful insects, each devouring as many as 700 in its lifetime. Their meals include caterpillars, leafhoppers, aphids, crickets, and beetles. However, they also go after beneficial bees and wasps. Mantid young overwinter in egg cases concealed within shrubs and hatch in spring. There can be as many as 300 per egg case. The young are pale yellow and ½ inch long but otherwise markedly resemble their parents. Young mantids suffer hunger pangs immediately and disperse throughout your garden or neighborhood in search of prey.

Yellowjacket wasps feed destructive caterpillars to their young and can be good plant pollinators too, visiting flowers as well as ripe fruit. Although yellowjackets sting primarily to paralyze caterpillars, they will also sting gardeners who swat at them, particularly if they are protecting a nest. One commonly seen type of yellowjacket makes a papery-appearing nest inside a stump or hollow log, so be careful when sticking your hand or garden equipment inside decaying wood. The wise gardener appreciates wasps and leaves their nests alone.

Ladybugs devour aphids. If you look closely in your garden, you may see one of these helpful creatures preying on pest insects.

Parasites

Parasites usually lay their eggs within the host insect, often within eggs or larvae. The hatching parasitic larvae feed on their hosts, destroying them. Many parasites are host specific, that is, they parasitize only one or a few kinds of insects.

Many parasitic wasp species, including the common $\frac{1}{64}$-inch-long trichogramma wasp, help out in the garden. A single trichogramma can lay eggs on as many as 100 moth and butterfly eggs. As soon as the tiny larvae hatch and begin moving, the parasitized eggs stop developing. Blackening of moth and butterfly eggs is a telltale sign of trichogramma activity.

Another common parasitic wasp is the braconid, usually seen as a little white cocoon attached to the back or side of a tomato or tobacco hornworm, cabbageworm, or gypsy moth larva. The adult female braconid glues its eggs directly on caterpillars; as the braconid larvae emerge, they begin feeding on caterpillar body fluids and eventually spin cocoons that turn into other egg-laying adults. Over 500 larvae can feed on just one hornworm. Adult braconids feed mostly on aphid or mealybug honeydew.

Many parasitic flies, such as the tachinids, resemble the common house fly, except that some are slightly larger. Instead of looking for kitchen table snacks, however, tachinids stay outdoors, feeding on flower nectar or honeydew. Adult females sometimes cement their eggs to the skin of host insects; at other times they place eggs on foliage so that the pests will eat them along with the leaf. Tachinid larvae feed on their hosts' innards, causing their eventual demise. Gypsy moths, variegated cutworms, sugarcane borers, sawflies, and Mexican bean beetles are among the larvae offering unwilling hospitality. Tachinid larvae also feed on adult grasshoppers, Japanese beetles, and elm leaf beetles.

Encouraging Beneficial Insects

Some gardeners attempt to increase the number of beneficial insects around their property by introducing purchased insects. Unfortunately, this tactic rarely works. The imports do not always stay around the garden, often dispersing far and wide; at other times they die of exposure or of hunger.

Repeated studies indicate that importing ladybugs and other predators works less effectively than is often claimed. Native species usually already exist where populations of prey can support them. Imported species tend to disperse almost immediately to reduce feeding pressure.

To encourage these parasites and predators to stay at home, you first of all have to feed them. This means that your garden must offer up a plentiful supply of pests to act as meals. For example, ladybugs thrive on aphids, each one eating as many as 50 an hour. Purchased ladybugs can arrive 4,000 to a container. Release these in your garden and 200,000 aphids had better be waiting, or your predators will starve to death.

Keeping ladybugs in your garden relies partly on timing. If you set them out too early in the season, aphids may not have hatched yet, or the supply may be skimpy. If there is no food, over the fence the hungry ladybugs go, dispersing until they die or find food. If your garden's aphid population increases later on, your purchased ladybugs will be nowhere in sight. They seldom, if ever, return.

You can encourage ladybugs to stay in your garden by making certain that adequate food is present when you set them out. Keep the bugs dormant until you notice a plentiful supply of aphids. Then release the ladybugs nearby. Handle ladybugs gently, placing them by hand at the bases of infested plants. Sun-down release and a protective mulch to hide in will also encourage your ladybugs to stay home.

You can also supply artificial food in the form of a sugar-water mixture. Combine 4 parts granulated sugar with 1 part water. Squirt this onto foliage with a mister to provide a temporary food source for ladybugs until their prey multiplies sufficiently to sustain them.

Praying mantids must also have an immediate sustaining food supply. Each egg mass contains as many as 400 eggs. If you purchase these, place them in the refrigerator, not freezer, for spring release when the weather warms up. Tie each egg case with thread to a twig as high off the ground as possible, and place each in a separate garden area. The young, upon hatching, are carnivorous and hungry and often attack each other. Those that survive attacks by their siblings, ants, and other predators disperse through your garden searching for food. Each praying mantid destroys hundreds of insects, including aphids, beetles, leafhoppers, caterpillars, grasshoppers, wasps, and bees, not all of whom act as garden pests.

If you lack praying mantid food in your garden, the creature does not mind going to the insect restaurant next door or down the block. Unless you want to import insect pests along with your mantid egg cases, there is no effective way to make a mantid stay in your tomato or strawberry patch.

Trichogramma wasps, which parasitize butterfly and moth eggs, can be another "natural" purchase. Commercially available in egg form, they arrive several thousand per container. After you place your purchase outdoors, hatching occurs. Adult trichogramma wasps deposit their eggs within host insect eggs, and the growing larvae feed on, and destroy, the host eggs. Knowing when your local butterflies and moths lay eggs is important here, as is placing trichogramma eggs near host egg masses. Once again, as with mantids and ladybugs, your garden must offer sufficient prey when you set out the trichogramma eggs or the wasps will disappear.

Other imported garden parasites and predators present similar problems. Releasing these insects will not cure all that ails your garden, but if you want to try them, considering the following facts should put you ahead of the game:

• Release beneficial insects only when prey is present, or they will starve.
• Release only predators and parasites that feed on the specific pests in your garden. Some have particular pest preferences; others are general feeders.
• Release parasites and predators before pests get out of control. They too need time to reproduce and do their job, especially if their larvae make up part of the insect control process.
• Regardless of when you see pests in your garden, imports will not breed until the sun is shining fairly consistently and the temperature stays at 70° F or above.
• Unseasonal weather may allow pests to multiply at a faster rate than the more sensitive predators, disrupting even the best-laid plans.

PATHOGENIC DISEASES

Much research focuses on controlling insect pests by introducing their pathogens (disease germs) into the garden. Whether fungus, bacteria, or virus, insect disease organisms pose no danger to people or wildlife, but they do control the targeted pest. One of the most effective and widely available such pesticides is *Bacillus thuringiensis,* usually called BT. This is a naturally occurring bacterial disease organism that infects most caterpillars. Gardeners can purchase BT in spray or dust form for use throughout the garden. BT is nontoxic to birds and mammals, and you can use it close to harvest time, following label instructions.

Leaf-chewing larvae (caterpillars) of butterflies and moths ingest BT as they feed on treated foliage, and the bacteria multiply in and destroy their digestive tracts. Initially, the caterpillar loses its appetite; it then gradually becomes paralyzed and dies. You will see the dried-up remains of tent caterpillars, for instance,

It's fun to release a package of ladybugs into your garden, but they won't stay there unless they find enough insect pests to eat.

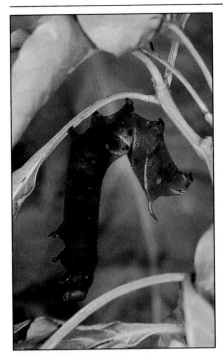

BT, an insect bacterial disease that is harmless to humans, destroys tomato hornworms and many other caterpillar pests.

dangling in the trees. Some gardeners assume that BT can't be working if the caterpillars keep moving for a while after foliage has been sprayed or dusted. Don't worry, however—they stop eating as soon as they are infected, and within three days they shrivel.

To get the best results from commercial BT, use it on young caterpillars before they are one-third grown. Many labels advise you to include a spreader-sticker in a BT spray; this helps the bacteria adhere to leaves. If it rains soon after application, you may need to respray. Check the product label for directions. Unfortunately, the bacteria do not persist in the soil, so you will need to apply it each year.

Milky spore disease is another naturally occurring organism that gardeners can purchase in dust form for lawn pest control. It infects grubs of Japanese beetles. After root-eating grubs ingest the bacterial spores, the bacteria multiply rapidly, reaching counts as high as 5 million per grub. A heavily infected grub has a characteristic milky white body fluid instead of its normal clear or slightly cloudy fluid. Infected grubs may continue to move about, but their life span becomes considerably shorter and they cease feeding. After infection, the dead grubs disintegrate, scattering bacterial spores in the surrounding soil. Other grubs ingest the spores, and the cycle starts over.

Milky spore disease has a couple of major limitations. It takes about three years for the spores to establish themselves, and that happens only if there are plenty of grubs in the soil to spread the spores about. Meanwhile, the grubs continue to damage your lawn. Also, the disease will not kill adult beetles, which can fly in from miles away.

For milky spore disease to be sufficiently effective, most entomologists recommend applying it to lawns and grassy areas communitywide. This requires considerable cooperation but brings results.

TRAPS AND BARRIERS

Gardeners use a wide variety of traps and barriers to keep pest insects out of the garden or under control. Some work, some work too well, some work partially, and some don't work well enough to be worth the effort.

Pheromone Traps

One form of trap that shows a great deal of promise is the pheromone-baited trap. Insects give off chemical signals called pheromones in order to communicate with one another. Certain odors act as danger signals, others mark the trail to a food source, and still others signal the insect's readiness to mate. Each insect species responds to its own particular pheromones. Entomologists have discovered how to harness synthetic pheromones to lure certain insects into traps. The majority of these use a female moth scent to attract males of that species.

The major problem with pheromone traps is that they tend to be overly effective. For example, in one test of sex-attractant power, a caged pine sawfly female attracted 11,000 males, not all of them from the immediate area. Japanese beetle pheromone and floral-attractant traps bring in beetles from as far away as 500 feet, many of them feeding and possibly laying eggs along the way.

Among the pheromone-baited traps now available are those specific for bagworms, leafrollers, peachtree borers, codling moths, Japanese beetles, lesser peachtree borers, rhododendron borers, California red scales, and gypsy moths.

An adhesive surface coats part of the trap, and the attractant pheromone may be in replaceable pellets or capsules. The victims fly right in, eager to mate. Instead, they become stuck on the adhesive. Because many insects are attracted to the color yellow, many pheromone trap containers have yellow landing pads.

Unfortunately, you can't assume that pheromone traps will end your insect pest problems. Currently available pheromone traps only work well enough to indicate that you have a pest problem— they won't trap all insects before they have mated or damaged plants. Commercial growers use pheromone traps to tell them it is time to apply insecticide. If they trap a troublesome pest, they begin a spray program; if they don't trap any pests, they won't spray. This saves the cost of insecticide and reduces labor.

You can use pheromone traps in the same way. For instance, set traps for codling moths in fruit trees when petals fall, and check them every two to three days for trapped moths. If, after three or four weeks you have caught fewer than 15 moths, no spray is needed. But if your catch is greater, you should probably apply pesticide. When moths no longer appear in the trap, control measures can stop, at least temporarily. Garden vigilance is always necessary, however, because some pests may not fly into the trap, and others may immigrate into your garden from other areas.

Sticky Traps

Some gardeners swear by certain sticky traps for controlling insect pests in fruit trees. These attract pests by their color and shape, not their aroma. You smear the traps with a sticky substance from a tube. Round, red balls lure apple maggot flies, which attempt to lay eggs in the applelike sphere—they get stuck instead. White triangles mimic apple blossoms, attracting tarnished plant bugs to their deaths. You will need one to six red spheres per tree, depending on the tree size, and four white triangles no matter what the size. If you have a quantity of fruit trees, all those traps can be expensive.

A new sticky trap product designed to catch whiteflies as well as the flying stages of aphids, leafminers, gnats, fruit flies, and leafhoppers (Ortho Whitefly Sticky Trap) relies on the insects' proclivity for the color yellow. A component color of green foliage, yellow acts as a lure for many foliage-eating insects. These sticky snares can be hung in infested plants, attracting the insects away from the foliage and trapping them on the sticky surface.

You can also encircle tree trunks with sticky bands, using them as a barrier to prevent caterpillars and other trunk-climbing pests from reaching the foliage to feed or lay eggs. Gardeners once used roofing tar as an insect-trapping sticky band, but now you can purchase specially created sticky-band traps for this purpose. Do not apply the sticky substance directly to the tree's bark, because it may injure the tissue beneath and even kill the tree. Follow the label instructions carefully. These usually advise you to wrap a 2-inch-wide band of masking tape around the tree trunk. (Fill any gaps between tape and bark with cotton.) Paint or spoon the sticky stuff onto the tape.

Sticky bands ensnare pest insects such as cankerworms, gypsy moth caterpillars, and adult cankerworm moths, which can crawl, but don't fly. These crawl up trees to lay eggs and feed, often returning to the ground at night or several times a day. The sticky band interferes with their progress.

Apply sticky bands in May and again in October to trap both moths and larvae. Destroy and replace the bands as they fill with insects, because dead pests can create a bridge over the barrier.

Light Traps

Light-attractant traps are sometimes recommended as another pest-catching alternative, although most entomologists do not advise them for home garden use. Light traps, which can be quite expensive, contain an internal light or lights in combination with a sticky surface, electrocuting grid, or fan that sucks bugs into a collecting container. Night-flying insects, such as codling moths and moths of corn earworms, cabbage loopers, hornworms, and cutworms, will be lured by particular colors in the ultraviolet spectrum.

There are several problems with using light traps in gardens. They attract only night-active insects; day-active insects are not affected. A second hitch occurs because insects will travel long distances to their favorite light color. Importing pests is not your goal, and if some don't make it to the trap but stop on the way, you can have more problems than when you started. Finally, light traps are indiscriminate, zapping both good and bad bugs with equal vigor. Some studies have shown that light traps destroy large numbers of beneficial insects. They're most useful for allowing commercial growers to monitor pest insect presence.

Other Traps

Other homemade traps that are useful on a small-scale basis include boards and flowerpots placed out at night as snail and slug traps. These moisture-loving pests feed at night and seek cool, damp shelter during the day. They hide under the boards and pots, and you can collect and destroy them each morning. Earwigs seem fond of hiding in rolled newspapers during the day. Set these out in the garden, and discard them each morning.

Some gardeners place a pie pan of beer in the garden to trap snails and slugs. Attracted by the yeasty aroma, the snails supposedly crawl in, absorb the alcohol, and drown. However, many slugs stagger away unharmed or fall in and crawl back out.

Barriers

Barriers may block pests from your prized plants, but they often require a lot of work. For example, trench barriers can be some help in keeping chinch bug infestations down, and aluminum strip-

ping around field borders deters some saltmarsh caterpillars.

On a smaller scale, scattering wood ashes around the bases of plants slows down some crawling insects that don't like to move over the harsh texture. Gardeners often employ sharp sand or cinders to ward off slugs and snails. These work fairly well until the stuff gets wet. Then hungry slugs and snails can produce enough slime to slide uninjured across the sharp barrier.

Another barrier you might consider, depending on your garden needs, is a homemade collar for protecting seedlings from cutworm ravages. Milk carton sides do fine, as do tin cans with tops and bottoms removed. To block soil-burrowing cutworms, both should be inserted 1 inch into the ground around seedlings as soon as you set them out.

GOOD GARDENING PRACTICES

Controlling insects by changing some of your gardening habits can help reduce pest problems.

Crop Choice

The easiest cultural control is to plant resistant varieties, those that are not often troubled or injured by insect attack. Some plants tolerate pest invasions with relatively little loss of crops, foliage, or flowers. Others repel insects by their taste or aroma.

If you have had a particular pest problem in the past, study your garden catalogs for pest-resistant varieties. When you buy seeds or plants at a nursery, you

may find information about pest resistance on the label. However, plant varieties that resist pests in one area may not have that resistance in another area, due to differences in soil, weather, rainfall, and many other factors. Ask a knowledgeable local nursery employee or call your county agricultural extension agent for information on resistant varieties.

Crop rotation involves not planting the same crop in the same place each season. Changing plant sites can be hard in a small garden, but you should try it if you have had a severe crop infestation in previous years. This is especially true of soil pests, such as nematodes and wireworms. Many insects lay overwintering eggs on their favorite plants or hibernate in weeds nearby. Rotating crops gives these insects a longer distance to travel for food supplies. Those with short-range mobility will be starved out or reduced in number.

If you don't have alternate sites because of your garden's size, vary your crops each year so that particular pests will not have an ongoing food supply.

You can also foil some insects by changing planting times or by planting varieties that mature earlier or later. Provide an insect's favorite food when it is not around. For example, seed maggots are most active in the cool, wet soils of early spring. If you delay corn, bean, pea, and melon planting until the soil warms up thoroughly, seed maggots do less damage, reducing your crop loss. Planting early-maturing summer squash rather than late-season squash permits harvesting before squash vine borers reach peak populations. Selecting late-blooming fruit and nut trees in areas infested by codling moths, which lay eggs in early spring, can save quite a bit of your crop.

Proper Soil Care and Composting

Soil tilling exposes soil insects to bad weather and predators, keeping the pest population down. Do not wait until

Opposite left: Boards or inverted pots will lure slugs, but be sure to empty these traps regularly, or they will provide staging areas from which slugs can eat plants. Opposite right: Three-inch-wide rings made of milk cartons or aluminum foil inserted 1 inch into the soil will help save your seedlings from cutworms.

spring to spade soil. Do it in late fall after you have cleaned the vegetable or flower bed. If you spade or overturn soil, preferably to 9 inches deep, you will bring up many grubs and pupae. This deep spading also buries other insects, such as grasshopper nymphs, beyond their emergence power.

Always keep your garden free of plant debris. Piles of decaying leaves, fallen fruit, or trash provide hiding places for many destructive insects, including codling moths, Colorado potato beetles, stink bugs, fall webworms, gypsy moths, spider mites, slugs, snails, ants, and spotted cucumber beetles. Insects also seek shelter in weeds, laying their eggs in the surrounding soil and on the weeds themselves. Weed-sheltered insects include stink bugs, chinch bugs, leafhoppers, weevils, curculios, Mexican bean beetles, Colorado potato beetles, and flea beetles. Other insects, such as walnut husk flies and cherry maggots, enter the soil from fallen infested nuts or fruit.

When you collect weeds and garden litter with the intention of composting them, you should not assume that accompanying pests and their eggs will be killed. If the internal temperature of the compost pile does not reach 140° F, you may merely be giving your bugs a comfortable place to spend the winter.

An iron pipe placed in the middle of a compost pile helps you check the internal temperature. If you have constructed a new pile properly, the pipe will begin to heat up in a few days. After a week, the pipe will be too hot to hold, signaling a compost temperature capable of destroying pests near the pipe. A few weeks later, your compost pile will begin cooling down as its oxygen supply, and thus its decomposition rate, decreases. When the temperature drops, turn the pile thoroughly. This allows air to reach all parts of the compost, causing it to begin decomposing and heating up again. Turning also mixes the ingredients, giving you a chance to place the outer layers in the center so that they can heat up too.

Insects cannot tolerate the heat of a working compost pile. If your compost pile does not get hot enough, it may be too small or too dry. Water lightly each time you turn the pile, but don't saturate the ingredients or the pile will smell like rotten eggs.

Healthy Plants

Some insects prefer plants that are weak or already ailing over healthy ones. Overfertilized plants have lush, weak growth that often attracts aphids and mites. Wet, soggy soil harbors seed maggots. Many mite species prefer water-stressed plants, often troubling plants grown where it is dry and dusty. An improper growing site can also create pest problems. For instance, lace bugs proliferate on azaleas grown in full sun, but not on those in light shade.

Properly planted, watered, and fertilized plants grow most vigorously and can often ward off insect attacks. The key is to provide the appropriate amounts of sun, fertilizer, and water—too much is often as bad as too little.

For cultural control to be effective, just one method will not do; you must employ several at once. Combining these cultural methods with careful insecticide applications gives you maximum relief from insect pests.

ENCYCLOPEDIA OF INSECT PESTS

This chapter describes the most common insect pests infesting garden plants. Use it as a reference, browsing through these pages to look for pests you have seen in your garden. You will find the pests discussed alphabetically by their common names. Photographs accompany each entry for easy pest identification. Each of the more than 60 entries tells you about several related pests.

When battling garden insects, it is important to identify the pest correctly. You may recognize the culprit by its photograph, but don't jump to conclusions. Read the beginning of the entry, which describes the damage the pest causes, the plants it infests, and other details, such as the seasons during which infestations usually occur. To help clinch your identification look for clues and descriptions under the section entitled The Pest.

If the pest you are trying to identify resembles one in a photograph but is not exactly like it, be sure to read the accompanying text, especially The Pest. The descriptions of different species given there may include the exact pest you are after, one that perhaps differs in color or size from the one photographed. This section also contains information about each pest's life cycle and reproductive habits, helping you time your control measures properly.

If you don't recognize the pest by a photograph, double check the photographs of beneficial insects on page 26. Rather than a pest, the insect could be a parasitic or predatory insect helping out by feeding on pest insects.

For more help in identifying a particular pest, try your county's cooperative

Eastern tent caterpillars prefer apple trees, but they readily feed on other fruit and shade trees.

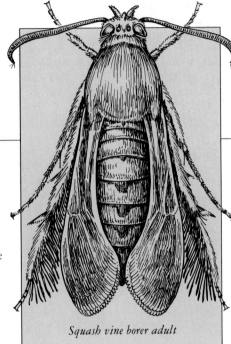

Squash vine borer adult

Here is a rogues' gallery of common insect pests. Photos give you a mug shot of each insect; the text explains the pest's modus operandi and tells you what you need to know to save your treasured garden plants.

agricultural extension service. It probably provides an insect identification service. You can take or mail in a sample of the insect pest and infested plant for a correct diagnosis. Or, seek advice from a knowledgeable person at your local nursery. Nursery personnel often know exactly what pests cause problems in local gardens.

After you have identified a pest, read the Control Measures section at the end of the entry to learn the best and most effective ways to rid your garden of the insect. Because you often use different insecticides for food crops than you use for ornamental plants, you will find control methods for fruits, vegetables, flowers, trees, and shrubs listed separately. The common name (generic name) of a recommended insecticide appears first; brand names of Ortho products containing that active ingredient and approved for use against the particular pest appear in parentheses after the generic name. You will find instructions for effectively using alternate control methods, such as traps and barriers, discussed in that section as well.

Be sure to read the first three chapters of this book before you begin control attempts. These describe in detail many of the control methods and insect life cycles and habits mentioned in the insect pest encyclopedia. The first chapter, "Insects in Your Garden," helps you better understand the pests you are trying to rid from your garden. There you'll read about insect growth and development and insect life cycles.

The third chapter, "Additional Methods of Pest Control," describes nonpesticide control measures in detail. There you'll find out which methods work successfully and which ones don't live up to their reputations. You'll learn about how to keep and attract beneficial insects and about when to release them into your garden for maximum effectiveness. "Using Pesticides Safely and Effectively," the second chapter, provides important safety information about using garden insecticides and application equipment. This chapter details everything you need to know about applying, storing, and disposing of insecticides. Read it before you purchase or begin handling garden chemicals. Your own safety and that of your family—and even your garden—may depend upon it!

ANTS

Except for the icebound ant-arctic and arctic areas, ants occur throughout the world. You most often see $\frac{1}{16}$- to $\frac{1}{4}$-inch-long brown, black, or reddish species, in both winged and wingless forms. However, ants can be shades of yellow, blue, green, and even metallic, and a few, such as the carpenter ant, can measure up to 1 inch long. Some ant species, such as the legionary ant and the fire ant, bite or sting severely, so you want to discourage them from setting up housekeeping in your garden.

To distinguish ants from similar-appearing insects, such as termites, note that ants have enlarged abdomens and narrow waists, whereas termites have parallel-sided abdomens and broad waists.

Most garden problems caused by ants occur indirectly from their habit of collecting and tending aphids, scale insects, and mealybugs, which they milk for their sugary honeydew by stroking their bodies. Ants actually carry these pests to their nests and transport them from plant to plant. Honeydew attracts

species also kill the grass surrounding their nests. They occasionally are guilty of stealing seeds or gnawing tubers and roots.

Lines of ants marching up and down tree trunks are usually a sign that aphids or other sucking insects are infesting the tree. Be sure to control the aphids along with the ants. Ants on peony buds may annoy you, but they do no harm. They are probably feeding on sap that is excreted by the buds.

The Pest

An ant colony consists of three castes: males, females, and workers. In general, winged males and females hatch once a year. These mate during a wedding flight from the nest, after which the males die and the females, called young queens, attempt to establish their own nests, usually in soil. However, ants also establish colonies in oak galls, under rocks, and in rotting trees and logs.

A queen who is establishing a new nest lays eggs that hatch into grubs, which she tends and feeds. These pupate eventually into wingless workers, which then care for the

To keep ant populations down, you must eliminate aphids, whiteflies, soft scales, mealybugs, and leafhoppers, all of which produce the honeydew that attracts ants and promotes ant colonies. (See the entries for these insects for the appropriate control measures.) Begin treatment at the first sign of insects, damage, or honeydew buildup.

To control ants that are infesting fruits, vegetables, lawns, flowers, trees, and shrubs, apply diazinon, or use a bait containing carbaryl (Ortho Bug-Geta Plus® Snail, Slug & Insect Granules) around listed plants.

Treat anthills in lawns with a diazinon compound (Ortho Diazinon Soil & Turf Insect Control, Ortho Diazinon Insect Spray, Ortho Fire Ant Killer Granules), chlorpyrifos (Ortho Fire Ant Control), or carbaryl (Ortho Liquid Sevin®). Repeat the application if new mounds appear. Reseed any bare spots after ants are controlled.

APHIDS, NAKED

More than 800 species of aphid have been identified, and they infest all kinds of plants. The more common ones will sometimes be named for their preferred plant host, such as green peach aphid, potato aphid, cotton aphid, bean aphid, and chrysanthemum aphid. Aphids are sometimes called green flies after their most common color, plant lice because they suck sap, and ant cows because ants sometimes milk them for honeydew.

Aphids feed by inserting a needlelike beak, composed of four stylets, into stems and leaves and then sucking out plant sap. They target new growth, which is juicy and tender, but victimize plants at any stage.

Aphids often seek out young, actively growing plant growth. Flower buds, like this rosebud, are a common target.

Heavily infested leaves yellow, curl, and become distorted. Aphids can harden buds and disfigure flowers. Plants may be stunted or killed. Some aphid species cause bark to crack and roughen, allowing the entrance of fungi, bacteria, and insects.

Aphids often cannot digest all the plant sap they ingest, and so they excrete the remainder as a sugary liquid called honeydew. Where aphid infestations are heavy, this shiny, sticky substance coats leaves and fruit and may become covered with unsightly sooty mold fungus. On trees such as tulip tree and maple, honeydew can become profuse enough to drip from the tree and create a mess below on a sidewalk or patio. Honeydew dripping onto parked cars damages the finish and paint.

In small numbers, aphids do no harm. They breed prolifically and often continuously, however, quickly reaching sizable numbers. Each female can produce 100 young during its lifetime, and the young mature and are ready to reproduce a week after birth. Most of the young remain to feed alongside their mother, so that populations seem to increase to damaging levels overnight.

Along with leafhoppers, aphids are the most common and widespread carriers of plant diseases. Aphids moving from plant to plant frequently

If you see many ants on a plant, look for the pests they are herding. Here ants tend a flock of aphids.

flies and wasps and may become covered with an unsightly black sooty mold fungus, which disfigures and shades foliage.

Ants can damage your garden directly by creating mounds which, if large enough, interfere with the use of yard equipment. Some ant

eggs that the queen continues to lay. Egg-hatching time varies according to the species.

Control Measures

Traps sometimes help in controlling ants. You might try a sticky adhesive band (see page 29) around tree bases to catch ants that are going after fruit or tending to their herds of aphids.

spread virus diseases, which can slowly kill a plant by reducing its vigor, health, and productivity. They transmit the virus when they inject their stylets into the plant.

The Pest

Aphids are slow-moving oval or pear-shaped, soft-bodied insects ranging in length from $1/16$ to $1/4$ inch. Most adults have no wings, but winged forms appear at specific times. Aphid body color varies and includes light green, dark green, white, pink, red, dark brown, black, blue, yellow, and combinations of these colors. Some aphids resemble mealybugs and sport a woolly coat. (See Aphids, Woolly, page 36.)

The aphid life cycle is complex; it seems to have evolved as a means of maximizing the reproduction rate. There is a male form, a female form, a stem mother form, and a winged form. Stem mothers are veritable aphid factories, producing live young, one right after another, without ever mating. The young nymphs, which are ready to give birth in about a week, can often be seen lined up behind the mother in order of birth, from smallest to largest, assembly-line fashion. When aphid populations become larger than their food supplies, the stem mothers give birth to winged aphids, which fly away to other host plants and establish new colonies.

Fertile males and females appear and mate only when cold weather approaches. The fertilized females lay eggs that overwinter and in spring hatch into stem mothers, which begin the cycle again.

Different species of aphid infest nearly all types of plants. Some species have a definite host or group of hosts, and others have a wide host range.

Examples of plants they commonly attack include apple, oak, pecan, maple, crape myrtle, stock, marigold, calendula, snapdragon, rose, strawberry, bean, spinach, pea, and Kentucky bluegrass.

In addition to laying eggs, aphids give birth to live young. This winged female is delivering a live nymph.

Control Measures

Normally, natural predators, such as hoverfly larvae, aphid lions, ladybugs, and braconid parasitic wasps, keep aphid populations from overrunning your garden. But when an aphid infestation becomes obvious, it is large enough to harm your plants, and control measures are necessary.

Some gardeners recommend spraying infested plants forcefully with a garden hose to wash off aphid colonies. Although this removes aphids, it does not kill them, and it may disperse the pests to other plants where they can begin new colonies.

Because aphids multiply so rapidly, be on the lookout for them as soon as growth starts in spring.

Examine new shoots and tender foliage in your orchard, flower bed, and shrub border. At the first sight of aphids, begin control measures. When you attack aphids with insecticides, it is important to cover foliage thoroughly with the spray. When applied in spring, systemics are especially effective in preventing aphids from becoming established on ornamentals. The plants absorb the pesticide, and it remains active for several weeks, ready to poison any aphid that dares take a nibble.

Many insecticides provide thorough aphid control in spray, dust, or granule form. The best choice depends on the kind of plant you are treating.

For ornamentals, a diazinon spray (Ortho Diazinon Insect Spray) is one choice. The systemic acephate (Orthene® Systemic Insect Control, Orthenex® Rose and Flower Spray) provides long-lasting control for listed plants. Malathion (Orthenex® Rose & Floral Dust, Ortho Malathion 50 Insect Spray) also controls aphids on roses and listed ornamentals.

For vegetables, your choice depends upon how long it will be until you harvest. Diazinon dust (Ortho Diazinon Soil & Foliage Dust, Ortho Fruit & Vegetable Insect Control), malathion (Ortho Malathion 50 Insect Spray), carbaryl (Ortho Sevin® Garden Spray), and pyrethrins (Ortho Tomato & Vegetable Insect Spray) control aphids and other pests.

On fruit trees, choose malathion, alone (Ortho Malathion 50 Insect Spray) or in a multipurpose spray containing a captan-malathion-methoxychlor mix (Ortho Home Orchard Spray). On citrus trees, use an oil-ethion combination (Ortho Citrus Insect Spray).

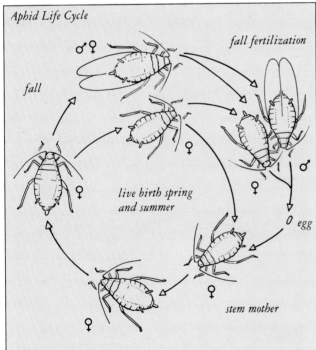

Aphid Life Cycle

fall fertilization

fall

♂♀

♀

live birth spring and summer

♂

♀

0 egg

♀

stem mother

♀

During spring and summer most aphids are female stem mothers, which give birth to live young without mating. Young are ready to reproduce in about a week, allowing populations to seemingly explode in a few weeks. As fall approaches, fertile males and females are born, mature, and mate. Eggs overwinter and hatch into the next season's stem mothers.

APHIDS, WOOLLY

Unlike most other species of aphids, woolly aphids infest only woody plants, attacking nearly all kinds of trees and shrubs. They often infest apple, pear, pyracantha, honeysuckle, mountain ash, hawthorn, alder, quince, pine, larch, maple, and elm. Severe infestations can cause great economic damage to forests as well as to home orchards and ornamental plantings.

Woolly aphids attack trunks, branches, roots, and sometimes foliage. These black insects are noticeable because they are covered with a white, cottony wax. Leaves of infested plants turn yellow, twist, and curl. Marble-sized growths, called galls, can develop on branches or roots where woolly aphids cluster to suck up plant sap.

Young plants severely infested with root aphids become stunted and may not survive. Because aphids interfere with the flow of water and nutrients from the roots, older plants with root galls

You might mistake woolly aphids for mealybugs, but if you push aside the fluff, you will see the familiar aphid form. These are apple aphids.

weaken and may die. They can also become weak enough to blow over in strong winds.

To check for root aphids, carefully pull away soil from around the tree's trunk and large roots. If present, the woolly aphids and galls will be clearly visible. Anthills often appear around trees infested with root aphids.

Like the naked aphids, woolly aphids excrete honeydew, a sweet, sticky substance that can drip down limbs. Honeydew not only attracts flies and wasps, but it can be a nuisance when it drips onto cars, lawn furniture, and patios beneath infested trees. Black sooty mold fungus often grows on honeydew, creating unsightly fruit and foliage. Sooty mold is not a disease, but it can become thick enough to block sunlight from leaves, further weakening the infested plant.

The Pest
Woolly aphids are small, sluggish, soft-bodied insects measuring $1/10$ to $1/8$ inch. Their black or purple bodies hide beneath a thick covering of gray or white waxy threads, resembling tiny cotton balls. You might mistake an infestation of woolly aphids for a mealybug invasion because a white cottony coat covers them, too. However, mealybugs have short tufts of wax along their body margins, whereas long, wavy wax strands cover woolly aphids. Woolly aphids cluster primarily at the bases of plants and on pruning cuts. Mealybugs live on leaves and stems, and you will see the insects wandering separately.

Woolly aphids reproduce in a manner similar to the more common naked aphid species, at the rate of many generations a year. Mated females lay eggs in bark crevices as cold weather approaches. In spring, overwintering eggs hatch, and young nymphs develop into wingless stem mothers, feeding where they hatch. Stem mothers do not require fertilization to reproduce, and they give birth only to female young. These nymphs mature and begin reproducing in approximately eight days, and so large populations can quickly infest trees.

In early summer, winged aphids hatch and fly off to start new colonies on nearby trees and shrubs. In the fall, sexual males and females are born, mate, and lay overwintering eggs.

Control Measures
Woolly aphids can be more difficult to control than naked aphids because their woolly covering protects them from pesticides and predators. Ladybugs feed on aphids from spring until fall, as do parasitic wasps in late spring and midsummer. But if woolly aphid populations threaten the health of your trees, you may need stronger control measures.

On ornamentals and fruit trees, a horticultural oil spray (Ortho Volck® Oil Spray) used as a dormant spray in early spring helps keep populations down by smothering the more vulnerable overwintering eggs. A more dilute oil spray used during summer effectively smothers mature insects. Oil sprays can be combined with other insecticides, such as malathion (Ortho Malathion 50 Insect Spray), to give more complete control.

With gall-inducing woolly aphids, apply insecticide during early summer and late fall to wipe them out during their vulnerable flying stage. A malathion spray, used alone (Ortho Malathion 50 Insect Spray) or in a multipurpose orchard spray containing a captan-malathion-methoxychlor mix (Ortho Home Orchard Spray) controls woolly aphids on fruit trees. Or use diazinon (Ortho Fruit & Vegetable Insect Control) whenever populations become noticeable. Be sure that you spray trunks and branches as well as foliage.

On ornamentals, use diazinon (Ortho Diazinon Insect Spray) or malathion (Ortho Malathion 50 Insect Spray), but if curled leaves give additional haven to

woolly aphids or if aphids infest roots, use a systemic, such as acephate (Orthene® Systemic Insect Control).

Although you cannot use a systemic insecticide on fruit trees to rid roots of woolly aphids, keeping the branches free of these insects reduces the populations on the roots. You can also make a soil drench of diazinon and pour it on the soil over the roots, according to the label directions. Reapply two weeks later if you still see root aphids. When planting new roses and shrubs, use a preplanting insecticide (Ortho Systemic Rose & Flower Care 8-12-4) to ward off woolly aphid infestation.

ARMYWORMS

After armyworms have eaten everything green in one area, they head out in troops to search for greener pastures. They will march from your lawn to your vegetable garden and then right over the fence to your neighbor's garden. After laying waste there, they may make a return visit to your lawn.

The Pest
Armyworm caterpillars are light tan to dark brown with yellow, orange, or dark brown stripes down the lengths of their backs. They range in size from $3/4$ inch to 2 inches long. Adult moths are tan or mottled gray with a wingspan of approximately 1 inch. They fly only at night.

Like the adults, armyworm caterpillars are active at night and on overcast days. In full daylight they hide in soil around grass roots. Because of their nocturnal habits, you may not notice their presence until feeding damage becomes extensive.

During a lawn infestation, you will see chewed grass blades and circular bare areas

Armyworms are marked with green, black, yellow, or orange racing stripes. Lawns and other plants disappear when these night feeders attack a garden.

that gradually become larger. The caterpillars, hatching from eggs laid on leaf blades, munch the blades right down to their bases. With heavy infestations, armyworms can completely strip a lawn in two or three days.

When armyworms attack corn, they feed on leaves, ears, and ear stalks. You will notice chewed leaf edges, and some leaves will be completely shredded. Those species that attack beets and lettuce destroy seedlings as well as skeletonize the leaves of mature plants.

Several generations of armyworms occur during the growing season. The first generation, beginning in mid-May, causes the most damage. Armyworms are especially numerous after cold, wet spring weather. Such weather slows the development of natural parasites, such as braconid and trichogramma wasps.

Armyworm moths migrate in fall from cold climates to warmer ones and return in spring to lay eggs on grass blades. The emerging caterpillars feed for several weeks and then pupate in topsoil, emerging as adult moths to start the cycle again.

Control Measures
Check your lawn in May for signs of armyworm infestation. If symptoms lead you to suspect armyworms, inspect grass blades on an overcast day to search for the actual pest. Spray immediately with chlorpyrifos (Ortho Lawn Insect Spray), diazinon (Ortho Diazinon Insect Spray), or carbaryl (Ortho Liquid Sevin®), or use a fertilizer spreader to apply diazinon granules (Ortho Diazinon Soil & Turf Insect Control). The systemic acephate (Orthene® Systemic Insect Control) will give protection for up to three weeks. Repeat as directed on the label.

At the first sign of armyworm damage to vegetables, use carbaryl (Ortho Sevin® Garden Dust, Ortho Sevin® Garden Spray) or diazinon spray (Ortho Fruit & Vegetable Insect Control). For best results, apply in early morning or late evening, when air temperatures are low and the air is still. Repeat as directed on the label.

BAGWORMS

Starting at the top and working downward, leaf-eating bagworms can completely defoliate a large tree. A bagworm infestation often kills evergreens, such as arborvitae and cedar, but may only slow the growth of a deciduous plant, which can grow a new set of leaves in midsummer.

Found from Massachusetts to Florida and all the way west to Texas and Oklahoma, bagworms attack box elder, black locust, basswood, apple, wild cherry, sycamore, elm, persimmon, poplar, maple, linden, and citrus; they are a frequent pest of most evergreens as well.

The Pest
You probably won't notice the pests themselves, but you will see the spindle-shaped bags they call home. These protective pouches, made of interwoven dead foliage, small twigs, and silk, reach about 2 inches long and dangle from twigs almost like Christmas tree ornaments. In winter each bag contains up to a thousand eggs. By May or June, dark brown caterpillars with white or yellow heads and black-spotted thoraxes hatch from the pouch and disperse throughout the tree. These small caterpillars can be blown to other trees, their silken threads acting like parachutes. Each larva begins weaving its own bag, using pieces of the host tree.

As leaves are devoured, the growing larva moves on, dragging its bag along. By late August, the 1- to 2-inch-long bagworm finishes feeding and attaches its bag to a twig. Inside the bag it pupates, and several days later an adult moth emerges from the pupa.

The adult female, resembling a white grub, stays inside its bag. The male, a small black moth with a furry body and feathered antennae, flies to a bag containing a female, and they mate while the female is still inside. After the female lays a mass of eggs within the bag, it dies.

Control Measures
Between October and May, you can try picking off egg-containing bags, but be sure to do a thorough job because each contains as many as a thousand eggs. Destroy the bags immediately, or place them in a tightly sealed container. If you discard bags in a compost heap or open container, the larvae will hatch and crawl away to affix themselves to any nearby shelter, including your house.

BT insecticide sprays, which contain bacteria pathogenic to caterpillars, will control bagworms. Use these sprays between late May and mid-July.

You may also be able to purchase pheromone traps with specific bagworm bait at a nearby garden supply store. Pheromone traps attract the adult male moth. They have some effect in reducing next year's population by preventing mating and egg laying, but they must be set out in August during bagworm mating season.

For thorough bagworm control, spray the entire plant, covering both sides of the foliage. On ornamentals or fruit trees, use diazinon (Ortho Diazinon Insect Spray), malathion (Malathion 50 Insect Spray, Ortho Home Orchard Spray), or carbaryl (Ortho Liquid Sevin®). On ornamentals, you can also use the highly

You can hand-pick and destroy bagworms from a small shrub, but to save a tall tree, sprays are usually necessary.

effective systemic acephate (Orthene® Systemic Insect Control, Ortho Bagworm Killer).

Pesticides control small larvae best, so begin applying insecticide in May in the South and in June in the North. Be certain that your plant is listed on the label of the product you plan to use. Spray again 10 days later if you still see active bagworms.

BARK BEETLES AND TREE BORERS

Insects that are often called borers attack trees and other woody plants by tunneling beneath their bark or boring into trunks and branches. The wormlike, boring or tunneling grubs may be the larvae of either bark beetles or clearwing moths; regardless of their origin, they cause severe damage to trees.

Infestations of bark beetles and borers result in dead buds, twigs, and limbs and sometimes even dead trees. A few species attack healthy trees, but most prefer trees and shrubs that are already weakened or injured from transplant shock, drought, overwatering, improper planting, mechanical injury, or the attacks of leaf-eating insects.

For instance, dogwood trees grown in lawns and gardens often die from borer attack brought on by severe stress. Native dogwoods grow as forest understory trees and prefer slight shade and even moisture. Planted in a lawn, a dogwood usually bakes in the summer sun, and its trunk suf-

Bark beetle tunnels make striking and deadly patterns under tree bark. Tunnels weaken the tree and let fungus in.

fers repeated injuries from bumps with the lawn mower. Dogwood trees that are injured and under water stress offer easy prey for borers. In contrast, borers seldom invade woodland dogwoods growing in ideal conditions.

Once you notice symptoms of borer infestation, the damage is usually already serious. And once they are established, borers are extremely difficult to eliminate. You will find that it is far easier to prevent attacks by these insects than to cure them.

Borers first announce their presence to the observant gardener by their small entry and exit holes in tree bark. On closer inspection of these holes, you usually see wood dust, frass (insect excrement), tree sap, or pitch nearby. The next symptoms may be wilting, yellowing, early leaf drop, or dying back of branches.

Some borers tunnel deep into a branch, reducing its strength until it becomes so weak that it snaps in a strong wind. Others tunnel and feed just beneath tree bark, impeding nutrient flow throughout the infested part. With severe attacks on trunks, an entire tree or shrub can die. Bark beetles also introduce fungus diseases, which can block the flow of both water and nutrients within the tree, causing its death.

The Pest

Hundreds of different borer species infest trees, shrubs, and herbaceous plants.

The very destructive bark beetles attack coniferous, ornamental, and fruit trees, often feeding from the top of a plant downward. Adult beetles are usually black, brown, or dark red and 1/16 to 1/4 inch long. Shothole borers, hickory bark beetles, and ambrosia beetles belong to this group, as well as the European and native elm bark beetles, which transmit the deadly Dutch elm disease fungus,

Both the adult beetles and their cream-white 1/16- to 1/4-inch-long grubs burrow into and destroy cambium tissue, the vital layer of inner bark responsible for trunk growth.

Adult beetles lay eggs in tunnels beneath the bark. Larvae hatch from the eggs and bore their own tunnels away from those of their parents, creating characteristic tunnel designs called galleries. These designs help identify the species of borer. You can observe these tunnels by peeling away a small section of infested bark. When fully grown, the larvae form cells within the tree bark, pupate over the winter, and then emerge as adult beetles in May or June.

The larvae of flatheaded borer beetles, such as honey locust borer, bronze birch borer, flatheaded prune tree borer, and flatheaded appletree borer, make flat or oval tunnels between tree bark and wood, cutting off sap flow and loosening the bark. As

Healthy trees are less likely to be attacked by bark beetles. Here, an adult bark beetle crawls amid its entry and exit holes—signs of damage inside.

the larvae feed, you may observe dark sunken areas on the bark at the infested site. The 1/4- to 1-inch-long adults have an attractive metallic luster; the larvae are yellowish white, legless grubs with large, flattened heads. In mid-May to mid-June, sun-loving adult beetles of some species crawl up and down the south sides of trees and mate. The females deposit their eggs in crevices of injured bark.

The larvae of roundheaded borer beetles, such as roundheaded appletree borer, hickory bark borer, locust borer, and poplar borer, make rounded, pencil-sized tunnels in the heartwood of a tree.

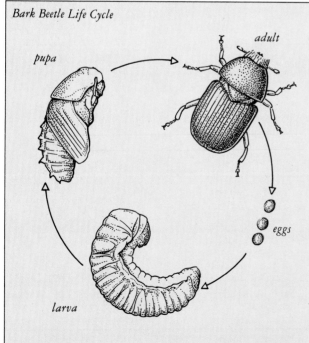

Bark Beetle Life Cycle

pupa

adult

eggs

larva

Adult bark beetles mate and then lay eggs in tunnels under tree bark. The eggs hatch into larvae, which make side galleries as they feed. The fully grown larvae form pupae, which emerge as adult beetles the following summer.

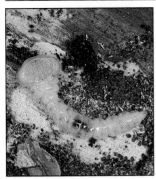

Flatheaded borer larvae eat random paths under the bark of trees and shrubs and then overwinter there.

The striped or spotted adult beetles vary in size from 1/4 inch to more than 3 inches long. All have long antennae, usually longer than their bodies. The larvae, usually yellowish white grubs, can reach a length of 3 inches and have large, rounded heads.

Clearwing moth larvae tunnel through the woody parts of many fruit trees as well as raspberry, cottonwood, grape, lilac, ash, clematis, dogwood, and rhododendron, among other common garden plants.

Although symptoms vary with the moth species, if you have peach, plum, cherry, apricot, or nectarine trees in your garden, you may already be familiar with the depredations of the very common peachtree borer. A gummy exudate and brown frass at the base of a tree or in a branch crotch are the first signs of the attack of this pest. The exudate increases as damage progresses. Repeated attacks over several seasons can kill the tree.

The adult moth begins laying eggs in June near the base of the tree. When the eggs hatch about 10 days later, the larvae bore into the trunk anywhere from 3 inches below ground to 10 inches above ground. Small trees seldom survive repeated infestations.

Control Measures
An ounce of prevention goes a long way in preventing borer infestations. Borers usually shun healthy, vigorous trees and shrubs and seek out weak or injured ones. Water deeply during drought, and fertilize annually. Plant trees and shrubs in appropriate light and soil conditions to avoid stress.

Prune in late fall or early winter to allow the wounds to heal when borer beetles and moths are not active; summer pruning offers fresh wounds for easy entrance. Dress large pruning wounds with tree paint (Ortho Pruning Sealer) to keep out insects.

Borers frequently infest injuries at the bases of trees caused by repeated bumping with a lawn mower or other equipment. It is a good idea to remove the grass surrounding lawn trees and replace it with a ring of shredded bark, ground cover, pebbles, or even bare ground.

With mild infestations, you can eliminate borers by pruning off branches and twigs that show signs of borer attack. Do this as soon as you see holes and frass. Burn or destroy the prunings to keep the borers from spreading.

In spring, metallic-colored flatheaded borer adults emerge and crawl on the sunny sides of trees. They mate and then lay eggs wherever bark is injured.

Some gardeners attempt to control borers by digging them out of infested trees with a sharp knife or by peeling back bark to expose the larvae. This can further damage a tree, however, so leave this type of treatment to a professional tree surgeon.

Lindane (Ortho Lindane Borer & Leaf Miner Spray) is one of the best insecticides for controlling clearwing moth borers that have infested orchard trees. If applied to the trunk, the vapors penetrate only slightly into the bark to reach tunneling borers. The insecticide may not get beneath the bark in sufficient quantities to kill all borers; however, it will kill borers as they emerge or attempt to invade. When you spray trees infested with peachtree borers, be certain that the insecticide covers the ground at the base of the trunk to eradicate the pupae or adults as they emerge from below ground.

Malathion (Ortho Malathion 50 Insect Spray, Ortho Home Orchard Spray) or carbaryl (Ortho Liquid Sevin®) applied to drench foliage and tree trunks forms a protective coating that adult beetles and moth borers ingest while chewing.

You can often prevent borer infestations by applying insecticides before the insect bores through the bark. For example, if one fruit tree in your orchard shows signs of borer attack, you should spray the remaining healthy trees to prevent the borers from spreading.

You may also want to routinely spray high-value trees that are prone to borer attack, such as birches, dogwoods, and fruit trees. Apply protective sprays when the adult beetles and moths are migrating and laying eggs. Because most borers overwinter in dormant form, winter control does not have much effect. You will want to spray any time from early March to early July, depending on the species of borer. Most tree borers emerge as adults from infested wood in spring and early summer and disperse to noninfested plants. The best treatment time depends on your region and the particular borer. For advice on exact timing, call your local county agricultural extension service.

BLISTER BEETLES

Blister beetles chew on flowers, vegetables, trees, and vines, eating both blossoms and foliage. Moving in swarms, they travel down vegetable rows, stripping one plant after another and sometimes destroying an entire crop. Their food preferences include tomatoes, potatoes, beans, beets, cotton, eggplants, peas, and melons; they also eat clover. Only adult blister beetles damage plants. The young larvae prey on insects, both beneficial and destructive ones.

Blister beetles are so named because their body fluids can cause painful blisters.

Adult blister beetles swarm through a garden, devouring flowers and vegetables. This is one insect not to touch—it really can blister skin.

If you suspect that the bugs chewing on your plants might be blister beetles, wear gloves before you handle them.

The Pest
You may see many types of blister beetles in your garden. The margined blister beetle is the most common. It has a slim, black 1/2-inch-long body with a narrow, gray band around each wing sheath. Other species have distinct body stripes on a light background, or they may be black, brown, gray, or bluish. All blister beetles have long, beadlike antennae, long legs,

and a head that is wider than the main body and separated from the body by a distinct narrowed "neck."

Reproduction begins as cold weather approaches, with each female depositing thousands of yellowish eggs, usually in clusters, in soil. The larvae hatch underground and go through six or seven distinct changes in appearance. First-stage larvae, with their large heads, large jaws, and long, slender, grasping legs, wander through the soil seeking and destroying grasshopper eggs. In some species, later larval stages may feed on bee eggs.

Leaf chewing begins when the adults emerge from the soil in June or July, and you should begin insecticide use at the same time.

Control Measures

Before modern insecticides made control easy, farm children would stir up plant-feeding blister beetles by beating on pans and swishing through vegetable foliage with leafy branches. As the beetles flew into the grass at the fence line, the grass was set on fire.

Today we use a captan-methoxychlor-rotenone dust (Ortho Tomato Vegetable Dust), pyrethrin-rotenone spray (Ortho Tomato & Vegetable Insect Spray), or carbaryl spray (Ortho Liquid Sevin®) to control blister beetles on vegetables. For best results, treat both upper and lower leaf surfaces. You can repeat as directed on the label if need be.

For blister beetles infesting ornamental plants, treat with a carbaryl spray (Ortho Liquid Sevin®, Ortho Sevin® Garden Spray) at the first sign of insects or damage.

Found almost everywhere that box elder trees grow, boxelder bugs also damage several other types of trees and often become unwelcome houseguests in the fall.

BOXELDER BUGS

Boxelder bugs suck sap of tender growth, flowers, and fruit, primarily on box elder trees, causing minor discoloration and deformation. They may also infest ash, maple, apple, pear, and plum trees. It is their habit of swarming on walls or venturing indoors in droves in the fall to seek hibernation sites, however, that usually starts homeowners looking for ways to control them.

Boxelder bugs do not feed indoors. However, they settle in closets, cracks in walls, and other sheltered spots for the winter, and their waste can stain curtains and furnishings.

The Pest

In early spring, the hibernating adults awaken and swarm outdoors, laying their eggs in cracks and crevices in tree bark. The bright red nymphs hatch shortly afterward and begin sucking sap from leaves and other tender plant parts. They feed until fall, maturing to ½-inch-long black bugs with red undersides and back stripes. One or two generations occur per year.

Control Measures

The first few warm days of spring and the last warm days of fall signal the time for boxelder bugs to swarm outdoors. This is the best time for you to take control measures. Spray susceptible trees with either malathion (Ortho Malathion 50 Insect Spray) or diazinon (Ortho Diazinon Insect Spray) as soon as you first notice the ½-inch-long bugs congregating. Thoroughly wet foliage and trunk. Repeat the spray if your trees become reinfested. Applying pesticide to trees reduces the number of migrating bugs in the fall, although it may not keep bugs from swarming into your home, because boxelder bugs can migrate from plants outside your property.

BUDWORMS

Budworms chew irregular or rounded holes in opening flower and leaf buds. These small caterpillars are the voracious offspring of many different species of bud moths. You will often find them in early spring hidden within rolled leaves or inside buds, which they devour from the inside out. Some species spin silken threads to tie the leaves together into a web for protection while they feed.

Budworm damage can be as minor as the annoying disfigurement of your azalea and rose blossoms or as major as the defoliation of entire trees. Some budworms destroy forests, causing untold economic and environmental loss. The most serious and common budworm pests are spruce budworm, larch bud moth, holly bud moth, blackheaded budworm, and tobacco budworm. These and other budworm pests do not necessarily limit themselves to the plant hosts after which they are named. They may do considerable damage to blackberry, apple, holly, spruce, balsam fir, hemlock, pine, larch, pecan, tobacco, rose, verbena, petunia, columbine, and many other plants.

In some plants, such as holly, budworms cause the tips of new growth to die and blacken. In others, death of bud tips causes tufts of branches to form.

The Pest

Budworm larvae usually hatch in early spring from eggs laid the previous year on twigs, evergreen needles, or garden debris. They immediately begin feeding by burrowing into expanding buds. After several weeks, they pupate, usually inside a silken web or case spun within a damaged bud or leaf. The small moths that result mate and lay clusters of eggs, which either hatch to produce a second generation or overwinter until spring.

Two kinds of budworms commonly infest roses and garden flowers: a green caterpillar with dark stripes along its body length, and another with whitish orange markings on its back. These are the larvae of bordered sallow moths.

Another common budworm is the offspring of the eyespotted bud moth. This ⅓-inch-long larva has a shiny black head and brown body. It overwinters in a small, silky, white case attached to a twig or bud and emerges to eat out buds in spring.

Eyespotted bud moth larvae also tie leaves together with silken threads; they then chew the undersides of leaves or make pits in developing fruit. If you have apple, pear, plum, cherry, or blackberry plants in your garden, infestations of eyespotted bud moth larvae can markedly decrease your fruit crop.

Spruce budworms begin activity when buds appear in

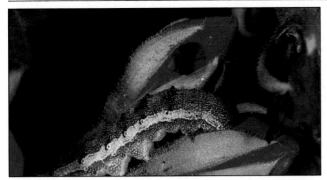

Budworms dash our hopes for beautiful flowers by eating into flower buds. Here, a budworm has eaten a hole in one geranium bud and is starting work on another.

spring. Initially they tunnel into old needles until they reach the center of opening buds. Later they chew off needles, webbing them together into a disfiguring mass. The larvae feed for about five weeks, pupating in silken cases on branch tips and emerging in several weeks as adult moths. These lay eggs in late July or August. Spruce budworm epidemics produce serious forest defoliation about every 10 years.

Control Measures

Sometimes, simply squashing budworms within their webs is enough to control the pests on small shrubs or flowers, or you can cut off and destroy infested buds and leaves. A large-scale invasion requires stronger measures, however.

To control budworm infestations in ornamental trees and shrubs in which you have had problems in previous years, a systemic spray of acephate (Orthene® Systemic Insect Control) applied just as buds begin enlarging and re-applied several weeks later is highly effective. The systemic remains active for two to three weeks and will wipe out hatching budworms. Repeat according to label directions, if necessary.

As soon as you see budworm damage on flowers or roses, usually in late spring, apply acephate (Orthene® Systemic Insect Control, Orthenex® Insect & Disease Control, Orthenex® Rose and Flower Spray) or a carbaryl spray (Ortho Liquid Sevin®),

which controls present insects and migrating pests.

Spray fruit trees with malathion (Ortho Home Orchard Spray, Ortho Malathion 50 Insect Spray) as soon as you see signs of budworms. Thoroughly cover branches and upper and lower leaf surfaces. Repeat, if necessary, following label directions.

For budworms on trees, you might also choose a BT spray, which contains the caterpillar disease pathogen *Bacillus thuringiensis*. Including a spreader-sticker additive in the spray helps the bacteria adhere to the leaves, where caterpillars will eat it.

Insecticides can be effectively applied from the time budworms emerge in early spring until they pupate in early summer, but the sooner you apply the spray, the less damage there will be. Insecticides applied after budworms pupate are useless.

Spraying with a dormant oil in late winter can reduce populations of hatching budworms. A light spray of summer oil on evergreens can help kill eggs and prevent them from overwintering.

Because your garden and landscape plants may be bothered by many different budworm species, if you have any doubt as to the proper treatment or timing for controlling a particular type, call your county agricultural extension agent. Describe the pest and what plant it is on to get specific recommendations.

CABBAGE LOOPERS AND WORMS

Two similar-appearing green caterpillars—the imported cabbageworm and the cabbage looper—cause serious destruction to plants in the cabbage family. Introduced to North America from Europe in the mid-1800s, the imported cabbageworm now infests gardens and farms throughout the entire North American continent. The cabbage looper also annoys gardeners everywhere on the continent.

The voracious imported cabbageworm does not limit its leaf chewing to cabbage; its diet includes the entire cabbage family. All members of the cabbage family (also called the mustard family) secrete mustard oil as a defense mechanism against herbivores. However, the defense doesn't work against the cabbageworm; a sniff of mustard oil merely whets its appetite. It will not feed on any plant lacking this aroma. This pest is particularly trouble-

some on cauliflower, Brussels sprout, broccoli, mustard, kale, kohlrabi, radish, and turnip, as well as nasturtium and sweet alyssum.

Cabbageworms are among the most economically injurious caterpillars. They begin feeding on the outer leaves of a cabbage, creating large, ragged holes. As inner leaves form, these too are attacked. Cabbageworms frequently hide deep within a plant, boring right into a head of cabbage, and mark their presence with unsightly dark green excrement pellets. If you do not eliminate them, your entire cabbage patch and related crops can disappear.

Cabbage loopers can be as destructive as cabbageworms, and they chew on the same crops, as well as lettuce, spinach, beet, pea, celery, parsley, tomato, potato, petunia, and geranium. When loopers destroy tomato foliage, the fruit becomes exposed to strong sun, which can cause sunscald, although the yield will usually not be affected.

You will see the round or irregular leaf holes quite

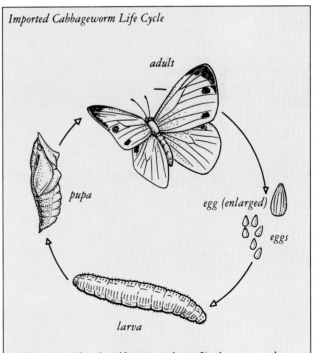

Imported Cabbageworm Life Cycle

adult

pupa

egg (enlarged)

eggs

larva

After mating, female cabbageworm butterflies lay eggs on the leaves of cabbage-family plants. Caterpillars (cabbageworms) hatch within 10 days and feed on the leaves, then pupate within a chrysalis. Adult butterflies emerge in a week or two.

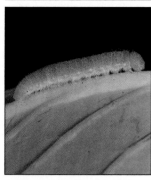

Velvety green, almost the same color as a cabbage-leaf midrib, one imported cabbageworm can devour an entire seedling in a single night.

clearly, and the greenish brown excrement marks the spot beneath a feeding cabbage looper.

The Pest

The imported cabbageworm that does all the damage is a fat, velvety, green caterpillar with a yellow stripe down its back and a broken line of yellow spots along each side.

Cabbageworm butterflies, the parents of imported cabbageworms, emerge from their overwintering pupae in very early spring. They are among the first butterflies to visit your garden each year, and you may notice them on sunny days chasing each other about. These bright white butterflies have a 2-inch wingspan. Two black forewing spots mark the females, and one spot marks the males. They feed on flower nectar and prefer white blossoms.

Just one day after mating, each female begins gluing from 60 to 100 eggs on the undersides of its host plant's outer leaves. The yellow eggs resemble ridged bullets and are each laid separately.

The larvae hatch within 10 days. Although they move sluggishly, it matters little because they are already on a host plant and they do not have far to travel for a meal. Three weeks later, now grown to 1¼ inches long, the cabbageworms begin to pupate. The worms attach

themselves by silken threads to plant leaves, fence rails, building shingles, or other nearby objects. Within a day, they are transformed into rolled-leaf shapes; their color often mimicks their location and ranges from dirty gray to yellow or green. Approximately one to two weeks later, out come new cabbage butterflies.

In the North, there can be three complete generations of these pests before winter. In the South, as many as six generations occur in one growing season.

The cabbage looper looks somewhat like the imported cabbageworm, but the looper is light green with white lines down its back, in contrast to the deeper green and yellow

Cabbage loopers are the jade-green caterpillars on cabbage-family plants that "loop," like their relative, the cankerworm.

stripes of the cabbageworm. The looper's habit of arching its back into a loop as it crawls provides another clue to its identification. The cabbage looper adult is a mottled gray-brown moth with a 1½-inch wingspan and a small silvery spot on its forewings.

Looper moths emerge from overwintering pupae in mid- to late June in the North, in early spring in the South. Each female lays about 300 single, greenish white, round eggs on a host plant's upper leaf surfaces. Small cabbage looper larvae emerge in three days. Two weeks later, the 1½-inch-long caterpillars weave thin cocoons in which

The cabbageworm butterfly is the adult of the imported cabbageworm. This is one of the few butterflies whose larvae are major garden pests.

they pupate. In another two weeks, the night-flying adult moths emerge.

Two to three generations occur each season in the North, and in the South there can be seven generations in a season. In some warm areas, loopers may be present all year long.

Control Measures

Some varieties of cabbage are more resistant to imported cabbageworm depredations than others. If you have had a problem, you might try planting 'Red Acre', 'Globe', or 'Savoy'. You can also try planting cabbage-family vegetables, which are often cool-season plants, as early as possible in spring to avoid the egg-laying butterflies.

Fine netting laid over crops when butterflies are about may also prevent eggs from being laid on your cabbages. Cleaning up garden debris and destroying old cabbage plants or properly composting discarded leaves also removes a source of overwintering pupae. Cleaning out cabbage-family weeds, such as wild mustard, reduces the number of pests visiting your garden.

Natural cabbageworm and looper predators and parasites include *Apanteles glomeratus* wasps, chalcid wasps, and *Bacillus thuringiensis*. You can take advantage of this last pathogen by spraying with commercial BT, beginning when caterpillars first emerge in spring. Repeat applications as needed.

When infestations threaten to cause serious damage to vegetables or flowers, as they often do, control imported cabbageworms and cabbage loopers with insecticides. Spray vegetable plants with diazinon (Ortho Fruit & Vegetable Insect Control), rotenone (Ortho Tomato & Vegetable Insect Spray), or pyrethrins (Ortho Tomato & Vegetable Insect Killer), or dust with carbaryl (Ortho Sevin® Garden Dust) or rotenone (Ortho Rotenone Dust or Spray). Many of these insecticides can be used right up until harvest; check the label for full instructions concerning your crop.

If a cabbage looper infestation spreads to your garden flowers, such as geraniums, carnations, chrysanthemums, and others, you can also choose an acephate systemic (Orthene® Systemic Insect Control), which is effective for up to three weeks. For best results, treat at the first sign of the irregular or round holes combined with ragged leaf edges that signal a looper attack.

Begin pesticide applications on vegetables in spring at the first sign of cabbage butterflies or worm damage. Repeat applications regularly according to container directions because several generations can occur in a year, and insect pests can fly in from neighboring areas.

CANKERWORMS

Cankerworms, also commonly called inchworms, swing from tree to tree on silken threads, rather like Tarzan of the defoliators. During some years, they become so abundant that you can hear leaves being crunched, and leaf shreds and caterpillar droppings fall down on anyone walking underneath an infested tree.

When not swinging around fruit and shade trees on silken threads, a cankerworm travels via a series of looping movements, drawing the rear of its slender body up to the front, forming a wide loop, and then stretching the front portion of its body forward. This movement accounts for the pest's many common names, which include, depending on where you live, measuring worm, looper, or spanworm.

The Pest

You will see two types of cankerworms in your garden; the moths of one appear in spring, and those of the other appear in fall. Caterpillars of both feed at the same time in the spring.

The spring cankerworm moths often appear on the first warm February day, or they may wait until early March. The wingless, 1-inch-long, gray females crawl up tree trunks to lay clusters of approximately 100 oval, brownish purple eggs under the bark. The gray, 1-inch-wide, winged males hide on tree branches or even in attics.

Spring cankerworm caterpillars hatch from the eggs about a month later, when the leaves are unfolding on trees. These very slender, ³/₄-inch-long pests can be green, brown, or nearly black, usually with green, brown, or yellow stripes on their backs.

In late May or early June, after a three- to five-week-long leaf-eating stint, spring cankerworms lower themselves to the ground and form pupae that overwinter below ground. Their silken trapezes may dangle from trees for a short while after the caterpillars have used them as escape ladders.

Fall cankerworm moths show up when most insects choose to hibernate comfortably. Moths appear in November or December, following freezing temperatures. The wingspan of the brown-gray males reaches 1¹/₄ inches, while the wingless females measure only ¹/₂ inch long. Female moths crawl up trees, where they deposit approximately 100 grayish flowerpot-shaped eggs in compact, single-layer groups on small twigs.

Fall cankerworm caterpillars hatch in March or April; they are brown above and green below, with three narrow, white body stripes. They feed on foliage, sometimes dropping to the ground on silken threads and then climbing up again to resume feeding. When fully grown, they drop to the ground and pupate in a silken cocoon 1 to 4 inches underground.

Spring cankerworms usually eat irregular holes in leaves, but during severe infestations they eat all but the midribs of leaves. They are troublesome on cherry, maple, hickory, oak, elm, and apple trees, although they have diverse appetites. Fall cankerworms prefer apple trees, but they also feed on oak, elm, apricot, cherry, plum, prune, and other trees, as well as rosebushes and rhododendrons growing near apple trees. By the end of their season, approximately May to June, the now-mature caterpillars may leave trees and begin eating holes in rhododendron or other shrub leaves.

Defoliation caused by cankerworms occurs early in the season, and trees usually grow new leaves by midsummer. One year's damage does not significantly harm a tree, but three years of defoliation in a row can seriously weaken it.

Control Measures

BT sprays, which contain a parasitic bacteria, give reasonably good control if applied to expanding foliage in March and April, when caterpillars hatch. Repeat applications, according to label instructions, if spring rains wash off the spray. This insecticide can take several days to control caterpillars, so you may see

The spring cankerworm is a kind of inchworm that feeds on many shade and fruit trees.

them still moving about while the bacterial disease takes its toll. Insecticide sprays will give you quicker and longer-lasting protection. Natural parasites include trichogramma wasps, which parasitize cankerworm eggs.

Sticky bands, such as Tanglefoot®, can be placed on trunks approximately 3 feet up from the ground in February to catch female moths crawling up to lay eggs. Banding alone does not provide satisfactory control, however, because female cankerworm moths will crawl over the bodies of trapped females, and because cankerworm caterpillars can avoid the bands by using their silken

threads to swing from tree to tree. Be certain to read instructions when applying any type of sticky band because some trapping substances injure tree bark. (See page 29 for safety tips.)

Even though healthy trees will leaf out again after cankerworm damage, you may still wish to use insecticides to protect valuable shade trees, new transplants, and fruit trees, especially if midseason defoliating pests appear. Spray at the first sign of feeding damage, when the insects are still small and easiest to control.

Spray fruit trees in late April or early May with malathion or a multipurpose orchard spray containing a captan-malathion-methoxychlor compound (Ortho Home Orchard Spray). Use an acephate spray (Orthene® Systemic Insect Control) on ornamental trees because these pests move into expanding young foliage.

Fall cankerworms tend to have marked population increases about every seven years. If you live in an area that has experienced serious problems in the past, check with your county agricultural extension agent for information updates.

To control chinch bugs effectively, treat the entire lawn, not just the dead patches left by the pest.

CHINCH BUGS

Brown-centered yellow patches in your lawn can signal chinch bugs at work. These sun- and heat-loving insects suck juices from grass blades and also inject a poison that causes blades to turn brown and die. The brown portions of your lawn are already dead, and you will find the chinch bugs feeding in the yellowing portion of the sickly patch. They will continue to move outward toward healthy green grass in ever-widening circles.

Chinch bugs occur throughout the United States; they especially favor St. Augustine grass, centipedegrass, and fine fescue, but they also attack Kentucky bluegrass, bentgrass, and zoysiagrass.

You can easily check to see whether chinch bugs are infesting your lawn. Cut out both ends of a tin can, and cut the rim off one end to sharpen it. Push the sharp end of the can 2 or 3 inches into the soil in a sunny spot on the edge of an area where yellow grass borders green. Fill the can with water. After about five minutes, both chinch bug adults and young will float to the surface. If you tug at dying grass infested with chinch bugs, it remains firmly rooted, unlike grass that has been attacked by grubs, which you can roll back as though it were a carpet.

The Pest

Chinch bugs are quite small, with adults ranging from $1/16$ to $1/4$ inch long, depending on the species. Most are black with white wings, each of which has a distinctive triangular black mark. Young chinch bugs look like smaller, wingless versions of their parents, but they are various shades of red with a white back stripe. They molt several times, becoming darker as they mature.

During winter, adult chinch bugs hibernate in tall grass, clumps of weeds, or lawn. When spring temperatures reach 70° F, they emerge, begin feeding, mate, and lay eggs near grass roots. The females can each lay several hundred eggs within two

Both adult (shown here) and nymph chinch bugs suck sap from lawn grasses, causing them to yellow and die.

weeks. Five weeks later the nymphs reach adulthood and begin to reproduce.

Two or three generations occur each year, and the pests continue feeding into fall. The greatest damage occurs in sunny areas during the hot days of July and August.

Where chinch bugs are a problem, inspect your lawn for damage once a week as soon as warm weather begins, as these insects can move across an entire lawn in several days. Look primarily in sunny areas, paying particular attention to the lawn bordering heat-reflecting sidewalks and driveways. Chinch bugs seldom attack shaded areas.

Control Measures

If you have had difficulty in the past controlling chinch bugs, the trick may be to treat your *entire* lawn, not just the yellowing patches. Because damage appears in patches, you may be tempted to do spot treatments. If you do, however, new yellowing areas sometimes appear because older nymphs and adults travel and set up residence elsewhere.

Insecticides for controlling chinch bugs come in both granular and spray form. Choose chlorpyrifos (Ortho Lawn Insect Spray, Ortho-Klor® Soil Insect & Termite Killer) or diazinon (Ortho Diazinon Soil & Turf Insect Control).

Just before spraying, irrigate your lawn thoroughly to bring insects to the surface. About 1 inch of water usually does the job. Then use a hose-end sprayer designed for lawns to apply the insecticide

according to the label instructions. For thorough coverage, evenly spray the lawn from side to side in one direction, turn 90 degrees, and spray again from side to side.

For granular insecticides, use a broadcast or drop spreader of the type designed for applying lawn fertilizer. Follow application instructions on the product label. Water the lawn deeply after you have applied granules to wash the pesticide down into the soil.

To prevent recurring damage from newly hatched nymphs, each generation of chinch bugs should be treated. In some areas, this can mean treating lawns every two months until frost. In southern Florida, you may need to repeat the applications throughout the year.

CICADAS

The noisy insects you hear but rarely see during warm spring and summer afternoons may be cicadas. Their annoying whirring song, which only males produce, emanates from vibrating membranes stretched over sound chambers located near the abdominal base.

Two species of these tree-dwelling pests cause serious damage to trees and shrubs: the periodical cicada, also called the seventeen-year locust and the dog-day cicada. Periodical cicadas have life cycles lasting 13 years in the South and 17 years in the North. This does not mean that you see them only every 13 or 17 years. Broods hatch every year, each having spent 13 or 17 years developing underground. Some broods are enormous, however, with as many as 40,000 cicadas emerging from beneath a single tree. These massive infestations can be predicted, but they vary in different regions.

American Indians used to regard cicadas as bad omens, associating them with crop loss. Cicadas damage trees but they do not devastate crops. Even today, however, people still often confuse the relatively benign periodical cicadas with the similar-sized but highly destructive locusts of biblical fame.

The periodical cicada appears for about a month and a half in early summer. The dog-day cicada appears during the hot dog days of July and August.

Dog-day cicadas do little garden damage. The periodical cicadas emerging in mid-May through June are the ones that may harm trees and shrubs; they prefer apple, oak, hickory, and dogwood.

Each female punctures as many as 50 splintery holes in twigs and small branches with its tough egg-laying organ. It then places 12 to 20 eggs in each hole. Multiple holes in the same stem or twig cause leaves to brown and twigs to break.

The Pest

Periodical cicadas are about 1 inch long with transparent wings that extend well behind their black bodies and red-orange eyes, legs, and wing veins. Except for their size, they do not resemble true locusts, which are grasshoppers. Grasshoppers are green, brown, or reddish yellow with long, highly visible legs.

The dog-day cicada is larger than the periodical cicada, has a black body, green wing margins, and numerous light markings on its chest and abdomen.

Adult cicadas live about six weeks. Eggs hatch in two months, and the ant-sized young nymphs drop to the ground and enter the soil. They burrow down to tree roots, remaining as far as 18 inches below ground until, years and many molts later, they emerge as mature adults. Each brood of dog-day cicadas spends two to five years developing underground. Periodical cicadas take 13 or 17 years to develop.

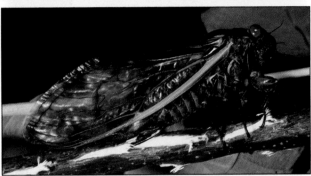

The males' noisy whirring may be all you hear and the nymphs' abandoned skins all you see of tree-dwelling cicadas. Dog-day cicadas (above) emerge annually in July and August. The more damaging periodical cicadas (below), which have red-orange eyes and wing veins, take 13 to 17 years to mature.

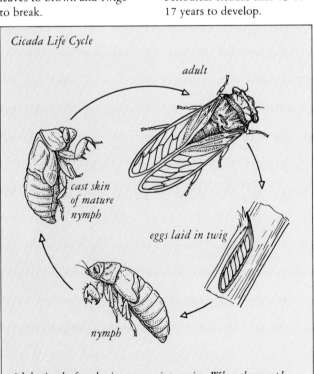

Cicada Life Cycle

adult

cast skin of mature nymph

eggs laid in twig

nymph

Adult cicada females insert eggs into twigs. When the nymphs hatch, they drop to the ground, burrow down, and feed on tree roots. After many years, the nymphs emerge from the ground, shed one last skin, and become adult cicadas.

Cicada nymphs suck sap from tree rootlets but do not do much damage. When ready for a final molt, the now 1-inch-long nymphs burrow upward, often leaving 1/2-inch-wide emergence holes in the ground. Crawling up stems or twigs, they shed their last nymphal skin revealing winged adults. You may notice the light brown, brittle, beetlelike shells in your garden. Four to five days after the final molt, adult males begin singing.

Control Measures

If the shrill chorus really bothers you, or if cicadas emerge in large broods, begin control measures within a few days of the first cicada noises. You want to eliminate the tree-inhabiting female before it has time to deposit eggs and injure trees.

Carbaryl sprays (Ortho Liquid Sevin®) effectively control cicadas when used according to label directions. Thoroughly spray the entire plant, including upper and lower leaf surfaces. Repeat the spray seven days later. Spraying is most effective in the evening, in the early morning, or during cool periods of the day, when insects are resting and are unlikely to fly away.

Avoid planting new trees, which are more susceptible to damage, in the several years before a large brood of periodical cicadas is expected to emerge. Also do not prune young trees heavily the winter or spring before such hordes arrive. Protect valuable shrubs with mosquito netting or inexpensive cheesecloth. If you see injured twigs and branches, cut them off and destroy them to prevent eggs from hatching.

CODLING MOTHS

Codling moths cause more wormy apples than any other pest. The larvae eat their way through apples, pears, plums, peaches, apricots, cherries, and other fruits. You will see small holes in fruit skin where the larvae have burrowed inside. A brown, crumbly excrement resembling sawdust may surround the holes. The combination of larval damage, early fruit drop, and rot, resulting from introduced bacteria and fungi, can completely destroy a crop.

Codling moth larvae also attack nut trees, especially walnuts. Early-blooming varieties are most susceptible. Symptoms include stained shells, holes at the bases of nuts, and premature nut drop.

This serious pest exists wherever apples grow. Codling moth damage becomes most extensive in years with warm, dry springs because the moths can lay more eggs. During cold, wet springs, the moths fly less and you will have less trouble with wormy fruit later on.

Other pests, such as apple maggot (see page 68), apple curculio (see page 51), and European apple sawfly maggot, cause wormy apples. You can be sure that your problem is codling moths if the larvae tunnel straight for the core. Codling moth larvae are whitish pink. Apple curculio worms are grayish white, apple maggots are legless and yellowish white, and European apple sawfly maggots are white or tan with brown heads and seven prolegs.

The Pest

The brownish gray codling moth, with a wingspread between $1/2$ and $3/4$ inch, appears from early to mid-May, when fruit trees are in full bloom. Large brown spots on wing tips and lacy brown lines on forewings distinguish this moth. Both the male and female fly at dusk, preferring dry weather and temperatures above 55° F.

The female codling moth deposits 50 to 75 eggs on leaves, twigs, and developing fruit. Eggs hatch in 12 days. The emerging brown-headed,

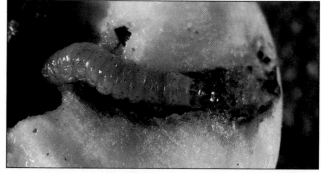

The worm in your apple is most likely a codling moth larva. This pest also burrows into many other fruits.

pinkish white larvae first feed on leaves, but they soon burrow into developing fruit near the blossom ends. They tunnel to the core where they eat both fruit and seeds. In about a month, the worms burrow out through the other side of the fruit, leaving a rotten core and a mass of brown excrement behind.

Now $3/4$ inch long, the larvae drop to the ground or crawl down tree trunks, find a sheltered nook, and spin cocoons. A second moth generation emerges from the cocoons and lays eggs in July. Second-brood larvae enter anywhere on the fruit.

In September, the new larvae spin cocoons in protected places, such as under bark or garden litter. Overwintering takes place in the cocoon phase, and in spring the codling moths pupate and adult moths emerge.

Control Measures

Dormant oil sprays suffocate overwintering larvae. Apply this type of spray to fruit trees in late winter before trees blossom. You can also use a lighter oil spray (Ortho Volck® Oil Spray) in combination with malathion (Ortho Malathion 50 Insect Spray) to wipe out eggs on twigs and tiny fruit. To be effective, the spray must be applied before the larvae hatch, just after petal drop.

Once codling moth larvae have burrowed into fruit, it is impossible to kill them. Insecticidal sprays give good control when applied just after a large number of larvae hatch.

The timing for this varies according to the year and the area, so you may want to check with your county agricultural extension agent for a precise time to spray. You usually have one to two weeks after the eggs have been laid to initiate successful controls. Accurate timing means that you spray more effectively and less frequently.

One way you can time insecticide applications is to lure moths with a codling moth pheromone trap. Inquire about this at major nurseries in your area. A pheromone trap contains rubber units impregnated with a sex lure that entices males into the trap, where they adhere to its sticky surface. You should set the trap at eye level in the branch canopy just before fruit trees reach full bloom. Be sure to replace trap liners whenever they are no longer sticky. Replace the pheromone every six weeks for maximum luring power.

Examine the traps at least once a week, removing trapped moths. If your traps contain fewer than 15 moths, no spraying is necessary. If you catch more than 15, spray immediately. Continue these weekly counts until you harvest all fruit. Traps used alone do not kill enough moths to prevent wormy fruit.

To protect uninfested fruit against the second generation of emerging larvae, spray with diazinon (Ortho Fruit & Vegetable Insect Control, Ortho Diazinon Insect Spray), malathion (Ortho Malathion 50

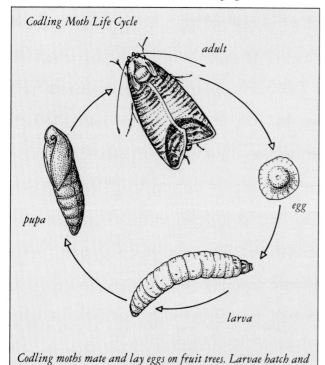

Codling Moth Life Cycle

adult

egg

larva

pupa

Codling moths mate and lay eggs on fruit trees. Larvae hatch and feed on both leaves and fruit. When mature, the larvae crawl down trees to pupate in cocoons. Adults emerge from cocoons in spring, followed by a second generation in midsummer.

Insect Spray), carbaryl (Ortho Liquid Sevin®), or a multi-purpose orchard spray containing captan, malathion, and methoxychlor (Ortho Home Orchard Spray). Because codling moths damage fruit continuously throughout the summer, spray at 10- to 14-day intervals as directed on the container label. Do not spray with diazinon or Sevin® until petals have fallen from flowers, because the pesticides can kill honeybees visiting the blossoms and thus prevent fruit set.

To control codling moths infesting nut trees, spray in spring with diazinon (Ortho Fruit & Vegetable Insect Control) when the nuts are ³⁄₈ to ¹⁄₂ inch wide. Repeat the spray six to eight weeks later. Once the larvae have penetrated the nuts, they will be impossible to control.

You can also try reducing codling moth populations by banding trees to catch larvae seeking cocoon sites. Place a band on each tree no later than mid-May. Use a 6-inch-wide strip of burlap or corrugated cardboard, wrapping this around the tree several times. If you use cardboard, the exposed ridges must be at least ³⁄₁₆ inch wide, and they must face toward the tree; otherwise larvae will not form cocoons within them. Remove bands once a week during warm weather, every other week during cool weather. Destroy all larvae and pupae under it, and then replace the band. Continue banding until you have harvested all fruit.

Regularly remove fallen fruit, nuts, and litter near tree bases where larvae pupate. Place fallen fruit in plastic bags, and destroy it. Scrape loose bark off trees during the dormant season, and remove any large weeds and rubbish nearby to eliminate possible hiding places.

Some trichogramma and braconid wasps parasitize codling moth eggs and larvae.

COLORADO POTATO BEETLES

After Colorado potato beetles, sometimes simply called potato bugs, finish chewing on your potato, tomato, eggplant, and pepper plants, the only foliage remaining may be a few mature leaves and stems. One Colorado potato beetle can reduce a plant's yield by 80 percent. Both adult beetles and larvae completely ravage foliage.

Emerging from the ground in midspring, overwintering adult beetles often hang around your garden even before their favorite plants sprout. They eat any leftover foliage from the previous season then fly to neighboring areas to search for food. But don't be reassured; they will probably return, depending on the pickings elsewhere. They do their worst damage just before and after your vegetable plants bloom.

The Colorado potato beetle originally lived on wild relatives of the potato vine in the Rocky Mountains, but spread to the domestic potato when it was introduced by settlers. In some areas of the country, infestations now reach epidemic proportions.

The Pest

With their black-striped wing covers, the bright yellow, ¹⁄₃-inch-long adult beetles are easy to spot. They make lengthy aerial journeys in search of an optimum food supply. Once they begin feeding, mating also commences. The females alight on the plant tops, while the males fly slowly and conspicuously overhead, seeking a mate.

When crops sprout, the females begin laying easily seen clumps or rows of orange-red eggs on leaf undersides. One female can deposit 400 eggs over a four- to six-week period. Plump red larvae with humped backs and black heads, feet, and side dots hatch 3 to 10 days later and start to eat immediately. Their color may change to pink or

orange when they mature. The larvae feed on the plant on which they hatched for approximately two weeks. They then descend, burrowing in loose soil or crawling along the ground randomly and for a considerable distance until they find a suitable burrowing spot.

Here, about 3 inches underground, each larva presses out a small oval cell and then pupates. In two weeks, an adult beetle emerges, looking and acting exactly like its parents. It begins another cycle of feeding, mating, and laying eggs, providing a second or even third generation within one season, depending on the area of the country.

Control Measures

If you have had prior damage from potato beetles, begin control measures when plants are only a few inches high. By this time, you may already see

Plump, brightly colored Colorado potato beetles can devastate a planting of peppers, tomatoes, eggplants, or potatoes.

the first leaf holes. Do not wait until the damage is extensive, or you may lose your entire crop.

Insecticide sprays and dusts destroy both the beetle and its larvae. You can use carbaryl (Ortho Sevin® 5 Dust or Ortho Sevin® 10 Dust) or diazinon (Ortho Fruit & Vegetable Insect Control). Pyrethrins (Ortho Tomato & Vegetable Insect Killer), which break down quickly, can be used very close to harvest time.

Reddish brown Colorado potato beetle larvae eat for two weeks, hibernate for two more, and then emerge as hungry adults.

Cover both upper and lower leaf surfaces with insecticide. Be on the lookout for marauding beetles, and repeat the treatment if needed. Carefully follow label directions concerning days until harvest after applying pesticides to vegetable crops.

Studies show that, given sufficient plants of a preferred potato variety, Colorado potato beetles will leave less tender-leaved potatoes alone. If you have a large garden, you might have enough room to include a trap crop of potatoes. Plant a patch of tender-leaf potatoes in the middle of a less-tender potato crop—the ones you will eventually harvest. (Check with your local nursery for varieties suitable for your area.) The tender variety draws the beetles away from the tougher-leaved ones. Expect to lose the crop of trap potatoes, and keep in mind that you may be increasing beetle populations for the next year.

Unkempt gardens provide feeding spots for Colorado potato beetles until your crops sprout. Pull up and compost or remove all garden plants after the fall harvest. A heavy mulch of straw laid around seedlings may prevent some beetles emerging from their underground chambers from finding open air and your vegetables.

Natural enemies of potato beetles include ladybugs, ground beetles, robber flies, spiders, daddy longlegs, parasitic tachinid flies and wasps, and domestic fowl.

CORN EARWORMS

Probably the most serious corn pest, occurring wherever corn grows, the corn earworm does not limit its meals to corn. The worm goes by other names, including tomato fruitworm, cotton bollworm, sorghum headworm, and tobacco budworm, named after just a few of the other plants it seriously damages.

Earworms severely stunt developing ears of corn, and harvested ears may be wormy and filled with excrement or

Corn earworms usually enter ears of corn through the tips. They may also eat other vegetables.

mold. The worms destroy pollen-yielding tassels and prevent pollination of the silks. Because each silk strand attaches to a kernel, for each unpollinated silk, one less kernel develops, often resulting in stunted ears called nubbins.

When earworms feed directly on kernels, molds easily enter and thrive, making any surviving kernels less appetizing. Parts without mold, however, can still be used at mealtime.

Corn earworms feed on foliage and eat through tomato fruits, encouraging mold to invade the damaged sites. Infested tomatoes are wormy and rotten, ruined for home use. These pests often move over to feed on neighboring vegetables such as cabbages, broccoli, beans, lettuce, and peppers.

The Pest

You will see the 1½-inch-wide adult moths flying at dusk or on warm, cloudy days from April until November, feeding on flower nectar. Dark lines mark their gray-brown forewings, and dark spots mark their white hindwings. The females each place up to 2,000 eggs on leaves of favored plants, with a strong preference for seedlings.

On corn, the moths lay eggs singly along the silks within the tassels. Emerging larvae start feeding at the tips of the ears and work down to the kernels, or they begin by boring through the husk. They may also chew ragged edges in young leaves.

On tomatoes, the moths lay eggs on the undersides of leaves. Upon hatching, the larvae immediately bore into ripening fruit, each leaving a small hole as an entry mark.

Corn earworms vary in appearance, so you may have difficulty identifying them by sight alone. Newly hatched larvae are tiny, black-headed, white worms. These grow rapidly, eventually reaching ¼ inch to 2 inches long. Mature earworms can be green, pink, yellow, or almost black, all with dark and light stripes and four pairs of prolegs on the abdomen.

Upon reaching full growth, the larvae drop to the ground, pupating in soil. Three weeks later, adult moths emerge. There can be as many as seven generations a year, and untreated crops often experience a population explosion of earworms in late summer if the year is warm and dry.

Control Measures

Light traps help commercial growers monitor the presence of earworm moths. These are rarely practical for home gardeners; you would have to search through the scores of trapped insects to identify the corn earworm moth. Also, with a small garden, light traps could attract earworm moths from neighboring properties.

You can best detect corn earworms by examining corn silks and other ripening plants daily for eggs, newly hatched larvae, and initial feeding damage. You must catch the earworms early, before they bore into ears and fruits, because once they bore into a fruit or vegetable, insecticides cannot reach them.

You should be able to keep your corn free of earworms by treating your crop with carbaryl dust (Ortho Sevin® Garden Dust) when 10 percent of the ears show silk and repeating the treatment three to four times at three-day intervals. If the infestation continues, repeat the dusting as necessary until harvest.

BT sprays, which contain a pathogenic bacteria, applied when corn earworms are young also help to reduce the pest population.

If you have a continuing problem with corn earworms, consider planting some of the hybrid corn varieties that are less vulnerable to earworm attack. Check your seed catalogs before selecting seeds.

On tomatoes, start pesticide treatment when flowers first appear or when fruits first set. Use carbaryl (Ortho Liquid Sevin®, Ortho Sevin® Garden Dust) or rotenone (Ortho Tomato Vegetable Dust). Fruitworm damage is most severe in late summer and fall, so if you have had tomato damage in prior years, plant varieties that blossom and ripen early.

To control earworms infesting your nonfood plants, spray with carbaryl (Ortho Liquid Sevin®) or acephate (Orthene® Systemic Insect Control). Treat all exposed plant parts, especially upper and lower leaf surfaces.

Because corn earworms overwinter as pupae in soil, sometimes as deep as 12 inches, deep spading destroys many of them and exposes others to predators and cold weather. To reduce populations in subsequent generations, remove all infested fallen fruits and vegetables from the ground, and destroy them. In the fall, clean up all garden debris and burn infested crops.

CORNSTALK BORERS

Among the multitude of insects that enjoy fresh corn are southwestern corn borers, European corn borers, southern cornstalk borers, stalk borers, and lesser cornstalk borers. These destructive pests primarily damage stems and foliage rather than the ears, but they prevent ear formation.

Along with the corn earworm, the European corn borer is one of the most troublesome corn pests, accounting for major losses of corn in both home gardens and farms. This pest also bores into sturdy-stemmed flowers, such as hollyhock, dahlia, zinnia, aster, chrysanthemum, and gladiolus. In addition to corn, vegetable hosts include potato, bean, pepper, onion, and tomato.

On corn, you will notice the initial damage as multiple small holes, called shotholes, in leaves. Broken tassels, bent stalks, and sawdust castings outside small stem holes also signify borers at work.

European corn borers tunneling into the sides of ears of corn weaken the ears until they drop. The tunneling of borers also creates openings for other insect pests and for fungi, which can cause stalk rot.

In potatoes and snap beans, larvae initially feed on leaves and then bore into the stems at leaf bases; their feeding kills the stems above. On pepper plants, larvae enter fruits at the cap ends, completing their development within the fruit. The resulting rot makes peppers distinctly unappetizing, although if you remove the blackened areas, the peppers are still edible.

European corn borers reproduce poorly during cool, rainy seasons. Infestations are heaviest when early summer weather favors egg laying. Very dry summers and cold winters also reduce the numbers of this pest.

The common stalk borer, a serious pest east of the Rockies, and the lesser cornstalk borer, a problem in the South, chew leaves until they are ragged. Stalks will not produce ears and become distorted and curled.

The southwestern corn borer and the southern cornstalk borer chew their way around cornstalk bases and bore into roots, often causing the stems to blow over during a moderate wind. The pests also chew corn leaves—even while they are still within the unfolding whorl. Chewed leaves look ragged.

The Pest

European corn borers overwinter as 1-inch-long caterpillars within plant stems or plant litter. After pupating in spring, they emerge as night-flying moths in early June. The female moths are yellow-brown with dark, wavy wing bands; males are similar but darker. During the day the moths hide under leaves or in nearby weeds. They fly and mate at night.

The females lay flat egg clusters on leaf undersides. Each female can lay up to 400 yellowish white eggs over a month-long period. The eggs hatch in a few days. The pale yellow or pale pink larvae have dark brown heads and two rows of small, dark brown spots down their bodies. They are 1 inch long when mature.

European corn borer larvae feed first on leaves and tassels and then tunnel into stalks, feeding for a month until they are fully grown. They pupate inside stems. Several generations occur per season. In northern areas, the first generation is complete by midsummer, and the second reaches full growth in time for winter hibernation.

The 1-inch-long common stalk borer caterpillar is grayish or light purple, and the 3/4-inch-long lesser cornstalk borer has brown stripes on a blue-green body.

The common stalk borer, most prevalent east of the Rocky Mountains, feeds within the stems of many kinds of plants, including dahlia, iris, aster, tomato, and hollyhock. In later stages, the caterpillar turns to corn, where it feeds in leaf whorls and then bores into the sides of stalks and burrows upward.

The caterpillars pupate in soil, and 1-inch-wide graybrown moths emerge in August and September. Each female can lay over 2,000 eggs, which overwinter on grasses and weeds, particularly giant ragweed. The common stalk borer produces only one generation per year.

The lesser cornstalk borer has two generations per year. In spring the yellow-brown moths with black spots lay eggs on corn leaves and stalks. The emerging borers feed on corn leaves and burrow into the lower 2 inches of stalk. After feeding for three weeks, the borers pupate in soil and repeat the cycle. Johnsongrass weeds may harbor lesser cornstalk borers.

Southern cornstalk borers and southwestern corn borers have two or more generations a year. Their straw-colored moths emerge in late spring and lay eggs on leaf undersides. The 1-inch-long borers are dirty white with dark brown spots. They may infest several plants before pupating for another generation. These pests overwinter in corn roots and stubble left in the field.

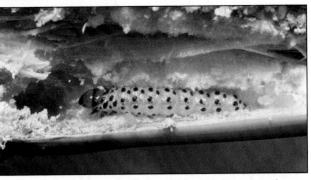

A cut-open cornstalk reveals the borer feeding within—a southwestern cornstalk borer.

Control Measures

The best prevention for European corn borers and southwestern cornborers is to wipe out the larvae by sprinkling diazinon granules (Ortho Diazinon Soil & Turf Insect Control, Ortho Vegetable Guard Soil Insect Killer) into whorls of corn plants when they are knee-high. Then carefully examine the plants, including the tiniest corn tassel, for evidence of live larvae or caterpillars feeding on leaves. You can reapply the diazinon granules on corn if your crop shows larval feeding damage, every seven days as needed. Corn can be picked immediately following the last application.

An alternative is to spray with rotenone (Ortho Rotenone Dust or Spray) or carbaryl (Ortho Sevin® Garden Spray) from the time plants are knee-high until they are full grown. Repeat treatments weekly or as necessary. Carbaryl can be applied up to harvest time, but stop rotenone use at least one day before harvest. On peppers, use carbaryl dust or spray.

Farmers use light traps to help monitor the presence of European corn borers. These are not recommended for home garden use. Researchers do not consider pheromone traps to be effective against European corn borers unless supplemented with other control methods.

BT sprays can be used against young corn borer larvae, but if you use insecticide afterward, you might eliminate any beneficial parasitic wasps feeding on the larvae.

Good garden sanitation goes a long way toward reducing subsequent populations because European corn borers, southern cornstalk borers, and southwestern corn borers hibernate in stems and flower stalks. Clean up all stalks and fallen ears after harvesting. Burn or destroy infested crops, rather than composting them.

If your garden has been bothered by European corn borers in previous years, planting corn in late May rather than early May helps your crop avoid peak borer damage, although yield may be reduced somewhat. You might also try planting resistant corn varieties. Some modern corn hybrids give good corn yields even when infested with borers.

By the time you see damage from cornstalk borers and lesser cornstalk borers, it is too late for any controls because the larvae are safe inside stems. But do make certain that your corn pest is not the controllable European or southwestern corn borer or the southern cornstalk borer by comparing the descriptions of the larvae given here.

To reduce populations of all kinds of cornstalk borers, remove and destroy all infested plants and garden debris. Eliminate nearby grasses and weeds where eggs or larvae of the pests can overwinter. The following spring, use an insecticide that contains carbaryl or diazinon to avoid reinfestation.

CRICKETS

You will find several species of cricket chirping in your garden from spring through summer. Many eat harmful insects, but several kinds, such as the field cricket, mole cricket, snowy tree cricket, and, very rarely, the Jerusalem cricket, harm garden plants.

During the day, field crickets hide under garden litter. They venture into your garden in late afternoon to eat newly emerging flowers and foliage.

The mole cricket becomes a damaging nuisance when it uses its large front legs to burrow in your lawn. This cricket tunnels in the top 2 inches of soil, cutting off grass roots. It

Field crickets can cause considerable damage to garden plants. They are especially fond of seedlings.

can tunnel 20 feet in a night, returning to its underground burrow during the day. You may see small soil mounds on your lawn, and the lawn will feel spongy underfoot. Large areas of grass can turn brown and die.

Snowy tree crickets chirp in unison. If one cricket stops, it restarts in time with the others. Its chirping rate changes with the temperature. You can calculate the temperature quite accurately by adding 40 to the number of cricket chirps you count in 15 seconds. This will give you the temperature in degrees Fahrenheit.

When young, snowy tree crickets eat aphids and other small garden insects, but they occasionally nibble on flowers

and fruit. Most garden damage occurs during fall egg laying when the females drill rows of deep punctures in berry canes or tree twigs to hold their eggs. The area beyond the punctures may later break off or die.

Although the Jerusalem cricket occasionally nibbles on potatoes, it also eats harmful insects. This beneficial cricket usually hides in soil or under rocks or garden litter, although sometimes it wanders indoors. Just usher it outside again, but since it can nip, use gloves or some other protection.

The Pest

The 1-inch-long, long-antennaed, dark brown field crickets overwinter in egg form in cold climates and in egg and nymph form in warm climates. Nymphs emerge in spring, taking twelve weeks to mature and reproduce. The females each lay 150 to 400 eggs in damp soil. One generation occurs each season in cold climates, and three occur in warm climates. Population explosions take place occasionally, sometimes caused by thunderstorms and other weather variables.

The shiny, wingless Jerusalem cricket is light brown with dark cross-stripes. It has a large head and very long antennae. The mole cricket is 1½ inches long and dark to tawny brown.

The ½-inch-long snowy tree cricket is pale green or brown. This cricket overwinters in egg form and produces only one generation per year.

Control Measures

No insecticide is currently registered for controlling snowy tree crickets. You can reduce their populations by pruning and destroying infested canes and twigs. Look for a 1- to 2-inch-long dotted line of pinhead-sized egg-laying scars on twigs. If you cut into these, you will find eggs inserted into the tissue.

Keeping lawns and grassy areas mowed and weeds removed, as well as eliminating plant litter, will reduce their populations by taking away their main hiding places. During population explosions, use netting to protect young trees. Use only yellow bulbs in outdoor light fixtures, because white lights attract crickets.

To check for mole crickets, mix 1 ounce of liquid dish detergent in 2 gallons of water. Drench 4 square feet of turf with the concoction. If present, mole crickets will come to the surface in a few minutes.

Control mole and field crickets with a granular bait containing propoxur (Ortho Mole Cricket Bait), which is specific for these insects, or use diazinon granules (Ortho Diazinon Soil & Turf Insect Control). Apply these with a lawn fertilizer spreader in July after eggs hatch and before cricket nymphs get a chance to do much damage. Mow grass and then water before applying insecticide, but then don't water for 36 hours. If infestation continues, treat again in late summer to early fall. Keep the lawn watered to encourage new root growth in damaged grass.

CUCUMBER BEETLES

A single cantaloupe plant can be home to 200 cucumber beetles. Pests that infest plants in the cucumber family, these beetles begin the spring season by chewing on emerging seedlings, often completely devouring them. Later on, they riddle leaves with holes, gnaw stems and fruits, and shred flowers. Their larvae destroy roots.

Cucumber beetles also transmit both bacterial wilt and mosaic virus disease. Rapidly multiplying wilt bacteria block a plant's water supply tubes, causing wilting during

This striped cucumber beetle is making a tender meal of a squash blossom.

day heat with apparent recovery at night, until the plant finally dies. If you break open an infected stem, you will find a slimy ooze filling the conducting tissue. Any fruit present shrivels. Leaves become mottled and wrinkled by mosaic virus. The stunted vines produce only warty, discolored, bitter-tasting fruits.

Of the many species of cucumber beetle, two, the striped cucumber beetle and the spotted cucumber beetle, commonly infest gardens. Both attack many kinds of plants, including ones in the cucumber family such as cucumber, squash, pumpkin, cantaloupe, and watermelon. The striped cucumber beetle primarily attacks cucurbits and bean. Its larvae feed on plant roots, often devouring the entire root system. The spotted cucumber beetle eats bean and cucurbits as well as asparagus, beet, cabbage, corn, eggplant, pea, potato, and tomato. It also eats flowers, including rose, dahlia, and aster, often choosing light-colored fall blossoms for feasting.

Cucumber beetles hibernate over winter under plant litter. At any time of year when the temperature exceeds 55° F to 70° F, depending on the species, the beetles come out for a picnic in the sun. In fall or winter, they find little to eat, so they fly from one garden to the next, searching for something edible. In early spring, seedlings and young growth provide ample food, and you will find cucumber beetles initially feeding on vegetable plants in your garden's outer rows.

The Pest

Striped cucumber beetles are slender, yellowish, 1/4-inch-long insects with three black stripes. Spotted cucumber beetles are similar in appearance but are pale green with 11 or 12 black spots.

After awakening from winter hibernation, cucumber beetles mate, and each female deposits 800 or more eggs in shady cracks and crevices around plant bases. White larvae with dark brown heads and tails hatch in 10 days and begin to eat plant roots. Infested crops grow slowly and, if they lack water for even a relatively short period, may suddenly die.

Two to six weeks after the larvae hatch, the mature 1/3-inch-long worms pupate, emerging three weeks later as adults. There are one to three generations per year, depending on the region.

Control Measures

Keep a watchful eye out for the first signs of germinating seedlings, and apply pesticide when you first see greenery. If cucumber beetles get to the seedlings first, they will devour them. Applying insecticide as a preventive before you see any beetles protects your garden from beetle-transmitted bacterial wilt and mosaic virus disease. Once beetles begin feeding, the infections may already be established, even if you wipe the beetles out.

Dust or spray susceptible crops as soon as you see the first green leaves on seedlings. You can choose rotenone (Ortho Rotenone Dust or Spray), pyrethrins (Ortho Tomato & Vegetable Insect Killer), carbaryl (Ortho Sevin® Garden Dust), diazinon (Ortho Fruit & Vegetable Insect Control), or an all-purpose insecticide containing a captan-methoxychlor-rotenone compound (Ortho Tomato Vegetable Dust). Read the container instructions

carefully, and repeat applications as needed. Some insecticides can be applied on listed vegetable plants almost up to the day of harvest.

If cucumber beetles infest nonfood plants, choose an insecticide with a carbaryl base (Ortho Sevin® Garden Dust). Repeat at weekly intervals if plants become reinfested.

Eliminate all cucumber beetle hiding places by cleaning up plant litter on a regular

Spotted cucumber beetles damage many crops, including corn and garden flowers.

basis. Destroy unwanted fruit rather than letting it remain on the vine as an added attraction. Start seeding your crop as early in the season as practical, so that seedlings get a head start on the beetles. You want vigorous plants before the temperature reaches a sustained 60° F or higher; that is when cucumber beetles emerge and stay around.

Because a rapidly growing, vigorous plant can withstand and outgrow beetle and larvae injury, prepare soil well and use fertilizer as recommended for the crop.

If you suspect that beetles in your area transmit disease, choose resistant varieties. Check your seed catalogs before choosing seed.

CURCULIOS

Several species of curculio ruin fruit and nut crops. Adult snout beetles feed on leaves and flowers and then puncture newly formed fruits and lay eggs inside. The punctures scar fruits badly; egg-laying punctures take the form of multiple small holes in fruits or characteristic crescent-shaped scars. Fruits become warty, scarred, or misshapen and often drop prematurely. Larvae may eat small fruits, such as cherries, entirely. Punctures on peaches and plums permit the spores of brown-rot fungus to enter, compounding the damage.

The apple curculio makes numerous punctures close together on apples, cherries, quinces, and pears. The plum curculio, a serious pest of stone fruits, such as apricots, cherries, nectarines, peaches, plums, and prunes, also injures apples. The punctures cause a crescent-shaped scar.

The pecan weevil and black walnut curculio cause nuts to shrivel and drop.

The Pest

Two generations of plum curculios can occur per year in the South, but only one occurs in the North. Adult curculios are weevils with prominent downward-curving snouts. They are about 1/4 inch long and dull brown with four bumps on their wing covers. Adults overwinter in debris or other protected spots, feed on spring growth, mate, and lay eggs.

Plum curculio larvae are grayish white, legless grubs with brown heads and curled bodies. They feed inside fruit for several weeks, often causing it to drop to the ground, where the larvae crawl out and pupate several inches underground. The adults emerge in about a month, feeding on fruit until low fall

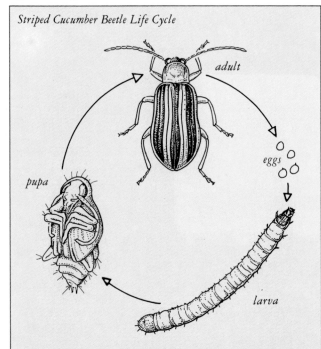

Striped Cucumber Beetle Life Cycle

adult

eggs

pupa

larva

Cucumber beetles hibernate as adults. In spring they mate and lay eggs. The larvae live in the soil, eating plant roots and pupating after two to six weeks. When the adults emerge three weeks later, they feed on leaves and flowers of garden plants.

The plum curculio lays an egg in a small puncture and then cuts a slit next to it, ruining plums and other stone fruits.

temperatures force them into hibernation for the winter.

The apple curculio and black walnut curculio produce only one generation per year. Otherwise, their life cycle closely resembles that of the plum curculio. The pecan weevil spends two years developing underground.

Control Measures
Once worms have infested fruits and nuts, there is no way to stop them from ruining the crop. However, picking up and destroying all fallen fruit every day reduces the number of larvae entering the soil and pupating.

Apply malathion (Ortho Malathion 50 Insect Spray) or a multipurpose orchard spray containing captan, malathion, and methoxychlor (Ortho Home Orchard Spray) to control beetles feeding on fruit or laying eggs. Spray when petals are falling from the blossoms or later in the summer when you see adult beetles feeding on fruit.

You may be able to collect curculios on a light-colored sheet spread out beneath an infested fruit tree. Gently strike the branches with a stick; many beetles may fall onto the sheet and play dead. Quickly stamp on the beetles to destroy them, or drop them into kerosene.

CUTWORMS

To see cutworms working, you will have to come out at night and peer at your garden with a flashlight. During the day, these wormlike caterpillars curl up into a ball about an inch below ground in small cells that they have dug underneath target plants or within a foot of target trees.

The over 2,000 species of cutworm include variegated, darksided, claybacked, black, yellowheaded, pale western, glassy, w-marked, greasy, and dingy cutworms, to name but a few. Each species belongs to one of several groups—surface, climbing, subterranean, or army—according to its feeding behavior.

Surface cutworms operate alone and sever plants, especially seedlings, off at ground level without eating much else the plant has to offer. Common early-season garden pests, they ruin vegetable and flower seedlings. Susceptible vegetables and ornamentals include corn, cabbage, onion, tomato, eggplant, bean, marigold, petunia, flowering tobacco, and dichondra.

Army cutworms work together in large groups and consume nearly all the foliage on a plant before moving on to the next. They have no plant preferences but eat whatever small plants they find in their paths.

Climbing cutworms ascend garden plants to chew on bark, leaves, buds, and flowers. In one night, one such cutworm can devour all but the stem of a young plant, moving on to other plants before daylight. Climbing cutworms sometimes crawl up fruit trees, grapevines, and blueberry bushes to eat leaves or buds.

Subterranean cutworms never come out of the ground at all. They live entirely underground and feed day and night almost exclusively on vegetable and grass roots, causing plants to wilt. The only way you will see these underground pests is by digging in the soil around the dying plant.

The Pest
The soft-bodied, hairless cutworm caterpillars can be various colors—most often gray, brown, or black. They are stout creatures, often growing to 2 inches long, and they curl up when touched.

You will see the first 2-inch-wide gray-brown cutworm adults, which are called miller moths, in April; they continue to appear until June. These night-flying moths sip

The larvae of various night-flying moths, cutworms frustrate gardeners by severing seedlings such as this corn plant.

flower nectar at dusk and flutter around outdoor lights. The females deposit egg clusters almost anywhere, including upper and lower leaf surfaces, twigs, and even the family clothesline. Each female lays from several hundred to 1,500 eggs.

Two days to two weeks later, the larvae emerge, drop to the ground, and begin feeding. Cutworms overwinter as pupae or half-grown larvae under rubbish or in soil or grass clumps. From egg to moth takes 30 to 45 days, with three or four generations possible each season.

Control Measures
Because some cutworm species can decimate an entire seedling stand overnight, do not wait until you have damage to take action if cutworms have been a problem in the past. Prevention is the best cure for cutworms. Apply preplanting insecticides to the soil to eliminate newly hatching larvae. For vegetables, sprinkle diazinon granules (Ortho Vegetable Guard Soil Insect Killer) onto soil before planting, working it in to a depth of 6 to 8 inches. These granules can be used when you are seeding or transplanting or around the bases of established vegetable plants according to label directions.

For cutworms feeding on food and nonfood plant foliage, apply diazinon (Ortho Diazinon Insect Spray, Ortho Diazinon Soil & Foliage Dust) in the early evening because cutworms are most active at night. In addition to treating leaves thoroughly, apply insecticide to plant bases, because some cutworms live in soil, and all hide there during the day. Cutworm control can be difficult, and treatment may be necessary on a weekly basis if destruction continues.

For lawns, use a chlorpyrifos spray (Ortho Lawn Insect Spray, Ortho-Klor® Soil Insect & Termite Killer). Repeat the treatment according to the label instructions.

Some gardeners reduce seedling damage with "cutworm collars" around each plant. Made of stiff paper, aluminum foil, tin cans, or milk cartons, these collars should be at least 2 inches high and pressed firmly into the soil about an inch or more below ground level. Cutworm collars are effective only against nonclimbing pests. To deter climbing cutworms, use sticky-band traps around stems and trunks (see page 29 for precautions).

Remove garden litter regularly so that moths do not have as many places to hide during the day. Cultivate soil thoroughly in September to expose and destroy cutworm pupae and larvae.

EARWIGS

The earwig seems to get blamed for a lot of damage that it does not cause. Although this insect, with its ferocious-looking pincer tail, does nibble ragged holes in flowers, foliage, and ripe fruit, it is really only snacking. An earwig's normal diet is garden fare you don't want anyway, such as decaying litter, rotting fruit, ants, snails, and aphids. Only occasionally does an earwig population get so large that you must consider control measures. Gardeners who want prize blossoms may wish to control small earwig populations, however.

During the day, earwigs hide under bark, fallen leaves, mulch, and stones, preferring cool, damp locations. Sometimes they snooze in the middle of flower blossoms or the holes left in fruit and vegetables by departing slugs, leading people to suspect that they made the initial hole. They feed at night.

Earwigs rarely bite people with their pincers, but it's still not a good idea to pick one up. And despite the folklore that accounts for their name, earwigs do not crawl into the ears of sleeping people.

A male European earwig, fierce as it looks, would rather hide than pinch a gardener.

The Pest
Earwig adults are slim, beetlelike, dark brown insects about $1/2$ inch long. A pair of sharp pincers adorns their rear ends, but they use these mainly for defense. They keep four leathery wings tucked tightly against their bodies.

Hatching in April from eggs laid the preceding fall, earwig young stay near their underground nests for about two weeks, appearing above ground in late April or early May. Except for being plumper, they look like pale brown versions of their parents. They go through several molts, or instars, before becoming full-grown adults.

The young mature by July. Pairing occurs in September, and egg clusters are placed from 2 to 6 inches underground in one cell of a communal nest. Unlike most insects, earwig females watch over their young. Any earwigs seen above ground in winter are usually males.

Usually, there is only one generation per year, but the overwintering adults may deposit a second batch of eggs in June, with nymphs hatching a few weeks later. Any overwintering adults will be gone by July.

Control Measures
Earwigs have several natural enemies, which include the parasitic fly *Bigonichaeta setipennis*, ground beetles, fungi, and mites.

Before you use an earwig insecticide, clean up garden litter and remove fallen fruit—both provide hiding places as well as food for earwigs.

Use the earwig's crawling habit to trap it on trees with a sticky band safely applied around lower trunks (see page 29). Make sure that no crevice is under the band and that no vine allows earwigs to crawl over it. You can also trap earwigs in homemade traps, such as upturned flowerpots stuffed with straw and rolled-up newspapers. The earwigs crawl inside to hide. Destroy the contents each morning.

If earwigs continue to be annoying, use a propoxur bait (Ortho Earwig, Roach & Sowbug Bait) around non-food plants and house foundations. Distribute the bait in late afternoon or early morning wherever earwigs congregate. Do not place bait

Earwigs are mainly scavengers, but they sometimes turn to tender plant parts, such as these flowers, for food.

in piles and, as for all insecticides, keep bait away from children and pets. You can bait from early May to the end of August. Repeat baiting as necessary because earwigs can come in from neighboring property.

On food plants, you can use diazinon (Ortho Diazinon Granules, Ortho Diazinon Insect Spray) or carbaryl (Ortho Liquid Sevin®, Ortho Sevin® Garden Spray). With sprays, use the fine mist setting on your sprayer, and treat during late afternoon or evening for

earwigs feeding on plants and grass. During the day, use a more forceful spray on any crevices outside the house that might provide hiding places. You can also apply a diazinon bait (Ortho Bug-Geta Plus® Snail, Slug & Insect Granules) to garden beds.

ELM LEAF BEETLES

The tiny larvae of this serious elm pest feed on the undersides of leaves, so you may not see the initial infestation at first. The larva devours a leaf from its underside, eating everything except the veins and the upper leaf surface, which turns brown. As damage continues into August from subsequent generations, dry, skeletonized leaves become obvious. Heavily infested trees have sparse foliage from premature leaf drop. Remaining leaves take on a rusty, reddish brown tint.

The larvae damage foliage more than the adult beetles do, but the beetles chew small, rough, circular holes in unfolding leaves before they lay eggs. Trees attacked in spring may grow new leaves, but these are eaten by the next generation of larvae, weakening the tree considerably. Three years of continuous defoliation can kill an elm tree.

Trees weakened by an elm leaf beetle infestation often become host to elm bark beetles as well. These carry spores of Dutch elm disease fungus. Leaves of fungus-infected trees turn yellow and then wilt and die. The fungus clogs a tree's sapwood, and eventually the entire tree dies.

Elm leaf beetles prefer American, English, Scotch, Chinese, and Camperdown elms over slippery, rock, and

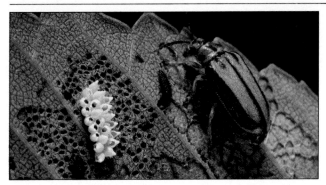

Elm leaf beetles, both adults and larvae, feed on elm leaves. The adults lay eggs on the leaves; several generations of beetles mature each summer. Adults hibernate during the winter.

winged elms, but they will attack almost all species when many varieties grow in the same area.

The Pest

Soon after breaking winter hibernation, the slender, 1/4-inch-long, black-striped, yellow-green adult elm leaf beetles fly to unfolding elm foliage, feed for a while, and mate. The females then lay orange-yellow teardrop-shaped eggs in double rows of 5 to 25 eggs on leaf undersides. Each female produces as many as 600 to 800 eggs over the course of several weeks. Older beetles may be darker in color and their stripes difficult to distinguish.

The sluglike larvae emerge in a week. After three weeks of voracious feeding, the now 1/2-inch-long, dull yellow, black-striped larvae drop or crawl to the ground. Gathering in large masses under tree litter or in crevices at tree bases, they transform into 1/4-inch-long, orange-yellow pupae. You may find masses of these bright pupae at the bases of infested trees.

Adults emerge 10 to 14 days later, return to foliage, and lay eggs for another generation. There can be one to five generations each year, with more generations occurring in long growing seasons and during warm weather.

In autumn, adult elm leaf beetles begin migrating into attics, cellars, sheds, and protected places outdoors, such as under loose tree bark and

house shingles. They can become quite a nuisance inside homes as they seek hibernation spots behind curtains, beneath carpets, between books, and in similar places. With spring, they reemerge, fly to nearby elm trees, mate, and begin laying eggs.

Control Measures

Proper timing is very important for best insecticide results. Examine leaf undersides for yellow eggs and young larvae in March and April in the South and in May and June in the North, soon after trees leaf out. Apply insecticides about three weeks after the leaves emerge, or when they reach full size, if you observe eggs and small larvae. A second application may be necessary two to three weeks later. Continue examining trees every two to three weeks for the rest of the summer, because reinfestations from neighboring trees can occur.

Foliage sprays of both carbaryl (Ortho Liquid Sevin®, Ortho Sevin® Garden Spray) and acephate (Orthene® Systemic Insect Control, Ortho Isotox® Insect Killer) give excellent elm leaf beetle control. Avoid applying carbaryl sprays when the temperature exceeds 85° F or when a long stretch of humid weather is expected.

Regularly remove and burn or destroy leaf litter during the growing season to eliminate pupae around bases of trees.

FALL WEBWORMS

When you see the branch ends of fruit, nut, and shade trees covered with loosely woven, dirty-white webbing, fall webworms may be the culprit. These pests spin webs in trees in early summer and again more prolifically in fall. Although they favor apple, ash, and oak trees, fall webworms attack over 120 kinds of fruit, nut, and shade trees, as well as roses and ornamental shrubs, throughout North America.

Several other caterpillars—tent caterpillars and uglynest caterpillars—spin webs in trees. You can control them in the same way you control fall webworms, although you may want to distinguish between them. Their nests provide the clue.

Tent caterpillars usually build nests in trunk or branch crotches, not at the tips. (See page 89 for more information

Young fall webworm larvae feed on leaves inside their ever-expanding nest. When mature, they crawl down the tree to pupate in ground debris.

on tent caterpillars.) Uglynest caterpillars make their nests on branch ends, as fall webworms do, but their nests appear thick and messy, being filled with excrement, leaf parts, and pupae. Cherry, hawthorn, and rose are favored feeding sites of uglynest caterpillars. Oak webworms feed only on scrub, red, black, and scarlet oaks. Mimosa webworms attack only mimosa and honey locust.

The Pest

The fall webworm is a fuzzy, pale green or yellow caterpillar measuring about 1 inch long. To distinguish the fall webworm from other web-spinning caterpillars, look for a dark stripe down the back, a yellowish stripe along each side, and a body covered with very long, silky gray hairs.

Two common kinds of fall webworms attack garden plants. The redheaded fall webworm has a red head with orange to reddish tubercles down its back. The blackheaded fall webworm has a black head with black tubercles on its back.

Groups of caterpillars make protective nests and feed within them. As they chew one leaf after another, their nests grow ever larger, until they have woven together the ends of several leafless branches. Blackheaded webworms create flimsy webs; redheaded webworms make larger, denser webs. When disturbed or threatened, fall webworms make jerky but rhythmic movements.

The caterpillars pupate over the winter as brown pupae within cocoons hidden beneath tree bark or garden litter. The adult moths emerge any time from mid-March to mid-April. These 2-inch-wide moths have a distinctive satin white color, brown wing spots, and tiny spots of red or orange at the bases of their front legs.

Female moths mate and soon lay globular white or golden yellow eggs in masses of 200 to 500 on leaf undersides. A protective layer of woolly scales covers each egg mass. Moths of the redheaded fall webworm deposit eggs in double layers in mid-April. Those of the blackheaded fall webworm deposit eggs in single layers in mid-March.

First-generation caterpillars hatch and feed from early spring to midsummer. They then crawl down trees to pupate in soil. A new cycle of

Fall webworms spin silken nests around branch ends. The pests rarely kill trees but can weaken them.

moths and eggs takes place, with the second generation of caterpillars feeding from August to September.

The fall feeders remain in their nests until midautumn, when they crawl down the tree trunks to pupate over the winter in the soil or in bark crevices. You will usually see these caterpillars moving about in groups.

The fall brood of caterpillars defoliates trees more extensively than the spring brood. Defoliation often includes several branches, occasionally an entire tree. Nests and defoliated branches are unsightly, but fall webworms usually do not kill trees, except in severe infestations. Early-season leaf loss weakens a tree's vigor and increases its susceptibility to other pests, however, so you might want to consider control measures.

Control Measures
Because fall webworms feed within their nests, you might want to cut out and destroy webbed branch ends as soon as you see them. Be sure, however, that pruning does not adversely affect the shape or productivity of the tree.

Spraying with BT insecticide, which contains a parasitic bacteria, works well in the early stages of an infestation, when caterpillars are small. Spring rains decrease the effectiveness of BT spray, so repeat applications, if needed, according to label directions.

You can also spray listed trees with carbaryl (Ortho Liquid Sevin®, Ortho Sevin® Garden Spray) or diazinon (Ortho Fruit & Vegetable Insect Control). A multipurpose spray containing a captan-malathion-methoxychlor compound (Ortho Home Orchard Spray) is a good choice for orchard trees. Use a tank-type or power sprayer to reach high branches, applying at the first sign of infestation. A high-pressure spray forces insecticide into webs and improves control.

On roses and ornamental trees and shrubs, you can also use acephate (Orthene® Systemic Insect Control).

You might also try a sticky band around tree bases to trap some of the descending caterpillars, thus reducing the size of future generations. (See page 29 for proper application techniques.)

FLEA BEETLES

If you encounter minuscule beetles that jump about like fleas when disturbed, you have met flea beetles. These pests eat multiple round holes twice their size in leaves of all kinds, but they prefer vegetable seedlings and young plants. Infested leaves quickly dry out and may wither. Drying often kills seedlings. Some plants, especially corn, have a scalded appearance caused by flea beetles eating away the upper leaf surface.

You may find various species of flea beetle in your garden, including alder, cabbage, corn, elm, mint, striped, sinuate-striped, palestriped, potato, redlegged, spinach, strawberry, tobacco, toothed, sweetpotato, grape, and horseradish flea beetles. Colors differ among species, and different species infest various parts of the country, but no garden is immune.

On dichondra, flea beetles do more damage than any other insect. At first, when the outside edges of your lawn turn brown, you might blame it on overfertilization or underwatering. As damage progresses toward the center of the lawn, you may look but still not notice any bugs. To see the tiny pests, spread a white tissue on the border between a damaged area and a healthy one. Flea beetles will hop onto the handkerchief then probably hop off again to continue their meal.

Potato flea beetles make those black spots and discolored pathways that you sometimes find when peeling potatoes for dinner. They also cause potato exteriors to become scaly. As soon as potato or tomato foliage appears, potato flea beetles arrive in droves to feed on them. They can also transmit potato viruses as they feed. Virus symptoms include stunted or dwarfed plants that have reduced vigor and productivity and distorted, mottled, or crinkled leaves.

Potato flea beetles also feed on pumpkin, eggplant, pepper, petunia, sunflower, violet, spinach, and primrose, among other plants.

Grape flea beetles wait on any nearby wild grapes or cultivated grapevines for newly emerging grape leaves. Next the flea beetles hop over to attack bud centers, destroying future grape canes. One adult beetle damages several buds, so if you have numerous beetles in your garden, both crop and cane growth will suffer. Grape flea beetles are most prevalent on neglected grapevines. They also feed on apple, plum, and elm trees.

Corn flea beetles make small holes in corn leaves, but they cause more damage by transmitting Stewart's wilt bacteria than by eating leaves. Corn plants infested with these bacteria become stunted and have long, wide, irregular streaks in the leaves. The leaves eventually turn brown and dry, and the plants wilt rapidly and then die.

Strawberry flea beetles go after your fuchsias and roses

Plants infested with flea beetles show characteristic pinhole feeding sites like the ones on this eggplant leaf.

as well as your strawberry patch. You will see damage before flowers appear, with leaves browning around many small, round shotholes.

True to its name, the spinach flea beetle feeds on spinach leaves, but it also likes beet leaves.

The Pest
The destructive black, 1/16-inch-long potato flea beetle overwinters as an adult in soil or garden litter. Emerging in May, the female lays about 100 white eggs near the soil surface close to a plant base. Tiny grubs emerge about a week later, depending on the weather. They feed on roots and tubers for two to three weeks. After pupating in soil for 12 days, the grubs change to adult beetle form. Because adult beetles can live for two months, there can be one to four overlapping generations per year.

Metallic, dark blue grape flea beetles are 1/5 inch long and start laying yellow eggs on buds, under bark, and on leaves in early summer. The black-spotted, light brown grubs emerge from June to mid-July, feeding for three to four weeks on upper leaf surfaces and causing lower leaf surfaces to brown. They then pupate in soil, emerging one to two weeks later as adult beetles. The adults continue feeding on new growth throughout the summer and then hibernate over the winter under garden litter. There is only one generation each year.

Corn flea beetles are $1/16$ inch long and brass colored. The $1/16$-inch-long strawberry

The adult flea beetle hops about when disturbed at a meal; the larva feeds on roots. This is the eggplant flea beetle.

flea beetles can be metallic green, golden bronze, or purple. Spinach flea beetles, comparative giants at $1/5$ inch, have yellow chests, greenish black wing covers, and black heads. Unlike most other flea beetles, spinach flea beetles deposit eggs in holes that they eat in plant stems. Emerging grubs are $1/4$ inch long, warty, and wrinkled. Two generations usually occur each year.

Control Measures

All flea beetles are quite susceptible to insecticidal sprays and dusts. Begin controls as soon as you first see leaf damage in the spring. For strawberry flea beetles, use insecticide one week or so before bloom. For grape flea beetles, use insecticide when the buds swell, repeating to kill grubs when shoots are 6 to 8 inches long.

Control flea beetles on vegetable and small fruit

plants by spraying with diazinon (Ortho Diazinon Insect Spray, Ortho Fruit & Vegetable Insect Control) or dusting with carbaryl (Ortho Sevin® Garden Dust). For vegetables, you can also use rotenone (Ortho Rotenone Dust or Spray) or a pyrethrins-rotenone compound (Ortho Tomato & Vegetable Insect Spray).

For best results with dusts, use in early morning or late evening when the temperature is low and the air is still. Treat both upper and lower leaf surfaces.

After applying pesticide, observe new growth carefully for continuing damage, and repeat the treatment at weekly intervals if necessary. Be certain that your plant is listed on the insecticide label.

On nonfood plants, use diazinon (Ortho Diazinon Insect Spray) or carbaryl (Ortho Sevin® Garden Dust). For flea beetles on grass and dichondra lawns, use chlorpyrifos (Ortho Lawn Insect Spray). Water the area before applying insecticide. Use a lawn sprayer (Ortho Lawn Sprayer); for best results treat the entire lawn. Repeat treatment once a month during the growing season.

Because flea beetles over-winter in garden litter, keep your garden clean and neat. Weed removal eliminates those alternate feeding sites that flea beetles use while waiting for seedlings to emerge. Always prepare the ground thoroughly before planting; quick-growing, healthy vegetable seedlings can often survive flea beetle attacks. Monthly fertilizer from March to September helps dichondra lawns fight off flea beetle damage.

When planting corn in areas that are subject to bacterial wilt, use the more resistant varieties, such as 'Apache', 'Aztec', 'Merit', and 'Silver Queen'.

FRUIT FLIES

The fruit flies that ruin fruit crops are larger than the tiny vinegar fruit flies you often see hovering over ripening fruit indoors. Although some, such as the cherry fruit fly, reach only $1/5$ inch long, the oriental fruit fly can be larger than a house fly. In between in size are the walnut husk fly, Mediterranean fruit fly, Caribbean fruit fly, Mexican fruit fly, apple fruit fly, and currant fruit fly.

Cherry fruit fly maggots are the cause of most "wormy" cherries. You see their damage as misshapen, undersized fruits, often with one side shrunken or decayed and turning prematurely red. In addition to cherries, the cherry fruit fly attacks pears, plums, and wild cherries.

Apple fruit fly maggots destroy apple, blueberry, plum, and cherry crops. In some states, infestation of unsprayed apples reaches 100 percent. The maggots tunnel through fruit, tearing the pulp into brown, winding galleries. Early apples become a soft mass of rotten pulp; later varieties have brown, crumbly streaks throughout and a pitted surface.

Walnut husk fly maggots tunnel through walnut husks, causing black decay on the surface of the shell. As they feed, the maggots excrete a dark liquid that stains the shells and may darken the kernels. Heavily infested walnuts are black on the outside, and the blackened areas are smooth and soft. If you break through the blackened areas, you can see the feeding maggots. They remain in the husk, never feeding inside the shell, although husk decay can allow molds to enter the shells and rot the nuts.

Some fly species cause walnut shells to become slimy and to stick to the nuts. Such walnuts can be unattractive, but they are still edible. Walnut husk fly maggots may also injure nutrient channels within developing nuts, caus-

Although walnut husk fly maggots can often be removed with the husk, they make the nuts unappetizing and may allow molds to enter and rot the nut.

ing kernels to shrivel. Some infested nuts drop prematurely, while others remain on the tree long after non-infested nuts have fallen to the ground.

These maggots prefer walnuts with thick shells, seldom attacking thin-shelled varieties or trees that are under moisture stress. Walnut husk flies also attack peaches.

Do not confuse walnut blight with walnut husk fly damage. Walnut blight, a fungus disease, results in rough, sunken, and cracked nutshells that are hard to the touch. Other insect pests also attack walnuts: Larvae feeding on mature nutmeats are not walnut husk fly maggots. They may be navel orangeworms, filbertworms, or codling moth larvae (see page 46). These pests attack the walnuts as well as the husks. Walnut husk fly maggots feed only on the husks.

Currant fruit fly maggots go after gooseberries as well as currants, causing red fruit that drops prematurely.

Oriental fruit fly maggots feed on about 250 different kinds of fruit, nut, and vegetable crops, including apples, apricots, avocados, bell peppers, cucumbers, grapes, grapefruits, lemons, tangerines, oranges, peaches, pears, plums, tomatoes, walnuts, watermelons, pineapples, papayas, and olives. Not only do maggots cause wormy fruits, but their feeding makes an open pathway through which decay organisms can enter, reducing the fruit interiors to rotten masses.

A foreign pest, the oriental fruit fly has successfully gained permanent residency in the United States only in Hawaii, but its importation to other regions remains a real possibility. The transportation of fruit trees and fresh fruit into areas subject to oriental fruit fly invasion is subject to strict quarantine, including mail quarantine.

The Caribbean fruit fly attacks citrus. Ripe fruits fall to the ground, each containing a small rotten spot and a tiny hole in the skin. Open the fruit and you will find a small white maggot just below the rotting area.

The Mediterranean fruit fly (see photograph, page 10) is the most destructive of the many kinds of fruit flies. Although the medfly, as it is often called, and the Mexican fruit fly occasionally make headlines when found inside the United States, so far strict quarantine laws have kept infestations of these foreign pests to a minimum. Effective

control measures—at a cost of millions of dollars—have been able to eliminate each outbreak. Both can attack over 100 types of wild and cultivated fruits.

Most medfly, oriental fruit fly, and Mexican fruit fly infestations begin with travelers bringing home maggot-infested fruits and vegetables. Once introduced, these pests can quickly threaten commercial farms and home gardens.

If you are suspicious that a fruit fly outbreak could be one of these pests, notify your county agricultural extension service immediately. Agricultural agents will place sex-attractant and feeding-lure traps in the area. An insecticide inside the trap kills the male flies on contact. These male flies can then be identified and counted to determine the extent of an outbreak.

The Pest

Adult cherry fruit flies are black with yellow borders on their chests, two white abdominal stripes, and dark wing bands. Emerging from overwintering pupae in early

June to mid-July, they fly to fruit trees and feed for about 10 days by scraping leaf and fruit surfaces and sponging up the liquefied sap.

The female flies lay eggs under the skins of young fruits. These hatch in three to five days, and the 1/4-inch-long white maggots develop inside the fruits for about two weeks, eating the interiors.

The striking wing patterns of an adult apple fruit fly are identification clues. The secret to control is to keep the pest from laying eggs in your apples.

When full grown, the maggots eat their way out of the fruits, drop to the ground, and spend their next six months as pupae 2 or 3 inches below the soil surface.

The adult apple fruit fly emerges in late June to early July. Slightly smaller than a house fly, the apple fruit fly is black with white abdominal bands and noticeable zigzag black wing bands. The female punctures fruit skin, laying eggs in the punctures. Within 10 days, these hatch into 3/8-inch-long white maggots. The maggots tunnel inside the fruits and remain in the ruined apples for about a week after the apples fall prematurely to the ground. They then leave the fruit to pupate in the soil.

Adult walnut husk flies are slightly smaller than house flies; they are brown with a yellow semicircle on their backs and have dark-banded, transparent wings. The first flies emerge in July and August, but others continue to emerge as late as October. Mating and egg laying begin

Premature apple fall is often due to apple fruit fly maggots. These pests turn apples to mush.

soon after adult emergence and may continue until fall.

The females puncture the husks of growing nuts and deposit about 15 tiny, pearl-colored eggs apiece just beneath the skin. The almost transparent 1/2-inch-long walnut husk fly maggots emerge about a week later and tunnel through walnut husks or under peach skins for several weeks.

When the nuts fall, the maggots drop with them and burrow into the soil. Here they change into pupal form and overwinter, looking somewhat like grains of wheat. Some walnut husk flies have one-year-long underground life cycles; others have two-year-long cycles.

The yellow-bodied, house fly–sized currant fruit fly has dark-banded wings. It emerges from overwintering soil-borne pupae in April or May. Each female lays up to 200 eggs, which develop into whitish maggots. The maggots feed for a few days after the fruit drops and then enter the ground to pupate.

The adult female oriental fruit fly, yellow with dark chest markings and clear wings, punctures fruit skin and then inserts its eggs, laying a total of 100 to 200 eggs. These hatch within three days, and the white-pink maggots feed within the fruits for 12 days. They then drop to the ground and pupate, emerging as adult flies approximately 37 days later.

Seldom seen, the 1/2-inch-wide brown adult female Caribbean fruit fly deposits

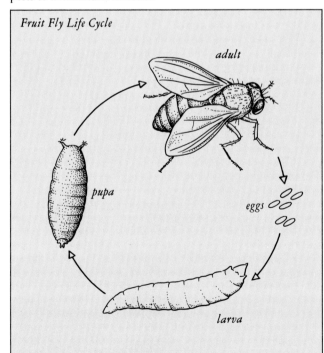

Fruit Fly Life Cycle

adult

pupa

eggs

larva

Adult fruit flies lay eggs near a plant that will later be a food source. Larvae (maggots) feed for one to several weeks and then pupate in the soil. Several generations occur each season. Generations that overwinter do so as puparia.

100 to 200 eggs in ripe fruit while it is still on the tree. Tiny maggots hatch two to three days later and feed inside the fruit for 7 to 10 days. During this period the fruit drops, and the larvae enter the soil to pupate. Another adult generation emerges two weeks later.

The Mexican fruit fly is larger than a house fly and is conspicuously marked in yellow and brown. The Mediterranean fruit fly has a similar appearance but is somewhat smaller, with a yellow abdomen marked by silver cross-bands and wings banded with yellow, brown, and black.

Control Measures

Once fruit fly maggots have infested fruits, it is impossible to kill them and still eat your harvest. The secret to controlling these pests and preventing wormy fruit is to eliminate the adult flies before they can lay eggs.

Because successful control depends heavily on accurately timed insecticide applications, you may want to check with your county agricultural extension agent for suggested spray times for your area.

Commercial growers sometimes judge when to spray for fruit flies by monitoring fruit fly presence and activity with traps. You can catch some fruit fly species with a sticky trap baited with pheromone or food attractant. Hang the traps in your fruit trees so that they are 2 to 3 feet above ground, and check them every other day to see what you have caught. Add new attractant and pheromone every six weeks.

Red spheres covered with a sticky substance will lure some egg-laying cherry fruit flies and apple fruit flies to their deaths. They land on the spheres, mistaking them for fruit, and get stuck.

Control fruit flies with a carbaryl spray (Ortho Liquid Sevin®), a multipurpose orchard spray containing a captan-malathion-methoxychlor compound (Ortho Home Orchard Spray), or a diazinon spray (Ortho Fruit & Vegetable Insect Control).

Treat cherry trees a week after you catch the first cherry fruit fly, again 10 days later, and then as often as flies appear in your trap. Spray apple trees when flies first appear and then at 7- to 10-day intervals until the beginning of September.

No insecticide currently available can be used to control Caribbean fruit flies on home citrus trees. Because mature and overripe fruit attracts the pests, pick fruit as soon as it matures. Dispose of fallen fruit daily, before maggots escape into the soil.

To control walnut husk flies, spray with malathion in mid-July and again two more times at weekly intervals, for a total of three applications. Spray the tree thoroughly, particularly the upper foliage. Do not spray after husks have begun to split. Malathion sprays kill adult flies but do not destroy eggs or maggots within the husks.

It is a good idea to destroy maggots in fallen walnuts before they can enter the soil to pupate. Pick up fallen nuts every day. (Any nuts not dropping because of maggot infestation may have to be knocked down.) Immediately place nuts in buckets and fill with water; let the nuts soak overnight. The maggots will drown, and the nuts can be safely discarded.

Good orchard sanitation can reduce next year's population of fruit flies. Apple fruit fly maggots remain in fallen fruit for up to a week before entering the ground to pupate, so remove fruit litter at least twice a week. Most other fruit fly maggots do not wait as long before abandoning the fruit for the ground, so it is a good idea to pick up and destroy fallen fruit every day.

GALL-FORMING INSECTS

A gall by any other name may be an oak apple, witches' broom, root knot, or crown wart. Galls are odd-looking growths or swellings on trees or garden plants. They take many different forms and are caused by many different kinds of pests, including some wasps, midges, aphids, psyllids, caterpillars, mites, beetles, and nematodes. Galls occur on leaves, flowers, buds, twigs, branches, roots, and even on acorns.

Gall-forming insects inject growth-inducing chemicals into plants when they lay eggs or feed, causing the cells of the plant in the injured area to change from a normal growth

This young adult cynipid wasp, which has just emerged from an oak apple gall, is ready for its first flight.

pattern to an abnormal one. The cells enlarge but do not undergo rapid division, like a cancer, until they surround the insect or its larvae. The insects feed on the host plants, spending at least part of their lives protected within the gall.

Each gall-making insect creates a gall of a unique size, shape, and color. Scientists can often examine a gall and tell you what type of insect formed it without ever seeing the pest inside.

Almost every type of plant can get some kind of gall, but they form most frequently on oak, elm, beech, eucalyptus, willow, and fig trees and on rose plants. There may be several galls on a plant, either all caused by the same insect species or each caused by a different type of insect.

You might want to differentiate between insect-caused galls and the rough, round, large crown galls that develop on roots, on stems near the soil line, at graft unions, and at the bases of tree trunks. Crown galls, caused by soil-borne bacteria, range from 1 inch wide to more than 1 foot wide. You see crown galls on rose plants, cherry trees, and berry vines, among others. To tell the difference between an abnormal crown gall and a normal tree burl, scoop a little out with a knife. The inside of a burl will be clean wood; the inside of a crown gall will have pockets of black, crumbly material.

Crown galls, burls, and insect-caused galls can exist together on the same tree. A professional tree surgeon can remove large tree galls. Although some insect-caused galls can look rather odd, most do not damage anything but a plant's appearance. However, certain species of phylloxera—tiny, aphidlike insects—create root galls in some varieties of grape that destroy the plant, and Hessian fly midge infestations create galls in wheat stems that sometimes stunt entire crops.

The Pest

The harmless large, brown, apple-shaped galls attached to oak tree twigs house immature cynipid gall wasps. These wasps, of which there are more than 600 types, also

Another wasp species makes the oak hedgehog gall. Experts can often tell the wasp species by looking at the gall it has made.

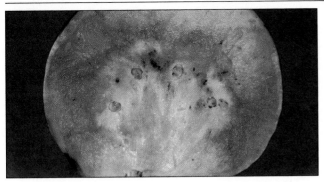

A section of an oak apple gall reveals the tiny wasp larvae that are feeding and maturing inside.

create spiny, star-shaped, flattened, or elongated galls on oak leaves and twigs. They seldom visit any other type of tree.

Mature female cynipid wasps pierce plant parts with their egg-laying organs, depositing a single egg inside each tiny hole. Accompanying the egg will be special fluids that cause gall formation. Emerging larvae produce substances that maintain gall growth, and they feed and live within this protected environment. At maturity, cynipid wasp larvae transform into pupae and then adults, at which point they chew their way out of galls. Depending on the species, there can be one or more generations a year.

Gall wasps seldom harm host plants, although some can disrupt the movement of water and nutrients through the affected part, reducing plant vigor.

Gall midges can cause over 700 types of galls. These $\frac{1}{16}$- to $\frac{1}{4}$-inch-long two-winged flies are relatives of the mosquito, but they don't bite. You may see gall midges in your garden on violets, spruces, pines, grapevines, honey locusts, cacti, and other plants, depending on where you live.

The orange chrysanthemum gall midge, which limits itself to chrysanthemums, lays 100 minute eggs on new shoots. Yellow, orange, or white maggots hatch in 3 to 16 days and bore into plant tissue. The resulting irritation causes many tiny, cone-shaped galls on stems and upper leaf surfaces. A group of galls has a knotted appearance. You will see twisted stems with distorted buds. Each life cycle takes about 35 days, and there are as many as six generations per year.

The dogwood clubgall midge, common on flowering dogwood, creates a club-shaped gall, $\frac{1}{2}$ to 1 inch long, on twigs. The adult midge places eggs on young shoots in late May, and the small, orange larvae remain in the galls until September, when they drop to the ground to pupate in soil. Treat by cutting off and destroying swollen twigs while larvae remain inside.

Cooley spruce gall adelgids (formerly called Cooley spruce gall aphids) feed on new growth of the Colorado blue spruce, oriental spruce, Sitka spruce, and Engelmann spruce. Eastern spruce gall adelgids (formerly called eastern spruce gall aphids) infest Norway, Engelmann, red, white, and black spruce. Adelgids overwintering on needles lay eggs at the bases of developing needles in spring. The young nymphs feed on the new growth and introduce toxins, which cause $\frac{1}{2}$-inch-long conelike galls to swell around the nymphs.

Initially greenish, the galls change to brown and come to resemble pinecones or pineapples. Each gall contains many chambers, with several young adelgids in each. Galls open in midsummer, and Cooley spruce gall adelgids migrate to Douglas fir for egg laying. (No galls form on the fir.) Eastern spruce gall adelgids fly to the same or to other spruces to lay eggs for a second, generation, which overwinters.

The presence of many galls can disfigure a spruce tree. Often, the growth of an infested tree slows, and some branches may die.

Elm cockscombgall aphids make galls that appear to be growing out of the leaves. These green, red-tipped galls grow to about $\frac{1}{2}$ inch high and $\frac{3}{4}$ inch wide and resemble cock's combs. Aphids in these galls produce honeydew, which drips under the trees.

The grape phylloxera creates galls on grape roots and the upper surfaces of grape leaves. It is the most destructive grape pest in the western states. Feeding phylloxera cause root rot and decay. Vines grow slowly and produce few grape clusters. Very often plants die.

The grape phylloxera's complex life cycle differs from region to region; California species form galls only on roots. Because grapes grown in the East have developed resistance to this pest, susceptible varieties can be grafted onto resistant rootstocks, providing cultural control in the West.

The common witches' broom gall, caused by mites and possibly a mite-introduced fungus, resembles a bushy clump of twigs among otherwise normal branches. It is most common on hackberry but also occurs on blueberry, cherry, spruce, pine, and fir, among other trees. This gall is most noticeable when trees are dormant. It does not harm the tree.

Control Measures

Although several parasitic wasps attack gall-forming insects, they are not always around when you bring susceptible plants into your garden. You may have a large number of galls and then, a year later, as parasitic wasps arrive, a much lower number.

Once a gall has begun to develop, you cannot stop its growth with insecticides. Contact insecticides work only during the brief period of adult emergence, and this time varies from year to year.

To control the destructive spruce gall adelgids, time insecticide sprays carefully. Apply pesticide to destroy the egg-laying adelgids in spring when new growth begins but before needles unfold. Spray

Midges cause the grapevine tomato galls that are enlarging these grape stems and leaf petioles.

again in late summer or early fall to wipe out the overwintering adelgids, which are not protected by galls.

For aphid- and adelgid-caused galls, appropriate insecticides include malathion (Ortho Malathion 50 Insect Spray), carbaryl (Ortho Sevin® Garden Spray), and diazinon (Ortho Diazinon Insect Spray). Read the container label carefully, and treat only listed plants.

Avoid planting spruce and Douglas fir together, because the Cooley spruce gall adelgid cannot complete its life cycle without the alternate host.

Do not prune out galls on mature spruces, especially those on the terminal leader; this disfigures the shape of the tree. You can safely prune out galls on young spruces, however. If gall branches on other trees become unsightly or numerous, cut them off and destroy the prunings. Prune and dispose of as many galls as possible as soon as you see them. This is the only way to get rid of the protected larvae or adults.

GRASSHOPPERS

Grasshoppers, often called locusts, do not become serious pests every year. Hordes emerge only during ideal weather conditions, such as after mild winters or cool springs that gradually warm up, or when drought conditions occur during the hatching season. Grasshoppers are most common in areas where annual rainfall averages 10 to 30 inches.

You may see any of the 600 species of grasshopper in your garden. Of these, only five damage gardens significantly. But whether you have

Grasshoppers eat a lot, are not choosy among plants, and often travel in large numbers, making them one of the most destructive of garden pests.

a few in your garden or thousands, you can be sure that they are chewing on any plant they can hop or fly to. Grasshoppers feed on weeds and then move over to field and garden crops. Seedlings disappear first. On more mature foliage, grasshoppers chew large holes around leaf margins. They can strip a tree or bush of leaves and then attack both bark and young shoots.

During severe outbreaks, grasshoppers can seriously damage vegetable gardens, lawns, flowering plants, and some shrubs and trees. On any garden crop, they are most numerous in rows adjacent to weedy areas, but they migrate inward as they deplete food sources. When food is scarce during grasshopper outbreaks, the pests eat dead vegetation, dead insects, and dead animals.

As grasshoppers grow, their hind legs and flight wings increase in length. They thus equip themselves for migration after they have eaten everything in sight. Some species of grasshopper migrate en masse when air temperatures rise above 75° F and are accompanied by a gentle breeze. Migratory grasshoppers can travel 25 to 50 miles in one day.

Grasshoppers feed during the day while the sun shines. They crawl over vegetation, eating continuously; they feed most heavily during the warmest parts of the day. At night they rest in foliage some distance from the ground, becoming active again only when the temperature warms up during the day.

Dry, windy weather encourages grasshopper development. Wet weather causes disease, and heavy rains sometimes bury nymphs so deeply in mud that they cannot escape. Grasshoppers do not drown easily, however. Both young and adults can be carried several miles by floodwaters, and they begin eating as soon as they hit dry land.

The Pest

Not all grasshoppers are green. Colors include pink, reddish brown, tan, white, yellow, brown mottled with red and gray, dark brown, yellow-brown, yellow with black wing marks, and greenish yellow. All have antennae, hind legs enlarged for jumping, and big eyes. They range in length from 1 to 2 inches, depending on age and species.

In August, September, and October, the mature female begins laying eggs in soil or any sod that can be found nearby. To do so it pushes its egg-laying organs into the soil. Into each 3-inch-deep hole go between 25 and 75 eggs surrounded by a gummy substance that hardens to form a case, or pod. The pod of a large grasshopper is about as thick as a pencil, somewhat curved, and about

1 inch long. The outer portion consists of a dried fluid to which soil particles, small stones, or portions of rootlets adhere. Each female can deposit up to a dozen pods.

Overwintering eggs hatch in spring, and the $\frac{1}{8}$- to $\frac{3}{16}$-inch-long nymphs begin feeding and hopping almost immediately. Initially white, they darken rapidly and in half a day can scarcely be seen when resting on the ground or on dead vegetation. They shed skins as they grow, sometimes molting five or six times. The old skins are sometimes left hanging from twigs or posts, where you may mistake them for dead grasshoppers.

After they hatch, grasshoppers reach adulthood in about 60 days, with mating commencing within a week of maturity. Egg laying starts three weeks later. Both adult males and females continue feeding until cold weather kills them. There will usually be only one generation each year, but in warm climates some grasshopper species can produce two generations.

Control Measures

Grasshoppers emerge in April, May, and June. During outbreak years, do not ignore the first nymphs or adults in your garden, because they act as trailblazers for the rest, which follow in groups. Insecticide controls include diazinon (Ortho Fruit & Vegetable Insect Control) for food plants and acephate (Orthene® Systemic Insect Control, Ortho Isotox® Insect Killer) for ornamentals.

Apply insecticides during warm weather, when grasshoppers do the most feeding. Repeat treatments weekly if plants become reinfested.

On lawns, use chlorpyrifos (Ortho Lawn Insect Spray, Ortho-Klor® Soil Insect & Termite Killer), applying it with a lawn sprayer (Ortho Lawn Sprayer). For best results, spray the entire lawn.

GYPSY MOTHS

Gypsy moth caterpillars, feeding in June and July, defoliate millions of acres of trees each year. They attack hundreds of kinds of trees and shrubs but prefer oak. Other favorite trees include alder, apple, basswood, birch, cherry, crabapple, hawthorn, linden, mountain ash, and willow. During periods of heavy infestations, which seem to occur about once a decade, whole forests and communities can be defoliated. By midsummer, instead of being lush and green, forested hillsides in the Northeast, where oak trees predominate, are brown and scorched looking.

When gypsy moth caterpillars infest trees in large numbers—as many as 30,000 caterpillars can infest a single tree, each one eating several leaves in its lifetime—you can hear the rainlike sound of their excrement dropping on the foliage below. Streets and the exteriors of buildings become blackened by crawling caterpillars, and a layer of excrement contaminates the ground beneath trees.

Although defoliated shade or fruit trees do not usually die the first year and may leaf out again by late summer, this double growth puts a great

Periodic outbreaks of gypsy moths defoliate whole forests, leaving susceptible trees leafless in midsummer.

deal of stress on trees, using up their stored food supplies. Infested trees may lose vigor. Deciduous trees that are over 50 percent defoliated several years running can be killed, especially if the infestation is combined with drought, mechanical damage, other insects, or disease. "Tag-along" insects, such as the twolined chestnut borer beetle, and diseases that prey on weakened trees, such as shoestring root-rot fungus, often invade trees that have been weakened by gypsy moths. These diseases cause most tree deaths in the years following gypsy moth defoliation. If evergreens, such as cedar, pine, hemlock and spruce, are defoliated even once, they usually die.

There were no gypsy moths in North America until 1868, when a Massachusetts naturalist interested in culturing silk imported them from Europe. He experimented by breeding domestic silkworms with several European silk-spinning caterpillars in an attempt to create a hardy hybrid that would eat almost anything. He imported several species, including the gypsy moth. Some caterpillars accidentally escaped from the breeding cages, and although the naturalist looked for them and even posted a notice, they escaped detection. Little did

he suspect the devastation that those few caterpillars would bring about.

In Europe the gypsy moth has many natural parasites and predators; in this country it has few. In 1890, just 31 years after the caterpillars escaped their Medford, Massachusetts, cage, the town began raising funds for gypsy moth control. Millions of dollars are now spent annually just trying to keep gypsy moths from destroying our forests.

Once confined to the northeastern states, the gypsy moth continues to expand its territory and has been found in the Carolinas, Florida, California, and Kentucky. The pest has several methods of travel. Because the moth attaches its egg masses to any rough surface, including lumber, trailers, trains, cars, packing boxes, and nursery stock as well as trees, the gypsy moth has proven quite a tourist, despite border inspections and quarantines.

The young caterpillars carry voyaging a step further—they have aerostatic hairs, which act like tiny para-

Female gypsy moths lay egg masses in August. If you see the velvety brown patches, scrape them off and destroy them.

chutes when a strong wind blows. They can travel from tree to tree, or in a stronger wind, as far as 12 miles away. As gypsy moth caterpillars age, they spin silk from their mouths like spiders do, which is what the naturalist originally wanted them for. They do not spin webs, however, but attach the silk to leaves, using it to swing about on trees and to cover their vulnerable pupal stage.

Gypsy moths have marked population swings, with extremely large infestations every 5 to 10 years within a given region. This varies with food supply, natural parasites and predators, and weather patterns. If you are worried about gypsy moth invasions where you live, call your county agricultural extension agent for more information.

The Pest

In early May, the ¼-inch-long, gray-brown, hairy young caterpillars hatch from their eggs and crawl up trees toward the light, feeding on new leaves. They feed at night, starting with the tree crown and working their way down. You probably will not notice the young larvae resting on leaf undersides during the day. If something disturbs them, or if they wish to move to a tree that still has leaves, they spin silken threads and then swing away on a lightweight trapeze.

As gypsy moth caterpillars grow, the tiny spots on their backs become more obvious. From the head down, the first

five pairs are blue, and the remaining six pairs are brick red. The brightly marked caterpillars are about 2 inches long when mature.

When the caterpillars are half grown, their habits change a bit. While a few always remain in trees during the day, the majority rest near tree bases during daylight, crawling up tree trunks to begin feeding at dusk and down again at the end of each night. The females molt six times and males five times before reaching maturity in late June or early July.

After spinning flimsy, transparent cocoons, the caterpillars harden into shell-like,

It is wise to control gypsy moth larvae while they are small because each can eat 5 to 10 tree leaves in its lifetime.

mahogany-colored pupae. These may be concealed in bark crevices and other dark places or may dangle openly from tree trunks, fences, or buildings.

Adult moths emerge approximately two weeks later. Males are gray-brown and resemble many native species; females are a distinctive creamy white with black-striped wings. The females' wingspan is approximately 2 inches. Males are slightly smaller. Neither female nor male moths eat after emerging from their pupae.

The females, who cannot fly, have a powerful male-attracting pheromone. Males, flying day and night, arrive to mate. Egg laying occurs shortly after mating. You will start to notice the highly visible egg masses around the

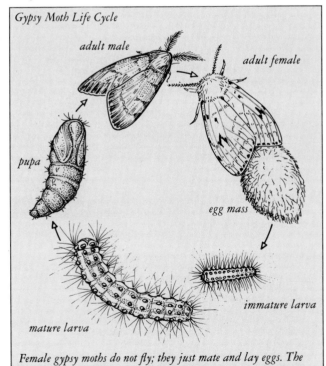

Gypsy Moth Life Cycle

adult male

adult female

pupa

egg mass

immature larva

mature larva

Female gypsy moths do not fly; they just mate and lay eggs. The eggs overwinter, with larvae (caterpillars) hatching in spring. The larvae eat tree leaves in June and July and then pupate in flimsy cocoons. Adult moths emerge two weeks later.

first of August. They are oval, brownish tan, dime- to quarter-sized, and covered with hair. Each contains from 100 to 1,000 eggs. Only one generation occurs per year. Adult moths die shortly after they have mated and produced the overwintering eggs.

Control Measures

In early summer, if you see tree leaves being eaten from the crown downward, particularly on oaks, a gypsy moth favorite, check for gypsy moth caterpillars on leaf undersides or at the tree base. If you do not stop the damage, an entire tree can be defoliated in several weeks. If you find gypsy moth caterpillars on one tree, check nearby trees as well because the caterpillars travel.

Spray infested trees with carbaryl (Ortho Gypsy Moth & Japanese Beetle Killer, Ortho Liquid Sevin®) or the systemic acephate (Orthene® Systemic Insect Control, Ortho Isotox® Insect Killer; the latter will also control mites). These pesticides kill caterpillars by immediately causing them to lose motor coordination and feeding ability.

It is best to spray in early spring, when the caterpillars are less than $\frac{1}{2}$ inch long and are most vulnerable, and before leaf damage becomes serious. Thoroughly spray the entire tree and the leaf undersides. Be sure to spray the trunk, where larvae frequently congregate. Repeat sprayings at weekly intervals if damage continues. You can use a hose-end, knapsack, or bucket sprayer for tree crowns up to 25 feet tall. For very large trees, you may want to call in a professional arborist. Do not apply insecticides when fruit trees are blooming and honeybees are about because insecticides can kill these pollinators.

BT sprays, which contain a pathogenic bacteria that paralyzes a caterpillar's digestive system, can be used on gypsy moth caterpillars. They will not harm bees and so can be used on flowering fruit trees. BT sprays do not last as long as other insecticides, nor do they eliminate as many caterpillars, but they are effective when infestations are not severe. You will have good results when the larvae are less than $\frac{1}{2}$ inch long. As a rule of thumb, apply BT when oak leaves are expanded halfway. Use two applications of BT and include a spreader-sticker in the spray, according to label directions.

To control larger caterpillars, your best tactic may be to encircle tree trunks with commercially available sticky bands (see page 29 for safety tips). These trap caterpillars crawling up or down during their daily journey. Change these bands as soon as they partially fill, because gypsy moth caterpillars will not avoid crawling over the bodies of their trapped siblings.

Another caterpillar-catching method—this one using wide burlap bands—dates back more than 50 years. You place the bands around tree trunks, the idea being not to trap the caterpillars but to give them an apparently safe daytime hiding place. You must then collect and destroy the caterpillars every morning.

To make an effective burlap trap, fold the burlap in half and drape it over a piece of string tied around the trunk about 5 feet from the ground. The burlap must be loosely attached and the bottom edge left free so that caterpillars can hide under the fold during the day.

Fold back the burlap flap each morning, and collect and destroy the caterpillars. Carefully inspect crevices and loose bark. Do not touch the caterpillars—some people are allergic to their hairs (which also blow about in the wind, causing allergies)—but gently scrape them off into a container with a stick or trowel. You can also wear gloves and pick them off by hand.

Drown the collected pests in rubbing alcohol, kerosene, or soapy water.

Before modern insecticides, control measures included painting gypsy moth egg clusters with creosote mixed with a small amount of lampblack for coloration. It is better for homeowners simply to scrape off the egg masses during fall or winter months and drop them into a container of rubbing alcohol or kerosene. These hairy clusters look almost as if they're covered with tan chamois or velvet, a help in identification. New egg masses are firm to the touch; hatched ones are soft and spongy.

Remove all objects and litter around the yard that might shelter gypsy moth larvae and pupae. Woodpiles are particularly attractive egg-laying sites for gypsy moths. Check these places carefully for overwintering egg masses.

Where gypsy moth caterpillars are a severe problem, do not mass-plant their favorite tree species, especially oaks, or you risk losing all of your trees. Choose trees less favored by the moth, such as ash, dogwood, fir, holly, horse chestnut, locust, sycamore, and tulip tree.

Natural predators include ground beetles, particularly the black *Calosoma scrutator,* or fiery searcher. These have some control effect and probably help keep the pest in check during normal years. One ground beetle can devour 10 gypsy moth caterpillars in a day. Some parasitic wasps and flies attack gypsy moth caterpillars and eggs. No current predator or parasite is capable of holding gypsy moth populations in check during years when populations explode, however.

Present research on gypsy moth control focuses on a gypsy moth caterpillar virus, sterilization techniques, pheromone lures, and growth-regulating insecticides.

HORNWORMS

If you grow tomatoes, you have probably already battled the repulsive, huge, green caterpillars known as hornworms. Both tomato and tobacco hornworms chew their way through foliage and fruit, primarily attacking plants in the nightshade family, such as tomato, pepper, eggplant, potato, tobacco, and petunia. They also infest geraniums and herbs. You can often find both species of these voracious pests working at the same time on your garden plants.

Other hornworm species are named after their adult moth stage; they are Abbott's sphinx moth larvae and achemon sphinx moth larvae, both of which infest grape and Virginia creeper; catalpa sphinx moth larvae, which occasionally defoliates catalpa trees; and whitelined sphinx moth larvae, which feeds on apple, beet, tomato, and other fruits and vegetables.

Hornworms feed primarily at night, often eating all the foliage and fruit of a single plant by morning, leaving only large stems as a remembrance of what grew there the

Hornworms eat not only leaves but the tomato fruit as well.

day before. Because each caterpillar consumes large quantities of foliage, it only takes a caterpillar or two on a plant to seriously injure it.

If you are observant, you may notice hornworm damage before the pest devastates your tomatoes. At 3 to 4 inches long, the hornworm should be highly visible, but it tends to stay partially concealed during the day, and the huge worm is the color of the leaves, so it is camouflaged. Look first for the hornworm's trademarks: large, dark green droppings littering the ground or foliage beneath skeletonized leaves. By doing a closer check, you can usually find the pest on a leafy branch directly above the droppings.

The Pest

The tomato and tobacco hornworms look somewhat alike in that they are both smooth skinned, hairless, and varying shades of green and sometimes brown. However, the tomato hornworm has eight V-shaped white marks on its sides and a black horn at the rear, whereas the tobacco hornworm has seven diagonal white marks on the sides of its body and a red horn at the rear.

When threatened, hornworms hold the fronts of their bodies erect in a stiff, sphinxlike pose. Folklore has it that their tiny horns can sting;

they can't. The only damage these caterpillars can do is to your garden.

Hornworms overwinter as 2-inch-long brown, hardshelled pupae about 4 inches deep in soil. The pupal cases have a distinguishing pitcherlike handle. In May or June, the adult moths emerge.

These 4-inch-wide gray moths with mottled brown wing streaks and yellow abdominal spots fly so rapidly, often hovering over flowers, that gardeners often mistake them for hummingbirds. They are often called hummingbird hawk moths, as well as five- or six-spotted sphinx moths and tobacco flies. You will see them primarily at dusk, sipping nectar from deep-throated flowers, such as petunias, with their extremely long tongues.

Each female moth places from 100 to 300 large, yellow-green eggs singly on the leaf undersides of host plants. The caterpillars hatch in a week and immediately begin feeding on foliage. They keep

Tomato hornworms have a black "horn," whereas tobacco hornworms have a red one. Both feed on tomatoes and related plants.

this up for four to six weeks, molting five times before they pupate again for another generation. Two or three generations can occur per year in the South, only one in the North.

The other hornworm species resemble tomato and tobacco hornworms. Abbott's sphinx moth caterpillars are about 2 inches long and chocolate brown. White striped and green or pinkish, achemon caterpillars grow to $3\frac{1}{2}$ inches long and have a black horn when young. The 3-inch-long catalpa sphinx moth caterpillar varies from black to yellow with a black horn. The $3\frac{1}{2}$-inch-long whitelined sphinx moth caterpillar is green with a yellow head and horn and pale, black-rimmed spots.

Control Measures

Because more than one hornworm per plant can severely affect a plant's yield, eliminate these pests as soon as they hatch and before they grow large enough to consume an entire plant in one meal. Begin looking for the pests in early to midsummer.

Fortunately, you have substantial help in controlling hornworms from two natural sources: trichogramma wasps, which parasitize hornworm eggs, and braconid wasps, which lay their own eggs inside hornworm caterpillars. When braconid wasp eggs

hatch, the larvae burrow into the caterpillar, feeding inside its body. They then move to the surface to pupate. You will see these tiny, white cocoons, which resemble miniature grains of puffed rice, lined up on the backs and sides of parasitized caterpillars. By the time the pupae hatch into tiny wasps, the hornworm is dead.

If you do not disturb parasitized hornworms, more braconid wasps eventually emerge to destroy other hornworms. Hand-pick and destroy any unparasitized hornworms you find.

If hornworm feeding threatens your crops, and there are no apparent parasites, use pesticides to control these pests before their appetite gets the best of your plants. A BT spray, which contains pathogenic bacteria, works effectively when the hornworms are small, as does a spray containing pyrethrins (Ortho Tomato & Vegetable Insect Spray). For larger worms, use carbaryl (Ortho Liquid Sevin®, Ortho Sevin® Garden Dust, Ortho Sevin® Garden Spray). Read the label carefully to determine harvesting time after treatment.

To control hornworms on nonfood plants, spray with acephate (Ortho Isotox® Insect Killer, Orthene® Systemic Insect Control). Repeat the spraying if reinfestation occurs, allowing at least 7 to 10 days between applications.

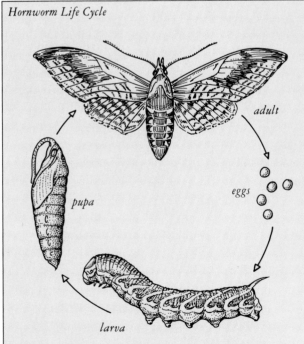

Hornworm Life Cycle

adult

eggs

pupa

larva

Adult hornworms are nectar-feeding moths. The females lay eggs on the leaves of host plants. After hatching, the larvae feed for four to six weeks, molting as they grow. The pupae, which have "handles" containing their tongues, overwinter.

LACE BUGS

Lace bugs, named for their lacy wings, should not be confused with the beneficial insects known as lacewings. Lace bugs severely damage trees and shrubs. They cluster on lower leaf surfaces, sucking plant sap.

White, yellow, or brown specks appear on the upper leaf surfaces of infested plants, and leaves often drop prematurely. Initially, you may not notice the damage, because lace bugs tend to attack large, leafy plants rather than

Lace bugs damage plants by sucking sap. Watch chrysanthemums, azaleas, and pyracanthas for pale or stippled leaves.

vegetables and annual flowers, which you probably inspect more closely.

Infested trees often develop white leaves, which turn brown by August. Continued sap sucking, combined with heavy infestations, greatly reduce the vigor of a plant, resulting in slowed growth. Reduced vigor means that a plant becomes more susceptible to damage from other insects, diseases, stress, or poor garden care. If heavy damage continues for several years, trees and shrubs can die.

Even if infestations seem light, the discolored leaves resulting from lace bug attack detract from the beauty of a plant. On evergreens, unsightly damaged foliage can hang on for more than a year unless it is removed.

Broadleaf evergreens, such as laurel, pyracantha, cotoneaster, azalea, and rhododendron, are commonly attacked. Hawthorn, quince,

sycamore, ash, hickory, mulberry, American elm, black walnut, and apple trees are favorite deciduous targets. You may also find lace bugs on the foliage and stems of chrysanthemum, aster, and scabiosa.

The Pest

Mature lace bugs are flat, ⅛- to ¼-inch-long, rectangular insects. Although their wings appear white at first glance, on closer inspection you will see dark brown to black markings. You can't disturb feeding lace bugs very easily—despite their wings, the adults seldom fly, preferring slow sideways movements.

Each female places clusters of 20 to 50 dark-colored eggs in irregular groups alongside leaf veins. Some eggs are attached with a sticky substance; others are partially inserted into the leaves. About four weeks later, young, dark-colored, wingless nymphs emerge.

The entire life cycle, from egg to adult, lasts about 30 days. Three to five lace bug generations can occur per year, depending on temperature and other environmental factors. Warmer climates support more generations.

Some lace bug species, such as azalea and rhododendron lace bugs, overwinter in the egg stage. Others, particularly those found on deciduous plants, overwinter as adults, hibernating in bark crevices, branch crotches, or similarly protected areas. Overwintering adults become active in spring as leaves begin unfolding.

In some southern states, overwintering eggs start hatching in February, building up to a dense pest population by March. In areas that have cooler springs, overwintering eggs hatch in April or May. The emerging nymphs begin to feed immediately.

Lace bug damage is similar to that done by leafhoppers. To differentiate, turn a leaf over; all lace bugs feed on leaf undersides. You may see flat lace bugs along with nymphs, skins left over from molts, and characteristic spots of brown or black excrement, which later turn a rusty color. You will be able to see this excrement clearly, and its presence differentiates between a leafhopper and a lace bug infestation.

From a distance, lace bug attack may also resemble mite damage. However, the spots caused by mites are smaller and, when you look closely, there will be no lace bug excrement, unless both pests are present.

Control Measures

Control measures should be applied before lace bugs cause unsightly, and destructive, damage. Inspect susceptible plants every two weeks during the growing season, looking for lace bugs on leaf undersides and for leaves with stippled black spots and a mottled, rusty appearance.

If you see only a few lace bugs, you can try washing them off with a strong stream of water from your garden hose. This does not kill them, however; it merely relocates them. Naturally occurring predators, such as lacewings, assassin bugs, spiders, and predaceous mites, may be present and provide control.

If insecticide control becomes necessary on ornamental plants, use carbaryl dust (Ortho Sevin® Garden Dust, Ortho Sevin® 5 Dust), diazinon dust (Ortho Diazinon Soil & Foliage Dust), diazinon spray (Ortho Diazinon Insect Spray), or acephate spray (Orthene® Systemic Insect Control, Ortho Isotox® Insect Killer). It may be necessary to repeat applications at 10- to 14-day intervals to maintain effective control.

When using dust, for best results apply it in early morning or late evening, when temperatures are low and the air is still. Because lace bugs feed on lower leaf surfaces, cover this area thoroughly with either spray or dust. For lace bug damage on trees taller than 25 feet, you may want to consult a tree specialist.

Cultural controls include removing plant litter where adult lace bugs might overwinter. A few lace bugs overwinter on weeds—for example, the chrysanthemum lace bug prefers goldenrod—so keep weeds out of your garden. Because large lace bug populations occur on azaleas and rhododendrons grown in sunny locations, if you have recurring attacks, you might try transplanting these shade-loving varieties to a less sunny spot and planting shrubs better suited to the location.

LEAFHOPPERS

Leafhoppers harm plants by inserting their piercing mouthparts into leaves and sucking out the nutritious leaf sap. As they suck, they inject salivary fluids that are toxic to susceptible plants. The toxic fluid can stunt new growth and discolor leaves. When leafhoppers suck out the green chlorophyll, small white or yellow spots appear on the leaves, giving them a stippled appearance. With severe infestations, leaves drop prematurely. Leafhoppers also transmit virus diseases, which can stunt or kill your plants.

Leafhopper damage is often very similar to the leaf burn caused by excess salt in the soil. Leaf edges turn brown, and leaf tips curl upward. To differentiate between salt damage and hopper burn, look in the folds or on the undersides of leaves for the wedge-shaped leafhoppers and their dark excrement or the empty white skins they cast off when they molt.

To check for leafhoppers, examine the undersides of stippled leaves for pale, shed skins and flightless immature nymphs.

On trees, leafhoppers puncture twigs while laying eggs and may completely girdle twigs, severely injuring or killing them. In addition, all leafhoppers excrete honeydew, a sugary substance that can coat leaves and become the home of the disfiguring sooty mold fungus, which attracts ants, flies, and wasps.

About 2,500 species of leafhopper occur in North America, and each species requires a specific host plant; taken as whole, they feed on almost every kind of garden plant. Of notable concern are the leafhoppers that suck sap from berry and vegetable plants such as cantaloupe, cucumber, tomato, pepper, eggplant, lettuce, bean, beet, potato, grape, and raspberry; flowers such as rose, aster, dahlia, geranium, nasturtium, pansy, and zinnia; fruit trees such as apple, peach, plum, apricot, and almond; and ornamental trees such as Norway maple, locust, elm, poplar, and willow.

The Pest

These very common 1/16- to 5/8-inch-long insects have slender, wedge-shaped bodies with small heads, large eyes, and wings that are held rooflike over their bodies. Adults and nymphs look almost alike, except that the young don't have wings. The most common colors are green, brown, and yellow, but some leafhoppers are beautifully marked with blue, red, yellow, orange, or black.

Leafhoppers have the curious habit of running sideways when disturbed. They also jump quite a bit, accounting for their common name, and adults can fly, so they can get around your garden quite a bit once introduced.

The very common rose leafhopper, found on roses, apples, cane fruits, cherries, currants, dogwoods, elms, grapes, hawthorns, maples, oaks, pears, plums, strawberries, and other plants, causes stippling, yellowing, leaf curl, and premature leaf drop. The punctures made during egg laying cause pimplelike swellings on twigs. When the punctures are numerous, plants become markedly weakened.

In the fall, right before the onset of the first frost or sustained cool weather, the yellowish white rose leafhopper females deposit eggs under twig bark and leaf veins. An inch of rose cane can contain close to 600 eggs. The punctures cause what appear to be small blisters on leaf undersides or pimply spots on twigs. Whitish nymphs with red eyes hatch from the eggs at about the beginning of May. These wander about the plant, finally establishing feeding sites on leaf undersides.

Molting to adult form occurs in the latter part of May and in June. Rose leafhoppers produce two generations a year, the second generation maturing in early fall and laying the overwintering eggs.

Although some leafhoppers are merely garden nuisances, rose leafhopper infestations can kill your roses and related plants. To identify these pests, note that they move forward, rather than sideways as most other leafhoppers do. Rose leafhoppers are most numerous in the northwestern states.

The apple leafhopper has a life-style similar to that of the rose leafhopper, except that there is only one generation a year. Its range extends from the north central states into the Pacific Northwest.

A similar species, the white apple leafhopper, is quite common in the central and eastern states. It can severely infest roses, apples, and many of the berry fruits, turning the leaves almost white. Fruits may be spotted from feeding damage and soiled with excrement. This pest has two generations per year, with young appearing in June and then again in August.

destructive virus diseases. On birch trees the potato leafhopper causes twig death as well as leaf distortion. On citrus this pest, often called bean jassid, punctures and scars the rinds of the fruit.

Potato leafhoppers usually do not overwinter in northern areas, but adults migrate in from the Gulf States during early to mid-May, when the weather warms up. They may feed on alternate host plants first and then move over to potatoes and lay eggs as the weather becomes warmer. Eggs are laid in stems and larger leaf veins; they hatch in six to nine days. Mature forms appear by the third week, with three to five generations possible per year.

The tiny grape leafhopper, colored pale yellow or white with red, blue, or yellow body markings, causes white leaf spots, which gradually turn brown. This sucking damage

Adult leafhoppers move fast, both leaping and flying when disturbed. Some species do little damage; others kill plants and spread disease.

The feeding of the light green potato leafhopper interferes with fluid conduction within leaves, causing a characteristic hopper burn. Initially, this shows up as a triangular spot of yellowing or browning on the leaf tips. The entire leaf margin then begins to roll inward, and leaves brown as they curl, with eventual leaf drop.

In addition to potatoes, this pest attacks dahlias, roses, apples, eggplants, rhubarb, snap beans, celery, soybeans, peanuts, birches, and citrus. Infestations seriously impair crop yield and flower production and often transmit

reduces normal vine growth, resulting in delayed fruit maturity and poor vine growth the following year. Leafhopper droppings can also mar the fruit, making it unappetizing.

Various generations of grape leafhoppers lay eggs within leaf tissue from spring until leaf drop in fall, with two or three overlapping generations occurring per season. Their egg laying accounts for the blisterlike swellings you sometimes see on the undersides of grape leaves. These leafhoppers overwinter as adults on fallen grape leaves.

The beet leafhopper, sometimes called whitefly in the West, is among the species that transmit plant diseases. This pale green to brown pest sometimes carries the very destructive curly top and tomato yellows viruses and attacks many garden vegetables. The beet leafhopper is primarily a problem in the western states, with damage being particularly severe on tomato crops.

Symptoms of beet leafhopper infestation include general yellowing, stunting, and leaf distortion. Besides overall stunting, curly top virus causes warty leaf veins; rolled, distorted, brittle leaves; and masses of hairlike roots on taproots.

The aster leafhopper, sometimes called the six-spotted leafhopper, is pale greenish yellow with six black spots. This leafhopper can produce as many as five generations per year. It transmits aster yellows virus to various vegetables and annual flowers, including aster, periwinkle, thunbergia, alyssum, cineraria, poppy, vinca, carrot, and lettuce.

The disease causes foliage to turn yellow, first along the veins. As the disease progresses, the plants become stunted, with very bushy growth and spindly branches. Aster flowers may be deformed and sickly green. Infested vines may lose their ability to climb.

The redbanded leafhopper, also called the scarlet-and-green leafhopper, infests blackberry and other garden plants throughout the United States. This colorful pest has a green body with bright red body markings and a yellow head, legs, and underside. One to three generations occur each season, and the pest overwinters in garden litter.

Control Measures

You often see leafhoppers out and about at night because they are attracted to incandescent and fluorescent light. Although light traps can attract and kill significant numbers of leafhoppers, this is not a proven control method. If you want to try such a trap, position it well away from the crop you are trying to protect.

Although insecticides control most leafhoppers, the white apple leafhopper has become resistant to most insecticides currently on the market. For insecticidal control of other leafhoppers on ornamental plants, spray with diazinon, (Ortho Diazinon Insect Spray), acephate (Orthene® Systemic Insect Control, Orthenex® Insect & Disease Control), disulfoton (Ortho 3-Way Rose and Flower Care), or malathion (Ortho Malathion 50 Insect Spray). Be sure to cover leaf undersides.

For leafhopper infestations on fruit and nut trees, use diazinon (Ortho Fruit & Vegetable Insect Control), malathion (Ortho Malathion 50 Insect Spray), or a multipurpose spray containing a captan-malathion-methoxychlor compound (Ortho Home Orchard Spray).

Leafhoppers attacking vegetables can be controlled with malathion (Ortho Malathion 50 Insect Spray), diazinon (Ortho Fruit & Vegetable Insect Control, Ortho Diazinon Insect Spray), carbaryl (Ortho Sevin® Garden Dust), pyrethrins (Ortho Tomato & Vegetable Insect Killer), or with an all-purpose vegetable dust that contains a captan-methoxychlor-rotenone compound (Ortho Tomato Vegetable Dust).

Be sure that your plants are listed on the container label whenever you apply any type of insecticide. On vegetable and other edible crop plants, pay particular attention to the harvesting dates after treatment.

Inspect plants every two weeks to determine whether additional spraying is needed. Do not spray more often then every 10 days. If you have had leafhopper damage in the past, particularly on prize plants, you may want to spray in the spring, when leaves first unfold, to prevent significant leaf damage.

Cultural control for leafhoppers includes cleaning up garden litter regularly to eliminate leafhoppers overwintering in protected areas. Removing and destroying fallen leaves in autumn is particularly important. This is most effective when the temperature is cold enough to discourage leafhoppers from flying away when disturbed. Eliminating weeds that harbor leafhopper eggs throughout the year also helps to keep down leafhopper numbers.

Before leafhoppers arrive in spring, some gardeners cover susceptible vegetable plants with a tight tent of cheesecloth or fine plastic netting to prevent the insect from landing and laying eggs. Leave this protective covering on for a month. Although the tent may keep out leafhoppers, it also shades plants, reducing growth and vigor.

Virus infections cannot be controlled with pesticides. Once a plant becomes infested with virus it becomes a source for disease spread. Your only control is to destroy all affected plants. Pull out stunted or yellowed plants, and burn or dispose of them in the garbage.

Some plant varieties are more resistant to leafhopper damage than others. Choose vegetable varieties with thick, tough leaves rather than thin, fragile ones. Likewise, some varieties are bred to be resistant to viruses. Check your seed catalogs before selecting vegetable and fruit varieties.

LEAFMINERS

Leafminer is a catchall name for the larvae of certain species of moth, beetle, two-winged fly, and sawfly. Although they are the larvae of quite different insects, leafminers all look very much alike, feed between the upper and lower surfaces of leaves, and hatch from eggs either deposited on a leaf surface or inserted into the leaf.

With its mouthparts acting like a scythe or shears, the leafminer tunnels between the top and bottom of a leaf, eating the interior. Some leafminer species make straight lines; others create snakelike tunnels. You can see blotch

You can see the brown shadows of serpentine leafminer larvae in the winding path they have eaten between leaf layers.

mines too, where the insect has gone around in a circle, oval, or fingerlike pattern.

Symptoms also include leaf tips that turn yellow and then brown. Leaves may be rolled, wrinkled, or skeletonized, or they may appear scorched or drop prematurely. Although many other pests, such as flea beetles, leafhoppers, and mites, cause some or all of the above symptoms, leafminer "etchings" distinguish this pest.

Leafminer damage is often only cosmetic, but infested plants can be terrible eyesores. Valuable trees can die from repeat attacks, and vegetable and fruit productivity can be reduced.

Boxwood leafminers form blisters in leaves by eating out the insides. Here, one side of a leaf has been cut away to show some of the larvae that did the damage.

The Pest

As many as 700 species of leafminer trouble garden plants in North America. The most notable of these are the birch, boxwood, columbine, chrysanthemum, holly, serpentine, and vegetable leafminers.

Leafminer larvae are about ¼ inch long with wedge-shaped heads that make traveling forward easier. They lack legs, eyes, and antennae. Leafminer larvae feed for varying lengths of time, depending on the species, but all eventually pupate within or just outside the leaves they infest. From these pupae, adult flies, sawflies, moths, or beetles hatch. Some mate and produce several generations a season; most others overwinter as pupae and hatch and mate in spring.

To determine which pest is causing the trouble, carefully observe the tunnel shape and location. Then observe the depth of the tunnel; different leafminer species tunnel mines at different leaf depths. Some create a full-depth mine, visible equally well from both sides of the leaf. Other species create lines that can be seen only on the upper or lower leaf surface. When looking at the mines, note also whether they are along the leaf edge or midrib and whether they start at the outer edge and proceed inward or meander between parallel leaf veins.

Hold the leaf up to the light and, using a magnifying glass, see if you can spot the leafminer working. Depending on the species, the head may move forward and back in a shoveling motion, or from side to side, like the motion of a scythe.

Observe the pattern and color of the frass, or waste product, which is quite characteristic of certain species. Frass spots can be straight, zigzag, spotted, located at one end of the mine only, centered, or tied way out of the way with silken threads.

Your local county agricultural extension agent can help you identify the type of leafminer that is infesting your plants.

Control Measures

Timing is crucial in controlling leafminers. Contact insecticides work only during the brief vulnerable flying stage of the adult or just after the larvae hatch but before they bore into the leaves. Once the larvae have tunneled into leaves, contact insecticides can't harm them.

A better plan of attack involves systemic insecticides, which plants absorb, thus poisoning the feeding leafminer within. Systemics can be used safely and effectively on ornamentals; on edibles, be sure to wait the recommended interval after application before you harvest.

Because controls for leafminers work best when properly timed, you will get optimal results by calling your local county agricultural extension agent or a knowledgeable nursery and asking for advice. Describe leafminer tunnels, location, frass, and the type of plant infested. The agent should be able to prescribe specific spray timings.

General treatment includes spraying flowering plants and ornamentals, beginning when leaves unfold in spring, with the systemic acephate (Orthene® Systemic Insect Control) or the contact poison diazinon (Ortho Diazinon Insect Spray).

On fruit trees and ornamentals, such as birches, dogwoods, peaches, apples, cherries, iris, and rhododendrons, you can use lindane (Ortho Lindane Borer & Leaf Miner Spray). Be sure to follow the precautions described on the label. The systemic acephate (Ortho Isotox® Insect Killer, Orthene® Systemic Insect Control) works well on holly, birch, lilac, and many other ornamentals. Diazinon (Ortho Diazinon Insect Spray) can also be used.

On vegetables or fruits, spray with diazinon (Ortho Diazinon Insect Spray, Ortho Fruit & Vegetable Insect Control). Begin when you first see white egg clusters under vegetable leaves, and repeat twice at weekly intervals to control subsequent generations.

If infestations on flowers and vegetables are light, destroy damaged leaves as soon as you see tunnels to prevent adults from emerging and laying eggs. It is also wise to rake up the fallen leaves of infested plants, especially trees and shrubs, because many leafminer pests overwinter there. Litter can be a continual source of reinfestation.

LEAFROLLERS

Most leafroller caterpillars roll leaves around themselves as they feed, creating a protective tube. Leaves under attack turn brown and die; heavy infestations weaken a plant. Leafrollers also chew on buds, blossoms, and fruit.

Many leafroller species damage garden plants. Some feed on only one type of plant; others choose a variety. The three most common and widely destructive leafrollers are the fruittree, obliquebanded, and redbanded leafrollers.

Besides attacking almost every kind of fruit tree, fruittree leafroller caterpillars also attack nut trees, oaks, ashes, birches, maples, locusts, box elders, elms, poplars, roses, and willows. They often feed within tightly webbed-together leaves, enclosing a small cluster of flower buds

Leafrollers make neat tubes in which they feed. They often wrap and eat flower buds, stopping fruit production.

and stopping fruit formation. They sometimes feed on tiny fruits, causing deep feeding grooves, often followed by premature fruit drop. On mature fruit, characteristic deep, bronze scars with roughened, netlike markings form. A heavy infestation can wipe out an entire apple crop.

Fruittree leafrollers also feed on tender new leaves, giving them a ragged appearance even when rolled into tubes. In severe cases, trees are partially or completely defoliated, with numerous silken

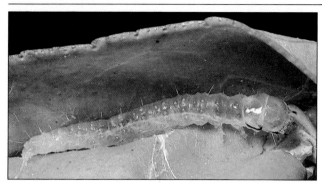

Opening a webbed leaf reveals the leafroller larva that has been feeding within.

threads covering the entire tree and ground below. Very active larvae frequently drop to the ground, defoliating grass and other plants growing beneath trees.

The obliquebanded leafroller is a serious pest of vegetables, flowers, and fruit and ornamental trees. The redbanded leafroller lives in the eastern states, attacking apple and other fruit and ornamental trees as well as vegetables and flowers.

The Pest

Overwintering eggs of the fruittree leafroller hatch into destructive larvae from March to mid-May in cooler areas. The caterpillars are green with brown heads and grow to be 1 inch long. These feed within rolled leaves and mature in 30 days. They then spin a silk lining inside the rolled leaves, within which they change into ¹/₂-inch-long brown pupae. Eight to eleven days later, adult moths emerge.

The ³/₄-inch-wide moths have brown forewings mottled with shades of brown and tan, and whitish to gray hind legs. When resting on tree trunks, their wings take on a bell shape characteristic of all leafroller moths, and their coloration blends in with the texture of the bark.

The moths fly during a three-week period in May or June, depending on the climate. Individual moths live only one week, just long enough to mate and lay eggs. Flat, irregular masses of 30 to 100 eggs laid on twigs and small branches receive a dark

gray or brown cementlike coating, which later turns white. After the larvae emerge the following spring, you can see the exit holes in the egg mass covering. One generation occurs each year.

Redbanded leafrollers overwinter as brown pupae; moths emerge in spring when apple buds open. Measuring ³/₄ inch wide, the moths have brown wings banded with red. They mate and lay eggs on tree bark. The larvae are green and are ¹/₂ inch long when mature. You will see them feeding inside webs on leaf undersides.

After four to six weeks, they form brown pupae within the webbed leaves. Two weeks later, the moths appear, mate, and lay eggs on foliage and fruit for a second generation in July. In some areas, a third generation occurs. Late-season larvae feed on fruit and vegetables, chewing patches on their surfaces.

Like redbanded leafrollers, obliquebanded leafrollers overwinter in cocoons, with ³/₄-inch-wide gray-brown moths emerging in early spring. These lay overlapping masses of green eggs on branches or occasionally the undersides of rose leaves.

The pale green, black-headed caterpillars grow to 1 inch long. These insects mine leaves first and then work inside rolled areas, often tying several leaves together. There are one or more generations per year, with damage continuing from April until November. They attack foliage in spring and fruit and foliage in summer and fall.

Control Measures

The key to controlling leafrollers is eliminating the very small larvae before they begin feeding or hiding inside leaves where pesticides can't reach.

A thorough application of dormant oil spray before buds open in spring often keeps leafroller populations in check. Cover every egg mass with oil spray to destroy caterpillars before they emerge.

Another choice is a BT spray, which contains a pathogenic bacteria, applied after the caterpillars hatch. This is most effective on young caterpillars. Apply BT first when flower buds show color. Some leaf feeding and damage may occur while the bacteria take effect.

On ornamental plants, you can spray in spring when you first see leaf damage with carbaryl (Ortho Liquid Sevin®) or acephate (Ortho Isotox® Insect Killer, Orthene® Systemic Insect Control). On fruit trees, use carbaryl (Ortho Sevin® Garden Spray, Ortho Liquid Sevin®) or diazinon (Ortho Fruit & Vegetable Insect Control).

Spray previously infested fruit trees in spring before you see damage. To ensure fruit set, begin when 75 percent of the petals have fallen and after bees have visited the flowers. Use carbaryl (Ortho Liquid Sevin®) or a multipurpose captan-malathion-methoxychlor compound (Ortho Home Orchard Spray). Repeat according to label directions.

A number of insects, including tachinid flies and trichogramma and ichneumonid wasps, parasitize leafroller caterpillars. Lacewing larvae and various beetles also prey on the caterpillars. When these beneficial insects are plentiful, leafrollers are not overly destructive. Commercial orchards often use pheromone-baited traps to monitor the presence of egg-laying moths. When adults are present, the grower begins a pesticide spray program. The pheromone must be replaced every six weeks.

MAGGOTS

Some two-winged flies zipping about your garden at up to 30 miles per hour may be laying eggs on or near your vegetables. From these eggs hatch small, white, legless maggots, which tunnel through seeds, seedlings, or fleshy plant roots, destroying them entirely or ruining them for table purposes.

The maggots of true flies that trouble gardens most often are the cabbage maggot, onion maggot, pepper maggot, and seedcorn maggot. (Other species of troublesome

If you see a cabbage-family plant wilting, even though it is well watered, dig just below the soil surface and look for cabbage maggots.

flies, such as leafminers, sawflies, and fruit flies, infest fruits and ornamentals. See pages 66, 77, and 56.)

Cabbage maggots feed on the roots of broccoli, radish, Brussels sprout, cabbage, cauliflower, and turnip. Infested cabbage wilts badly during day heat and may take on a bluish cast before dying. These maggots also spread black leg fungus, which causes seedlings to rot. Cabbage maggots live primarily in the North, causing serious damage in cool, moist weather in spring and fall.

The aromas of onions, shallots, chives, and garlic bring the onion maggot fly into your garden, if it has not overwintered there from the previous year. Cool, wet weather favors its development, and it tends to be a pest, like the cabbage maggot, in northern states.

In spring, maggots feed on seedling onions, causing significant crop loss. Surviving plants grow slowly. Leaves become flabby and faded. Their feeding permits bacteria to enter bulbs, causing bacterial soft rot. In late summer, maggots often attack onions right before harvest, causing storage rot. Pepper maggots leave your harvest infested with a wormy interior or cause fruits to decay or drop prematurely. The flies lay eggs on developing fruits of pepper, eggplant, and tomato, troubling vegetables in the East and Midwest.

Seedcorn maggots live throughout North America and in warmer climates may be active all year. These tiny maggots chew on corn seeds as well as seeds of lima bean, green been, squash, cucumber, onion, pea, cabbage, beet, radish, and potato. They also infest sprouts of these plants.

The maggots burrow and feed within sown seed, often leaving you with only the seed coat as a reminder of what you planted only a short time before. Those seeds surviving attack may emerge as "snakeheads" with only one leaf or none instead of the normal two.

The Pest

Cabbage maggots are the larvae of cabbage flies. These pesty flies measure ¼ inch long and are large winged and ash gray with black stripes and bristles. Female flies deposit 60 banana-shaped white eggs at the bases of plants or within their bulbs. The white, blunt-ended, ⅓-inch-long maggots hatch in 2 to 10 days, dispersing up to 6 inches deep in the soil. When they find a suitable root they tunnel inside.

Approximately 19 to 32 days after hatching, cabbage maggots form ¼-inch-long brown pupae 1 to 5 inches below ground near the infested plant. These become adult flies in two to four weeks. A third generation follows in another five weeks. This generation overwinters as pupae in soil, emerging in May.

The onion fly looks somewhat like the cabbage fly except that it has indistinct brown stripes on its chest.

Onion maggots can kill onions suddenly. Leeks are a relatively resistant alternative crop.

This fly appears in May, and the female lays eggs near the soil surface or behind leaf sheaths. Each female may deposit up to 450 eggs in its 45-day life span.

Maggots hatch in 2 to 7 days. Like cabbage maggots, onion maggots are white, blunt ended, and about ¼ inch long. There can be three generations of onion maggots a year. The last generation overwinters as late-stage maggots or pupae in soil near infested plants.

Seedcorn maggots overwinter as maggots or pupae in soil, plant litter, or manure. The ⅓-inch-long gray-brown adult flies emerge from pupae in May to July, depending on the climate, and lay eggs in soil or on seeds and seedlings. Maggots are yellowish white and grow to ¼ inch long. First-generation maggots are particularly destructive during cold spells, which slow seed germination. There are three to five generations a year.

Pepper maggots hatch from eggs laid by ⅓-inch-long flies emerging from overwintering pupae in mid- to late summer. The maggots are white at first, maturing to yellow. Only one generation occurs per year.

Control Measures

Control of cabbage and onion maggots is purely preventive and should begin when you plant seeds or transplant seedlings. (Once growing plants become infested, wilt, and turn yellow, nothing can be done.) It is best to apply a soil insecticide because its relatively long period of effectiveness wards off maggot attack when seedlings most need it, permitting seeds to germinate and plants to establish sturdy root systems. Such sturdy young plants can resist any later infestations.

Mix diazinon granules (Ortho Diazinon Soil & Turf Insect Control, Ortho Vegetable Guard Soil Insect Killer) or diazinon dust (Ortho Diazinon Soil & Foliage Dust) 4 to 6 inches into the soil before sowing seeds or transplanting seedlings. Control lasts about one month. Repeat treatment 7 to 10 days after plants emerge.

You can also spray foliage with diazinon or malathion when flies are active to prevent egg laying. Correct timing for this spray is difficult because flies may be active at

Root maggot damage stunts cabbage-family plants by destroying roots. Left: a healthy plant; middle and right: two stages of root maggot damage.

different times, depending on the climate. But many gardeners observe that first-generation cabbage flies emerge when sweet cherries bloom, and second-generation cabbage flies often appear when the common daylily has been in bloom for a week.

Some gardeners try to prevent flies from laying eggs in crops by covering seedbeds or transplants with a cheesecloth tent. The cheesecloth should have a minimum of 24 threads per inch. Construct the tent so that it extends 6 inches beyond the bed and has no gaps. Leave the tent on

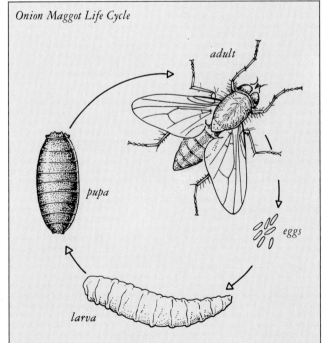

Onion Maggot Life Cycle

adult

pupa

eggs

larva

Onion flies hatch in spring from pupae in the soil and lay their eggs on or near onion plants. The larvae, called maggots, feed on the onions and then enter the soil to pupate. The insects overwinter as late-stage maggots or as puparia that resemble grains of wheat.

until the plants have passed the seedling stage and have developed sturdy root systems, but keep in mind that the cloth shades plants, slowing their growth.

Crop rotation helps control onion maggots. Plant other crops for several years running in places where onion maggots have been a problem. Plant onions well away from previously infested plots.

Destroy all maggot-infested onions as soon as you see them, and remove garden litter on a regular basis to cut down on reinfestation.

Keep developing fruits of peppers, eggplants, and tomatoes dusted with malathion or rotenone to prevent pepper maggot flies from laying eggs.

Cultural controls help ward off seedcorn maggot attack. When you select seeds, keep in mind that colored seeds have more resistance than those with white seed coats. Because seedcorn maggots do the most damage in wet ground and during cool weather, do not plant too early. It is best to wait until the soil has warmed thoroughly. Sow seeds no deeper than necessary, because you want to promote rapid germination and growth.

If you use manure or other organic material to fertilize your crops, add it to the soil four to six weeks before planting so that any seedcorn flies attracted to the garden will not find germinating seeds on which to feast.

You can effectively treat seeds with insecticide before planting. In a small jar, mix together the contents of one seed packet with ¼ teaspoon of an insecticide powder containing diazinon. Shake carefully until the seeds are thoroughly coated. (Wear rubber gloves when you are planting insecticide-treated seeds.) You can also use a diazinon spray on the row just after sowing.

If seedcorn maggots destroy a nontreated crop, try replanting immediately with insecticide-treated seed.

MEALYBUGS

Female mealybugs congregate in masses in the crooks of leaves and on the stems and roots of many kinds of garden plants, especially woody plants such as fruit trees and ornamental trees and shrubs.

Mealybugs feed in the same manner as their scale insect relatives, by inserting hollow stylets into plants and using these "straws" to suck up nutritious fluids. Affected plants wilt, yellow, become

Mealybugs are similar to scale insects but form a covering of waxy threads instead of a shell. Clustered to feed, they look like cotton fluff.

stunted, and occasionally die. These pests trouble greenhouse plants and warm-climate gardens most often, but several species are occasional pests in the North. Some mealybug species also inject toxins or transmit viruses, which can do serious damage even when only a few bugs are present.

During heavy infestations, large mealybug colonies form on fruits, limbs, or trunks. On fruit trees, you will see discoloration and pitting on mature fruits and premature dropping of young fruits. Mealybugs cluster at the stem ends of fruits and are very difficult to dislodge. They also frequently gather where two fruits touch.

Mealybugs secrete honeydew, so you will see this on surrounding leaves and other plant parts. Honeydew soon turns dark gray and moldy from sooty mold fungus.

The Pest
A relative of scale insects, the mealybug armors itself with powdery-looking, waxy threads instead of a shell. An individual mealybug is a thread-covered oval, segmented bug measuring about ¼ inch long. The pest often resides in obvious cottony-looking clusters, however.

Female mealybugs each lay as many as 600 orange or yellowish eggs in white, cottony egg sacs kept hidden under their protective coverings. Some mealybug species give birth to live young as well. These also initially hide under a protective covering.

Young, pale yellow nymphs, called crawlers, scatter over a plant before settling down and growing their waxy armor. They can also be carried some distance by air currents. Mature mealybugs stay close to their homes and move very slowly. Mature females, although slow moving, continue to wander about plants even after their covering has completely formed.

All stages of female mealybugs live on plants at the same time, with three or more

A black coating of sooty mold often forms on plants infested by mealybugs. The mold lives on honeydew, which the insects secrete.

overlapping generations possible each year. Female crawlers shed their skins three times in the six to eight weeks it takes them to reach maturity. Some of these discarded skins become matted together with a secretion of cottony wax threads to form the mature insects' covering. This covering

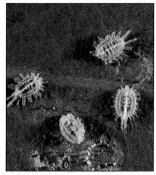

Some mealybugs are decorated with long, waxy filaments. All damage plants by sucking sap.

becomes somewhat resistant to insecticide penetration.

Immature male mealybugs initially look like immature females, but in two to four weeks they form a small, cottony cocoon, from which they emerge as winged males seven to ten days later. You usually do not see the tiny, winged, gnatlike adult male mealybugs. After male nymphs become winged males, they mate, then live for only a few days longer.

Control Measures
For minor infestations, you can try spraying plants with a strong stream of water to dislodge and wash away the pests. But a major infestation requires a pesticide.

On fruits and vegetables, choose malathion (Ortho Malathion 50 Insect Spray) or diazinon (Ortho Diazinon Insect Spray, Ortho Diazinon Soil & Foliage Dust), which can also be used on ornamentals. Repeat spraying if the tree becomes reinfested.

Thorough coverage of all plant parts is necessary—you must spray the stem, leaf undersides, and plant base. Because mealybug infestations occur primarily on the insides of trees, pay special attention to this area when spraying. Use strong pressure to penetrate foliage.

Do not spray fruit plants when they are in full bloom, because control measures can decrease populations of pollinating bees. After applying the pesticide during harvest season, closely follow the label recommendations concerning the number of days you must wait to harvest.

On fruit trees and deciduous ornamentals, you can also control mealybugs with a dormant horticultural oil spray (Ortho Volck® Oil Spray), which smothers overwintering eggs. Use a more dilute summer oil spray during the growing season. On many plants, a summer oil spray, alone or combined with malathion (Ortho Malathion 50 Insect Spray), gives good results.

On ornamental plants, the systemics acephate (Orthene® Systemic Insect Control) or Di-syston® (Ortho Systemic Rose & Flower Care 8-12-4) provide effective control of leaf-feeding mealybugs, whose protective coating can make them difficult to eradicate with contact sprays. Spray with acephate two or three times at 7- to 10-day intervals for thorough control, or apply Di-syston® granules every six weeks.

MEXICAN BEAN BEETLES AND BEAN LEAF BEETLES

The Mexican bean beetle is a ladybug relative, but instead of eating bean pests as ladybugs do, it eats bean leaves. When you first see this pest, you might be tempted to leave it alone, thinking it a beneficial predator. When in doubt, count spots. The highly destructive copper-colored Mexican bean beetle has 16; the orange ladybug has 12. If you see beetles with three or four spots feeding on bean foliage, your pest problems may be bean leaf beetles instead of, or in addition to, Mexican bean beetles.

Both the larvae and adults of the highly destructive Mexican bean beetle feed on the leaves, pods, and stems of green beans, lima beans, cowpeas, and soybeans. The pests chew on leaves, eating the tissue between leaf veins, which

If you see a four-spotted beetle on your beans, you have an infestation of bean leaf beetles. You won't find their larvae on leaves; they feed on the roots.

gives leaves a lacy appearance. Heavily infested foliage turns brown and becomes skeletonized. Beetles may infest beans at any time during the growing season.

Bean leaf beetles eat foliage, but the larvae, unlike those of Mexican bean beetles, feed on bean plant roots. Seedlings attacked by bean leaf beetle larvae may turn yellow and wilt. Pull them up and you may see slender, white larvae feeding on the roots. Bean leaf beetles attack peas, beans, cowpeas, and soybeans.

The Pest

The 1/4-inch-long, coppery, 16-spotted adult Mexican bean beetles overwinter in garden litter and woody areas, becoming active in early spring through midsummer. Each female deposits about 500 oval yellow eggs in groups of 50 on leaf undersides. Emerging in 5 to 14 days, the larvae begin feeding immediately.

The distinctive yellow larvae have harmless forked spines sticking out all over their bodies. In about two to four weeks, they reach 1/3 inch long. Mature larvae attach themselves to the undersides of leaves and pupate, emerging as adult beetles in about 10 days. Between one and four generations can occur per year, with female beetles ready for egg laying within two weeks after hatching.

Bean leaf beetles are pale yellow to dull red with three or four black spots and a triangle on their backs. Their shield-shaped shells are rimmed with black. They overwinter as adults and become active in May or early

June. The females lay orange eggs in the soil at bases of plants. Slender, white grubs hatch in 10 to 14 days and feed on roots for about 20 days until they reach 1/3 inch long. They pupate in the soil, and adults emerge in about a month. One generation occurs each year in the North and as many as four generations in the South.

Control Measures

Both hard rains and hot, dry summers reduce the numbers of Mexican bean beetles. Some bean varieties are more resistant to attack than others;

The bane of beans, Mexican bean beetle adults and larvae eat lacy patterns in the leaves.

check your seed catalogs before selecting seeds.

Use carbaryl dust (Ortho Sevin® Garden Dust) or a diazinon spray (Ortho Diazinon Insect Spray, Ortho Fruit & Vegetable Insect Control) to control Mexican bean beetles. Pyrethrins (Ortho Tomato & Vegetable Insect Spray or Killer) can be used a day before harvest. Diazinon, carbaryl, and pyrethrins also control bean leaf beetles.

Be sure to apply pesticide to the leaf undersides, where beetles feed. Early treatments to control adults can prevent the more damaging larvae from becoming a problem. Mexican bean beetles can be strong fliers, so be alert for new infestations, even after using controls.

Remove and destroy all garden litter after harvest to reduce overwintering spots for adults.

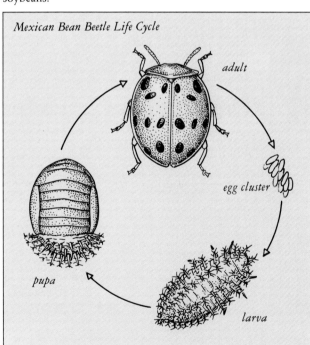

Mexican Bean Beetle Life Cycle

adult

egg cluster

larva

pupa

In spring, Mexican bean beetle adults feed on bean leaves, where they also lay eggs. The larvae feed on bean leaves, pupate, and hatch into adults. Several generations may occur per summer, with the adults overwintering in plant litter.

MILLIPEDES

Because millipedes commonly make their homes in gardens, living in soil and plant debris, many gardeners think of them as insect pests. However, they are neither. Scientists do not classify millipedes as insects, because, rather than having six legs, as all insects do, millipedes have from 30 to 400 legs. (Despite their name, they don't have a thousand legs!) And they seldom cause major garden problems, because their food fare usually consists of dead, not live, plant matter. Some species even act as beneficial predators, eating other soil insects.

However, if a drought follows rainy weather, millipedes may turn to plants as a source of water. Once they have tasted fresh plants, they usually don't return to their normal diet of decaying material.

Millipedes sometimes feed on the underground portions of beet, carrot, parsnip, turnip, and potato plants, as well as bean, corn, and pea seeds. If tomatoes, strawberries, cucumbers, squashes, and melons lie on damp ground, millipedes may damage the fruit. They also sometimes eat leaves close to the ground, such as those of cabbage, cauliflower, and lettuce. They can cut off seedlings at ground level, too. Holes made by millipedes permit fungus diseases to enter your crops. If millipede damage becomes excessive, you will want to consider control measures.

The Pest

Millipedes are somewhat similar to earthworms and wireworms and are often confused with centipedes. All can be brown, pinkish brown, or gray and, depending on the species, measure between $1/2$ inch and $1^1/2$ inches long. Two pairs of short legs are attached to each of their many body segments. Their bodies are rounded and hard shelled, and they coil up like a spring when touched.

Wireworms, offspring of the click beetle, also have hard coverings, but they have only six legs and do not coil up when disturbed. Wireworms can be destructive and should be controlled (see Wireworms, page 93).

The earthworm, another noninsect, has bristles, not

Millipedes often coil up when you disturb them, unlike centipedes, which scurry away.

legs, but you usually cannot see these without a magnifying glass. When you disturb an earthworm, it will form a temporary C shape or S shape, not a coil. Earthworm tunneling benefits your garden, loosening soil and making it easier for rainwater and nutrients to reach plant roots.

Centipedes, in contrast to millipedes, have flattened bodies and 30 or more legs. They have long antennae. Most centipedes measure about 1 inch long, but some reach 8 inches.

Some gardeners confuse the slow-moving millipede with the fast-running centipede just because both have many legs. The centipede will benefit your garden by eliminating snails and other pests, however. A centipede uses poisonous claws to paralyze prey. Its sting causes a reaction similar to a bee sting, so handle one with gloves or not at all.

During the summer female millipedes deposit translucent egg clusters in or on the soil. Each female lays as many as 300 eggs. Young millipedes emerge a few weeks later, looking much like their parents but smaller and with fewer legs. These young live through the winter, producing a new brood the following year. Millipedes usually live for one or two years, but some species can live as long as seven years.

Control Measures

When you see wormlike creatures near or in your garden, especially near damaged or weak plants, try to determine what they are so that you know whether to encourage or control their activity.

Some millipedes can give off a smelly brownish protective fluid or spray when disturbed. This fluid can cause skin inflammation and eye damage. Use caution, and do not pick them up with your bare hands.

The best way to control problem millipedes is to keep your garden free of decaying plant matter. With their usual food source unavailable, the pests simply will not be around in large enough numbers to bother your crops.

If millipedes abound, however, you might try placing an old window screen on the ground under their favorite plants, such as unstaked tomatoes or strawberries. Cut slits in the screen, carefully bringing the plants through. This keeps the fruit off the ground where millipedes live. Pick fruit as it ripens. Overripe fruit invites millipedes.

You will also see millipedes on lawns. They do not do much damage there because they feed primarily on decaying matter. However, after a heavy rain they can congregate in large numbers and start migrating across the ground. This happens most often in spring and fall.

Garden millipedes sometimes wander into houses and garages. If this happens, you may have to use controls on your entire lawn, plus your home exterior and interior, to eliminate the invasion.

For lawn millipedes, apply diazinon granules (Ortho Diazinon Soil & Turf Insect Control) with a fertilizer spreader. You can also use these granules at planting time to control millipedes on most vegetables. A diazinon spray (Ortho Diazinon Insect Spray) can be used on lawns, fruits, and vegetables. Sprayed around patios, windows, and foundations, it will prevent millipedes from coming into your house.

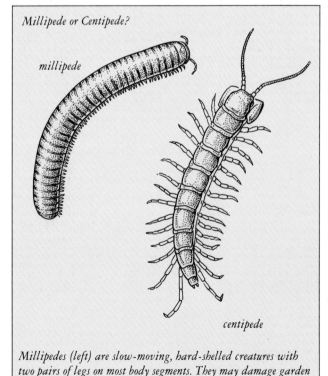

Millipede or Centipede?

millipede

centipede

Millipedes (left) are slow-moving, hard-shelled creatures with two pairs of legs on most body segments. They may damage garden plants. Centipedes (right) are fast moving creatures with one pair of legs per body segment; they help control pests.

MITES

Spider mites sometimes spin a fine silk over leaf surfaces, but they do not weave typical spider webs, because they are not spiders, merely spider relatives. Being spider relatives means that spider mites are not insects, either. Lacking true jaws and with eight legs and compound eyes, they are more closely related to ticks and spiders than to insects such as aphids and mealybugs. But plant pests they are and major ones at that.

Spider mites puncture leaf undersides with two needlelike stylets and suck out both water and food-producing green chlorophyll. You may not notice mite damage until it is moderately severe. Each mite feeding site creates a tiny white dot; numerous punctures eventually cause the entire leaf to fade and take on a speckled or stippled appearance. As an infestation worsens, leaves begin to shrivel, turning yellow or bronze.

With increasing damage, leaves die and drop off. On citrus, fruit may drop as well as leaves. Plants suffering marked leaf damage one year lose vigor and may not bloom properly the following year.

There are hundreds of mite species, with many color variations and plant preferences. Some limit themselves to certain plants, and others infest anything that's green and growing. Mite infestations often include a mixture of several species.

There seems to be a mite named after just about every plant in your garden, including the apple rust mite, bamboo mite, bulb mite, carmine spider mite, citrus bud mite, clover mite, cyclamen mite, cypress mite, European red mite, fuchsia mite, honey-locust spider mite, privet mite, southern red mite, spruce spider mite, strawberry spider mite, tomato russet mite, and two-spotted spider mite. You will sometimes hear all of

Use a hand lens to check for mites. Most species spin a fine web in which they feed and lay small, round eggs.

them lumped into the category of red spider mites, although that is not really an accurate description, because some are not spider mites and others are not red.

Start inspecting susceptible plants, especially those previously infested, for mites in the spring, looking closely at both upper and lower leaf surfaces. Examine leaves closest to the ground first, because many mites overwinter near the ground, crawling onto the nearest available feeding area after spring emergence. Many mite species initially cluster near leaf veins and then expand their colonies to other leaf parts.

Because most mites are only $\frac{1}{60}$ inch wide—about the size of a period on this page—you might have difficulty seeing them, particularly early in the season. One easy way of checking out a possible infestation is to hold a sheet of white paper beneath a suspect leaf or branch tip and then tap the leaf. If red, greenish, blackish, orange, or yellowish bugs the size of grains of salt drop onto your paper and start crawling around, you have diagnosed your problem.

Because many mites spin webs, you can also look for these as a diagnostic clue. Mite webbing, much finer than real spiderwebs, will consist of irregular strands located on leaf undersides or running from one leaf base to another, acting as a mite highway. Late in the season, entire

leaves may be covered with webs, especially those on plants that are indoors or outdoors where there is no wind.

Beneath this white silk sheath, which sometimes makes the leaf underside look as if it has been dusted with powder, you may see hundreds of mites running to and fro. With a magnifying glass, you can also see, depending on the species, transparent, cream to bright red-orange eggs and the cast-off skins from molts. These give the leaf underside a grainy appearance. Mites on juniper, pine, and other conifers produce very small amounts of webbing, so don't use this as a clue with needled evergreens.

Conifer spider mites proliferate during cool spring and fall weather. Most other mite infestations are worst in hot, dry weather, particularly when temperatures soar to 90° F. The pests can become serious on plants grown in dusty, dry garden sites. Underwatered

especially when growing conditions favor mite population explosions.

Mite populations can also increase following pesticide use to control other insect pests, such as aphids. When other pests, which compete with the mites for food and space, are eliminated, the mites often increase due to more favorable conditions.

If you have never noticed mite damage in your garden before, you may wonder how these tiny insects traveled to your yard. Mites can only crawl short distances, and they don't fly, but they are so small and light that a spring or summer breeze can transfer them from plant to plant or over the fence. They may even drift from your outdoor garden to your houseplants through an open window.

The Pest
Mites vary in color. The very common red spider mite, which infests just about any

Sometimes mite webs completely encase leaves, as they have this eggplant leaf. Underwatering often leads to problems with mites.

plants and those suffering from moisture stress due to low humidity or lack of rain are most often attacked. Cool, wet conditions discourage hot-weather mites and keep populations in check.

Natural mite predators include predaceous mites, some spiders, lacewings, thrips, certain species of tiny black ladybugs, and some beetles. Although these help to keep mite populations down, mites multiply so rapidly that they can reach damaging levels despite numerous enemies,

garden plant, can be yellow, orange, cream, greenish, or red. The twospotted spider mite, another general feeder, is pale yellow to pale or dark green and has two dark spots on its back. The almond mite can be rusty brown, olive green, or reddish. The jumping mite, which feeds on grain and grass, has a yellow body. The cardinal mite, highly destructive to ash trees, is bright red.

All mites are tiny, but some, such as the plum and pear rust mites, can only be seen with a microscope. Some

Tomato russet mites look more like minute yellowish worms. They cause tomato leaves to turn russet or brownish.

have a wormlike appearance, and although they feed like spider mites, they also cause plant galls or blisters. Cyclamen mites, only ¹⁄₁₀₀ inch long, cause severe leaf wrinkling and bud curling on strawberries and snapdragons and other flowering plants.

Life cycles for the different species of spider mite are similar, except that a few species overwinter as adults whereas most overwinter as eggs. If a female mite has been fertilized by a male, 80 percent of the offspring will be female. Unfertilized female mites can also deposit eggs, but when these hatch they will all be male. In southern areas, many mite species reproduce throughout the year, slowing down a bit in the colder months.

Each female spider mite deposits from 3 to 30 eggs per day, for a total of 100 to 300 eggs during its approximately month-long life span. The eggs hatch into six-legged larvae in one to eight days. These feed for 10 to 32 days, undergoing two nymphal stages before molting for the final time into eight-legged adult mites.

Mites produce many generations per year, the exact number depending on the species. You usually do not see mites after September except in very mild climates. Cyclamen mites, however, do prefer cool weather and seldom emerge when it is hot.

Control Measures

Where mite populations are large, several insecticides can provide excellent control of most mite infestations. Pesticides, however, kill only adults, not eggs, and are effective only if repeated for several weeks. An insecticide specific for mites is called a miticide.

For controlling mites on fruit trees, use a diazinon (Ortho Fruit & Vegetable Insect Control) or malathion spray (Ortho Malathion 50 Insect Spray, Ortho Home Orchard Spray), which control other insect pests as well. For citrus choose an ethion–petroleum oil compound (Ortho Citrus Insect Spray).

On ornamental plants, spray with acephate (Ortho Isotox® Insect Killer) or malathion (Ortho Malathion 50 Insect Spray). Mites can develop a resistance to pesticides, so it is best to alternate miticides if repeat applications become necessary.

On vegetables, use a sulfur dust or spray (Ortho Flotox® Garden Sulfur) for partial control of spider mites or tomato russet mites. Sulfur burns some vegetable plants, however, including cucumber, grape, melon, and squash. Do not apply sulfur dusts in very warm weather (above 90° F). Instead, use wettable sulfur. Sulfur is a less effective control when the temperature drops below 70° F. Do not use sulfur within 30 days of using an oil spray.

You can also use diazinon (Ortho Fruit & Vegetable Insect Control, Ortho Diazinon Insect Spray) or malathion (Ortho Malathion 50 Insect Spray).

For effective mite control on both edible and ornamental plants, you should repeat pesticide applications at the intervals recommended on the container label. This is usually three repeat sprayings at 7- to 10-day intervals. Your first spraying usually kills

adult mites or makes them stop feeding; the second destroys those weakened by the first spray and any that have hatched since the earlier spraying.

Spray both upper and lower leaf surfaces as well as all other plant parts that may harbor mites. A fine spray gives the most thorough coverage on most plants. On dense foliage, however, a coarse spray penetrates best.

A horticultural oil spray (Ortho Volck® Oil Spray) can be used as a control on woody plants. Be certain to read the insecticide container label carefully, checking that your plant is listed. During the winter, use a dormant oil on deciduous trees to kill mite eggs. During the growing season, oil sprays destroy mites at varying stages. Summer oils are most effective with several applications made one to two

Fuchsia mites have recently arrived from the fuchsia's South American homeland to devastate many North American gardens. Fuchsia breeders are working to develop resistant plants.

weeks apart, but do not repeat if high temperatures coincide with high humidity.

You can apply most oil sprays with a garden hose-end sprayer (Ortho Spray-ette® 4) or any tank-type or power sprayer. Because oil works by suffocating mites, it will only be effective if you spray all plant surfaces.

If plant health is not seriously threatened, you can significantly reduce initial mite populations by hosing down infested plants with a fine, hard water stream from your garden hose. Hold the

hose nozzle 4 to 8 inches away from infested leaves, and wet them completely, including the undersides. The mites will be killed and will cause no further damage. Water does not destroy the eggs, however, and sprays may miss some mites despite your best efforts, so repeat the hosing every other day for at least three weeks.

When considering control measures, do not confuse damage caused by mites with that caused by other insects, such as leafhoppers (see page 64) and tarnished plant bugs. All suck plant juices and cause stippling, but these insects cause larger stipples and have six legs compared to the mite's eight. They also do not spin webs.

If you are not certain whether your plant has a mite infestation, bring an infested shoot or twig to your county agricultural extension agent.

Because mite damage will be most severe on plants suffering from water stress, keeping your garden well watered and mulched will ward off mites. During periods of summer drought, do not water only your vegetable patch and flower beds, but be sure to water trees and shrubs deeply as well; and don't ignore any "durable" ground covers beneath trees. The tree roots may rob the ground-cover of moisture, leaving it susceptible to mites, which may then spread to the tree. Once mites have injured a plant, nothing will bring back green color to the affected areas. However, by controlling mites with insecticide or other measures and giving the plant adequate water and fertilizer, you can often restore some of its garden appearance. With proper treatment, unless the damage is quite severe, you may be able to coax new leaves into appearing, although these may be smaller and yellowish for a while.

NEMATODES

Microscopic worms called nematodes living in soil may be impossible to see, but you can't miss the damage they do to garden plants. Unfortunately, nematode damage to roots resembles injury caused by diseases and other soil and pest problems.

Root damage prevents root systems from supplying above-ground plant parts with sufficient water and nutrients. Plants become stunted, wilt, discolor, fail to thrive, and occasionally die. Trees may suffer from dieback. Some nematodes transmit ring spot and other viral diseases. Their root punctures also pave the way for root-rot fungi and wilt-causing bacteria.

Most nematodes are root nematodes, attacking root systems and causing knotty growths or black spots on plant roots. Root nematodes live inside roots and infest all kinds of garden plants, including lawn grass, but they are particularly widespread on vegetables and flowers.

Damage to lawns includes slow growth and sparse grass patches that gradually turn yellow. In hot weather blades may wilt. Main roots can be short, or you will see many roots growing from one stem. Like all nematode problems, lawn damage will be most severe in southern states and in moist, sandy, loam soil.

Foliar nematodes attack buds and foliage rather than roots. Brown or black areas between leaf veins signal the initial invasion. The discoloration rapidly spreads, and leaves eventually wilt, brown, and hang limply from the stems. Lower leaves suffer more than those well above the ground. Foliar nematodes commonly trouble aster, begonia, chrysanthemum, cyclamen, dahlia, delphinium, fern, phlox, verbena, and zinnia.

You need to distinguish between root knots caused by nematodes and the nitrogen-fixing nodules normally found on bean roots. You can

These tomato roots show the disfiguring effect of root nematodes.

remove nitrogen nodules with your thumbnail without harming the root. Root knots grow from the plant itself, and you can't remove them without tearing the root.

To be sure that your garden problem is caused by nematodes, you will need to have a lab test performed. Contact your county agricultural extension service for exact instructions. You will probably be asked to dig up some of the roots of the ailing plant and place them in a plastic bag with some of the surrounding soil. Seal the bag tightly to keep the soil moist, and take or mail it to the testing lab as soon as possible.

Root nematodes reach your garden through contaminated equipment, water, soil, and transplants. Once in your garden's soil, they travel independently fewer than 3 feet per season, but they get much farther by hitching rides on your garden shovel or shoes. Splashing water spreads foliar nematodes from leaf to leaf. Both overwinter in soil and contaminated plant debris.

The Pest

Most nematodes are colorless, round worms measuring $1/50$ to $1/10$ inch long. Each female root nematode lays 300 to 3,000 eggs in a yellow-brown, jellylike mass on roots. Larvae develop within the eggs and begin feeding immediately after hatching. An entire life cycle takes about a month. Both eggs and larvae overwinter in soil or root galls.

Foliar nematodes spend the winter in plant buds and

then slither up wet stems through a film of water to reach the leaves. The nematodes are so tiny that they can enter through the stomata (pores) of the leaves. The female foliar nematodes lay eggs, which hatch and grow to reproductive age within two weeks.

Control Measures

Once nematodes have infested plants, there is no pesticide that can control them. The only sure way to get rid of nematodes is to destroy infested plants and then fumigate the soil. Professional pest control operators have several powerful nematocides from which to choose. Homeowners can use meta-sodium (Vapam®), a chemical available for home gardens.

Because soil fumigants kill all living organisms in the soil, including nematodes, fungi, bacteria, weed seeds, and plants, you must be careful when using them. Do not use where roots of desired plants grow into the treatment area.

When using a soil fumigant, follow label instructions explicitly. You will need to till the garden bed, apply the diluted nematocide with a watering can, and water it in with a sprinkler. After a week, break up the soil again to let the fumes dissipate, or wait two to three weeks before planting.

By rotating crops, you may be able to prevent nematodes from building up to high levels in the soil. If nematodes have infested your tomatoes, for instance, check with your county agricultural extension

agent for advice about replanting with a resistant tomato variety or an unsusceptible crop. If nematodes do too much damage in one area, stop gardening in that spot for a year or two.

Be sure to destroy—not compost—all nematode-infested plants. You can safely take tip cuttings to propagate foliar nematode–infested plants if only the lower leaves appear brown.

Because nematodes can survive for three or more years in plant litter and soil, practice good sanitation measures. Clean up your garden beds at the end of the growing season, and burn or otherwise discard suspect plants any time of year.

To slow foliar nematodes, pick off and destroy all browning leaves and the two leaves directly above them. Try to avoid wetting foliage when watering.

Healthy, vigorous plants are less likely to succumb to nematode attack. Keep plants growing vigorously with proper fertilization, watering,

You can tell which parts of this field have the most nematodes. Root damage has stunted the corn in the foreground.

and pruning. Till soil regularly during the summer, turning it to expose nematodes to heat and drying.

Purchase only top-quality plants from reputable nurseries, or you may be importing infested soil. When bringing plants in from a friend's garden, avoid sickly looking specimens. Look for root knots or dark and bushy roots, which can indicate the presence of nematodes.

PARSLEYWORMS

The parsleyworm, also called the celeryworm, may be one pest you will tolerate in your garden. That's because it is the larva of the beautiful black swallowtail butterfly. The large butterfly visits your flower beds, feeding on nectar, but the caterpillar feeds on parsley, carrot, dill, turnip, and celery foliage.

The mature caterpillars can consume a lot of leaves, stripping all foliage from the stems. They do no serious harm unless large numbers of them infest your vegetable or herb garden.

The Pest

The parsleyworm overwinters as a brown, cocoonlike structure called a chrysalis, from which the yellow-, blue-, and orange-spotted black butterfly emerges in spring. The butterfly has a 3-inch wingspan and tail-like projections from the hind wingtips.

The females lay single white eggs on host plants. Small brown larvae hatch and mature into brilliantly colored

The parsleyworm, the larva of the black swallowtail butterfly, eats parsley, carrot, and dill, but is seldom a serious pest.

green caterpillars with white- and yellow-spotted black bands across each segment. When disturbed, two fierce-looking orange horns emerge from the caterpillar's head for a few seconds.

Two to four generations can occur in a season. In the South, parsleyworms overwinter as butterflies.

Control Measures

Hand-pick caterpillars when you first observe stripped foliage. You will easily spot the mature caterpillars, but look carefully for tiny, newly hatched ones.

If large numbers of parsleyworms infest your garden, spray with BT, which contains bacteria pathogenic to caterpillars, to control young pests.

PSYLLIDS

Psyllids, sometimes called jumping plant lice, take off into flight with a hop. These aphid relatives land on boxwood, apple, pear, blackberry, fig, tomato, potato, hackberry, magnolia, yaupon, laurel, and other edible and ornamental plants.

Psyllids feed on mature leaves, new leaves, and developing buds. You can often find these insects tucked inside cupped terminal leaves from March until June. Any buds within these leaves usually die. Depending on the plant and psyllid species, foliage may survive or turn brown and then black, possibly shriveling and dying by midsummer. No new growth occurs on branch tips with damaged buds.

If you peel the cupped leaves open, you will see the immature psyllid within. You may see adults, resembling tiny flies, jumping on the leaves or flying around the infested plant.

Some psyllids transmit viral diseases or cause a toxic reaction, such as psyllid yellows, when feeding. On many plants, serious damage comes not from psyllid feeding but from diseases transmitted by these tiny insects.

The pear psylla is the most damaging pear pest in the United States. It also attacks quince and occasionally other plants. In addition to removing nutrients from leaves and stems, the pear psylla pro-

Check plants' growing points for cupped leaves that may house psyllids. The bud damage they cause distorts new growth.

duces saliva containing viruses or toxins damaging to plant tissue. Some pear varieties are quickly killed by this.

Honeydew often covers pear psylla nymphs. It can be so profuse that it completely covers the pear tree, including the bark. The sooty mold fungus that grows on the honeydew darkens the tree and causes fruit russeting.

Potato and tomato psyllid nymphs cause psyllid yellows. Leaflet bases turn yellow and roll upward. End leaves develop a reddish or purplish discoloration. Older leaves brown and die, and stems don't grow. Infected potato shoots have swollen bases and small, distorted leaves.

Some psyllids, such as the hackberry psyllid and laurel psyllid, cause plant galls. These nipple-, crater-, or blisterlike growths form on leaf undersides. (Other gall-forming insects are discussed on page 58.)

The nymphs of some species, such as those of the boxwood psyllid, produce waxy threads that form a protective web. This web can become so thick that it resembles a cotton ball.

The Pest

Psyllids are $1/8$- to $3/16$-inch-long, gray-green insects with long antennae, long hind legs, and mouthparts developed for piercing and sucking. Different species have different life cycles.

The $1/10$-inch-long, reddish brown, transparent-winged pear psylla resembles a miniature cicada. It overwinters as

an adult, becoming active when temperatures rise above 50° F. The female begins laying eggs immediately on twigs, bark, or buds. Each female lays 200 to 300 whitish yellow eggs. After trees have begun leafing out, eggs may be laid on leaf undersides along the midrib.

Yellow-brown pear psylla nymphs hatch in 20 to 30 days and begin feeding on young leaves. They mature by mid-June and lay eggs on new foliage. Three to four generations occur each year.

The $1/10$-inch-long adult tomato and potato psyllids appear in early spring after overwintering on weeds. Adults are green, later turning black marked with white. When air temperatures reach 80° F, the females deposit bright-yellow stalked eggs on leaf undersides. The flat nymphs, which emerge in 4 to 15 days, are initially yellow and then green with a fringe of hair. Three generations can occur per year.

Control Measures

During the growing season, pear psyllas can be difficult to control. It is best to inspect all rapidly growing terminals for adults and eggs before flowers bloom. When you find adults or eggs, wait to apply pesticide until nymphs hatch.

On fruit trees, use malathion (Ortho Home Orchard Spray, Ortho Malathion 50 Insect Spray) or diazinon (Ortho Fruit & Vegetable Insect Control).

For vegetables, choose diazinon (Ortho Fruit & Vegetable Insect Control) or malathion (Ortho Malathion 50 Insect Spray). Apply as soon as you see the first psyllid nymphs or adults feeding on plants, because psyllid yellows can develop even if only a few psyllids are present. Repeat the spray as noted on the product label.

Spray nonfood plants with acephate (Orthene® Systemic Insect Control, Ortho Isotox® Insect Killer). Thoroughly wet buds in early spring to penetrate curled terminal leaves, which protect immature psyllids. Repeat two weeks later.

Once galls form around leaf-gall psyllids, insecticides cannot penetrate. You may want to cut out deformed shoots and dispose of them. On previously infested fruit trees and ornamentals, use a dormant oil spray (Ortho Volck® Oil Spray) in early spring before buds enlarge.

SAWFLIES

The sawfly, a relative of bees and wasps, does not sting, it saws. The female uses its egg-laying apparatus like a saw to cut holes in leaves or needles, where it deposits eggs. The resulting small caterpillar- or wormlike larvae feed on foliage or fruit. Most larvae remain on leaf surfaces, but a few tunnel into leaves (see Leafminers, page 66) or fruit.

Many sawfly species trouble fruiting and ornamental trees and shrubs. Some of the most common species are discussed here.

If there is a small, rounded hole in a ripening green cherry, that's the entrance of the cherry fruit sawfly larvae. The culprit will be inside, near the pit. You won't see larvae in ripe red cherries, because any infested fruits will have dropped before then. In fact, if enough fruits have fallen, you won't see any ripe red cherries at all!

The cherry fruit sawfly larva chews on cherry, plum, and prune pits, stopping fruit development. The adult cherry fruit sawfly times its appearance to coincide with fruit formation. On sunny days you can see this fly buzzing about flowers on the topmost branches of fruit trees just beginning to bloom. The female moves from one tree to another, searching for fruiting trees at the right flowering stage.

The pear slug, common in gardens, is another sawfly larva. It looks like a small slug, down to the slime covering. The pear slug feeds on upper leaf surfaces, leaving only a brown lower epidermis and a lacy network of veins. Favored targets are pear, cherry, hawthorn, mountain ash, plum, and quince.

Roseslugs feed on roses. Initially, they skeletonize upper leaf surfaces, leaving behind their telltale shiny slime trails. They then proceed to eat holes in what remains of the leaves.

Redheaded pine sawfly larvae work in groups, feeding on needles of many types of pine as well as tamarack, larch, and spruce. These larvae prefer young pine trees, often

Several species of sawfly attack conifers. Here, white pine sawfly larvae feed in a mass, a habit characteristic of all such sawflies.

commencing an attack on older leaves at branch ends. However, they will feed on young foliage and even chew holes in tender bark when leaves become scarce. In large numbers they can strip one

portion of a tree or even the entire tree. The affected part usually dies.

The similar European pine sawfly attacks pines, eating new unfolding needles before moving on to older foliage. The green larvae blend into the needles and are not obvious until they have wrought serious damage.

The Pest

After the blackish females and reddish brown males mate, adult female cherry fruit sawflies insert their shiny, white, kidney-shaped eggs into the green, leaflike sepals covering flower buds. The dark-headed, whitish, C-shaped larvae emerge in four days, at about the same time petals fall. They bore into the small fruit, eating the soft, undeveloped pit. Within a few days, they molt, exit, and find another fruit.

One larva feeds on three fruits in a three-week period. When it reaches full size, it drops to the ground along with injured cherries. Working its way a few inches into the soil, it forms a papery cocoon. Only one brood occurs per year. The larva remains in the cocoon during summer, fall, and winter, emerging in early spring.

The shiny, black, $\frac{1}{5}$-inch-long adult pearslug sawfly appears in spring and again in late summer, each time inserting small oval, flattened eggs in leaves. Yellow sluglike larvae emerge in one or two weeks and feed on upper leaf surfaces. They turn greenish as they excrete slime and mature. You will see the first brood from April to July and the second from July to September, depending on where you live. Adults overwinter in cocoons in soil.

Black roseslug sawflies emerge in April and May; the females lay white eggs in slits they cut in rose leaves. The whitish green slugs reach $\frac{1}{2}$ inch long when mature and have a bristly covering. A life cycle requires only 30 days, and there can be as many as

six generations per year. Pupation occurs in whitish or brownish cocoons hidden in leaf litter during the summer and in soil during the winter.

Redheaded pine sawfly larvae have reddish orange heads and six rows of black dots. They grow to 1 inch long. Two generations occur each

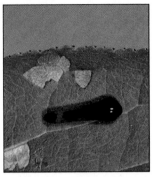

It looks like a slug, but the pear slug is the larva of a sawfly. Shown here on cherry, it also eats leaves of pear, hawthorn, and mountain ash.

year, with larvae present in late spring and again in late summer or fall.

European pine sawfly larvae are green with black heads. They mature into gray-green worms with a stripe down their backs. The worms pupate in late summer, and the emerging adults lay overwintering eggs.

Control Measures

To control sawfly larvae on nonfood trees, spray with acephate (Orthene® Systemic Insect Control, Ortho Isotox® Insect Killer) or lindane. For leaf-eating larvae, spray when new spring foliage appears; repeat following the label directions.

On fruit trees, use a multipurpose captan-malathion-methoxychlor compound (Ortho Home Orchard Spray). For sawfly larvae on fruits, spray when most of the flower buds are in the prebloom stage, because no eggs are laid after flowers show color. Wet the branches, trunk, and ground near the trunk with the spray. If you delay spraying until after petal fall, you may obtain some control, but some fruit will be damaged.

SCALES

Destructive scale insects often go undetected. These mealybug cousins camouflage themselves not under woolly threads but beneath brown or gray shells. They remain stationary on twigs or leaves, looking as natural as a bump on a log. Yet scales can, if numerous enough, destroy a plant in a very brief time.

Even close inspection of malformed and bumpy branches often does not bring these extremely common pests to your notice. The brown color of most scales blends right into bark color, so many gardeners assume the bumps form a normal part of the branch. They attribute leaf yellowing or other symptoms to aphids or some other obvious insect.

Most gardeners expect insects to move. Adult scales do not move—another technique of their camouflage. Once affixed to a feeding site, females gradually lose the use of their legs and never move again. Males are immobile too, except when winged, fertile forms develop for mating.

Gardeners often separate these pests into two categories: hard-shelled scales and soft-shelled scales. Actually, mature females of both types have equally tough insecticide-resistant covers. The difference lies in how the shells attach to the insects.

The shells of hard-shelled scales, often called armored scales, are made of waxy, gland-secreted fibers and cast-off skins from earlier molts. To assure symmetrically formed shells, scale insects may rock, rotate, or pivot while applying their coverings. The resulting shells can be quite impenetrable.

The hard shells of armored scales can be separated from the insects beneath. Soft scales do not have separate shells, but adult females that have laid eggs have chitin-coated bodies that are as hard as the shells of their armored cousins. Otherwise, the two kinds are similar.

A mature scale insect settles down at a permanent feeding site, inserting its two hollow stylets like anchors into the plant tissue. It sucks plant sap through these straws and never moves again. Some species of scale also inject a toxin while they feed. The feeding site can be any part of a branch, fruit, or leaf, but a leaf stem (petiole) is the most common location. Initial symptoms of scale infestation include yellow leaves. Leaf crinkling, stunting, browning, and leaf drop soon follow. Bark, when heavily attacked, can split and drop off.

Soft-shelled scales excrete honeydew, a sticky, sweet liquid composed of undigested plant sap. This often drips onto foliage, where a black sooty mold fungus grows on it. Copious amounts of honeydew can cause an entire plant to blacken, and sidewalks and other surfaces below become coated with honeydew and sooty mold.

Unfortunately, scale damage mimics the injury caused by many other insects. If you are unsure of what is causing the problem, look carefully for scales. Unlike other insects, scales do not disappear after they have done their damage. Living or dead, they remain attached to the plant; you can scrape the dead ones off easily with a fingernail. When scraped off, all hard-shelled and soft-shelled scale species leave behind white, circular outlines of wax where they were attached to the plant. Live ones stick more firmly and are juicy when squashed.

Once you are aware of the clues, you will notice fruit damage from scale infestation more easily. Look for depressions or soft brown to black spots around the bumps. These result from the withdrawal of nutrients and fluids by the insects.

Over 3,000 species of scale attack plants in North America. Just about every type of fruit, shade, and evergreen tree can suffer from scales. Shrubs, ground covers, and, less often, flowers and vegetables as well as houseplants, can get scales.

San Jose scale, which seriously injures most kinds of

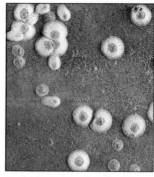

Look closely to tell scales from normal bumps on your plants. Armored scales have shells made of a secreted waxy substance and cast-off skins from earlier molts.

fruit trees and small fruits, as well as ash, linden, hawthorn, lilac, and willow, occurs throughout the country. Oystershell scale, occurring in all climates, commonly infests apple, apricot, plum, grape, raspberry, boxwood, mountain ash, lilac, beech, maple, oak, pachysandra, camellia, and viburnum. Brown soft scale troubles greenhouse plants and gardenia, camellia, fern, and oleander, as well as many other fruit trees and ornamental shrubs and flowers in the South. Prevalent on several species of euonymus, euonymus scale can be quite destructive, especially in northern areas. The European fruit lecanium is the most common soft-shelled orchard scale, infesting most fruit trees and many ornamentals.

Cottonycushion scale, accompanied by a large, fluted white egg mass, may be the easiest scale to spot. This Australian import destroys citrus and many ornamentals in the South.

The Pest

Scales come in a multitude of colors. In addition to the common brown, scales can be dark red, black, yellow, white, gray, pink, green, or glassy and transparent. The often pinhead-sized adult scales are round or oval and measure $1/100$ to $1/4$ inch in length.

Some hard-shelled scales overwinter as eggs protected in soft white sacs beneath the

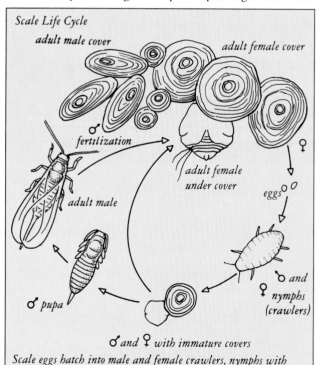

Scale Life Cycle

adult male cover

adult female cover

fertilization

adult male

♂ pupa

adult female under cover

eggs

♀

♂ and ♀ nymphs (crawlers)

♂ and ♀ with immature covers

Scale eggs hatch into male and female crawlers, nymphs with legs. These crawl briefly before becoming stationary and growing hard shells. Males pupate beneath their shells and emerge as winged adults. They mate with stationary females, then die.

protective shell-like covering. These hatch in late May or June, and as many as a hundred tiny six-legged, yellowish crawlers emerge from beneath each shell, wandering about for a few days until they find suitable settling sites. Some hard scales overwinter as nymphs protected by their shells. Most soft scales overwinter as nymphs hidden in bark crevices.

Newly hatched crawlers usually journey only a few feet, but they can also travel further via wind, birds, and water droplets. Once settled, the female crawlers insert feeding stylets, molt several times, and lose their legs and antennae while they form their protective coverings.

You seldom see winged adult male scales; they are few in number and quite small. (However, the white, needle-shaped shells of male euonymus scales are numerous and quite obvious.) After male nymphs have molted several times, they emerge from their shells as winged, gnatlike adults and lose their ability to feed; they mate and then die.

Various species produce one to several generations a year. Nymphs will be active in early summer and again in August or September. In warm climates some scales reproduce the year around.

San Jose scales are grayish or brownish pinhead-sized bumps. In large infestations, they may completely encrust the branches of fruit and ornamental trees and shrubs. They are disclike in shape, and each has a tiny yellow nipple in the center. Under the coverings or shells, the saclike females are bright yellow. They produce two to six generations a year, depending upon the climate.

Oystershell scales are long, curved ovals resembling miniature gray-brown oyster shells. If you remove the covering of one, you can see the yellowish female by using a magnifying glass. In large numbers, these scales can

encrust branches of fruit and ornamental trees. One or two generations occur per year.

European fruit lecaniums resemble small, shiny, brown turtles lined up along twigs. Sometimes they are covered with a white powder. They overwinter in an immature stage, with crawlers emerging from beneath shells from late May through June. One generation develops each year.

The female brown soft scale lays one or two eggs every day for about a month. These hatch quickly, and nymphs mature in two months, forming soft, greenish brown shells with a marbled effect. This scale excretes abundant honeydew.

Euonymus scales produce two generations a year, one in May and another in August. Stems and leaves may be encrusted with the dark brown shells of the females, which lay orange-yellow eggs beneath the shells. The white, needle-shaped shells of the males may also blanket infested stems and leaves.

Control Measures

Scales are among the most difficult insect pests to control. The key to controlling them is to apply pesticides when the crawlers are moving about the infested plants. The waxy shells of adult scales provide them with excellent protection from contact insecticides. You will have the

Although it is just as tough as that of an armored scale when mature, the shell of a soft-shelled scale is not a separate structure but the insect's exoskeleton.

greatest success if you strike before the crawlers begin secreting their protective covering.

Although the exact timing varies with the species, most scales have a crawler stage in early summer; others have a second brood in late summer or early fall. Spraying crawlers when they are still tiny and shell-less wipes them out. Hard-shelled scales become quite resistant to pesticides shortly after the crawlers settle and become wax coated. However, most soft-shelled species can be killed by insecticides throughout the growing season, so spraying can prevent additional damage.

You will find that a 10X magnifying glass is of great help in accurately identifying the various scale types and life stages. Use it to check scale-infested branches once or twice a week throughout the growing season. Apply insecticides when you see crawlers hatching, and repeat sprays according to label directions until you observe no new crawlers.

If scales infest new plant growth, it is important to apply pesticide to prevent further injury. Control measures are not necessary, however, if scales remain on older growth but new growth appears healthy and uninfested—the scales are probably dead. If you are not sure, pry up the scale shells with your fingernail or a metal nail file, and use a magnifying glass to peek at the scale's chambers to see whether it is inhabited.

Many insecticides control scales. On leaves of ornamentals, you will have the best results with a systemic such as acephate (Orthene® Systemic Insect Control, Ortho Isotox® Insect Killer). This has some effect against mature scales because plants absorb the pesticide and deliver it to the feeding scales through sap. Spray three times at 7- to 10-day intervals.

On fruit trees, choose carbaryl (Ortho Liquid Sevin®, Ortho Sevin® Garden Spray),

diazinon, (Ortho Fruit & Vegetable Insect Control, Ortho Diazinon Insect Spray), or malathion (Ortho Malathion 50 Insect Spray). When spraying fruit trees with a carbaryl

Cottonycushion scale is a pest of greenhouse plants and many fruits and ornamentals. Fluted egg masses form the "cotton" that gives the pest its name.

spray, you might also want to include a miticide, such as dicofol in your treatment plan, to prevent any resultant spider mite buildup. Ask your garden shop staff whether this is a problem in your area.

If plants have been infested with scale in previous years, you can do preventive spraying during the dormant season, either using spray oil (Ortho Volck® Oil Spray) alone or combining it with carbaryl, acephate, diazinon, or malathion (Ortho Malathion 50 Insect Spray). Apply the spray in late winter, before buds swell, to smother scales overwintering in mature female form, scale eggs under the now-dead female's covering, and scales still in crawler form. Oil sprays applied at a reduced rate in summer control soft scales well.

Because several different species of scale can live on one plant, and because some have more than one generation per year, a repetitive spray program achieves the most success with serious infestations. Spray every two to three weeks for a total of three applications, or spray whenever crawler generations appear. Whatever insecticides you use, be certain that all infested plant surfaces receive a thorough spray covering.

SCARAB BEETLES

The large scarab beetle family includes the Japanese beetle, June beetle, and rose chafer—some of our worst garden pests. Adult beetles chew holes in foliage, fruits, and flowers, and their larvae devour grass roots.

Japanese beetles begin by eating small holes in the upper or lower sides of leaves. The holes gradually widen to form a lacy skeleton with only the leaf veins remaining. Leaves may turn brown and fall off. Foliage on even large trees can be completely skeletonized. From a distance, severely injured trees appear to have been scorched by fire.

Adult beetles attack more than 250 kinds of plants. Favorite targets include roses and plants in the rose family, such as peach, quince, apple, cherry, and kerria. Preferred flowers include zinnia, African marigold, and hollyhock. Deciduous shade trees such as birch, chestnut, elm, linden, and horse chestnut are frequent victims, but evergreens usually escape. Boston ivy, Virginia creeper, grapevines, and basil also attract this pest.

Japanese beetles get around, capable of a sustained flight of 5 miles. They fly during the warm parts of the day, often a little after 1 p.m., feeding from the top of a plant downward, regardless of whether it is a 50-foot-high tree or a 6-inch-tall flower stem. It's not that the tops have better flavor; they merely have maximum sun exposure.

Japanese beetles are gregarious insects; a group will congregate around a single rosebud, devour it, and then move on to another. Over 100 beetles may feed simultaneously on one young apple fruit.

The equally destructive larvae, called white grubs, feed on grass and sod roots. In severe infestations, there can be more than 50 Japanese beetle grubs per square foot of soil. Lawn damage consists of dead or balding patches. Grub-damaged turf has no roots, so you can be certain that grubs did the harm if you can roll back the brown grass like a carpet. If it is firmly rooted, then another pest is the cause.

Unlike the Japanese beetle, the June beetle flies only after

June beetles eat the leaves of many kinds of trees. Night feeders, they may fly into a house if the lights are on.

dusk. You will often see it flying about shade trees, particularly oaks, in summer. It is attracted to porch lights and often bumps repeatedly into brightly lit windows. This beetle is a clumsy flier, moving along in the air as if uncertain of its course. If it finds a landing spot near a light, it just stays there, facing the light. During the day it remains hidden under grass or in plant litter.

This common beetle has various nicknames, including May beetle, June bug, and daw bug. There are over 200 species of June beetles, all with similar life-styles. The adults feed on foliage of ash, apple, birch, elm, walnut, blackberry, poplar, oak, willow, and other trees. A few species attack roses.

The grubs eat grass roots and are serious lawn pests. They also chew on the roots of strawberry, corn, beet, and onion plants and burrow their way into potato tubers. Small plants may become permanently stunted or may wilt and die. Large plants have better resistance to attack but may also suffer if numerous grubs feed on their roots.

Rose chafer grubs also chew on grass roots. The damage resembles that done by June beetle and Japanese beetle grubs, except that chafers infest lawns only in sandy regions.

Rose chafers devour the areas between leaf veins, leaving lacy skeletons. You will see the beetles in swarms feeding first on flowers, especially roses and peonies.

They then move on to other flower, vegetable, or berry plants. In some areas, they severely damage elms. Rose chafers also attack apple, cabbage, cherry, dahlia, foxglove, grape, geranium, hollyhock, peach, poppy, wisteria, and other plants.

The Pest

The larvae of Japanese beetles are plump, brown-headed, grayish white, 3/4-inch-long grubs that feed at grass root level. They usually curl into a C shape. Adult beetles are pretty, 1/2-inch-long insects with shiny metallic-green heads and copper-colored wing covers.

In early morning on clear, warm days, males fly low over the ground searching for newly emerging females. The males land where they smell the powerful female sex pheromone and start crawling toward their goal. Many may reach the same female at once, with others continuing to arrive.

After mating, the females burrow 2 to 4 inches deep into soil, at night or on a cloudy day, to deposit one to four eggs apiece. They markedly prefer well-kept lawns for this. They then crawl back out again to feed for several days and return to the soil to deposit a few more eggs. Each female deposits approximately 50 eggs in this manner. The males continue eating steadily or flying about looking for something to eat.

Grubs hatch about two weeks after the eggs are laid; they feed on grass roots near

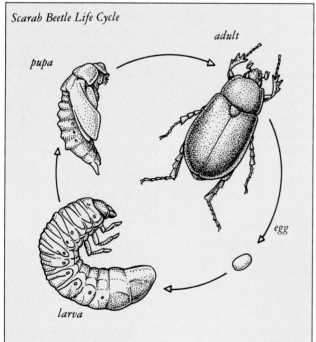

Scarab Beetle Life Cycle

pupa

adult

egg

larva

Scarab beetles lay eggs in the soil in summer. These hatch into larvae called grubs, which feed on plant roots. The larvae burrow deeper in winter and pupate in late winter or in spring. Adults emerge in early summer and feed on foliage, flowers, and fruit.

the surface until fall and then burrow 10 inches or more into the soil to spend the winter. In spring they return close to the surface, feed on grass roots for a few weeks, and then pupate and emerge as adult beetles from mid-June to mid-July. Adults feed until October.

The 1-inch-long, reddish brown or black adult June beetles emerge from the soil in May, June, and July. In late summer, each female deposits as many as 200 eggs in soil, preferring soil with plenty of grass and weeds. Strawberry beds can be another target area. Each egg goes in a separate cell 1 to 8 inches below the soil surface. The grubs

The larvae of several kinds of scarab beetles eat grass roots. Infested turf can often be rolled back like a carpet to reveal the culprit grubs.

hatch in about three weeks. They look somewhat like Japanese beetle grubs but are larger, measuring $\frac{1}{2}$ to $1\frac{1}{2}$ inches long, and their small underbody spines form an elliptical pattern. June beetle grubs feed on roots until fall.

June beetles typically have a two-year life cycle in southern states, whereas in northern areas the life cycle can take three years. Grubs spend the winter underground and then tunnel upward in spring, feeding on roots all summer. The next autumn they move down again, going 8 inches deep, where they pupate. The following spring, adult beetles emerge from the soil.

The slender, tan, long-legged, $\frac{1}{2}$-inch-long rose chafer emerges in late May or early June. It feeds for about a month and then, in mid- to late summer, the female lays eggs in sandy soil. The grubs hatch in one to two weeks.

Rose chafer grubs resemble June beetle grubs but are lighter colored, smaller, and slimmer. Like the other scarab beetle grubs, they feed near the surface and then tunnel downward for the winter, going 10 to 16 inches deep. They move upward again in spring and feed for a while before pupating close to the soil surface. They emerge as beetles in June.

Control Measures

Similar control methods work for all kinds of scarab beetles. Because they pupate deep in soil, spading garden beds in summer and fall kills some larvae and pupae and exposes others to birds. Avoid putting crop plants in soil that was recently used as lawn, because grubs may damage the plants. If you are going to garden in such an area, spade or till the plot in fall. Then till or spade regularly until planting time.

Popular Japanese beetle traps use sex attractants and floral aromas to lure beetles. The beetles land on the trap's smooth surface and then slide off into a plastic bag trap. These attract beetles so efficiently that beetles from as far as 500 feet away arrive at the trap, meaning that you may lure your neighbor's beetles to your garden. Many of these become trapped, but they might stop on their way to eat holes in your roses or lay eggs in your lawn.

If you use a trap, place it at least 100 feet away and downwind from the plants you want to protect. Empty the bag regularly because decaying beetles repel live ones. Renew the pheromone according to label directions.

Light traps attract June beetles. Like all traps, there are pros and cons to this method. Many insects, some beneficial, can be attracted to and killed by light traps.

Milky spore disease, caused by the pathogenic bacterium *Bacillus popillae*, may be applied to lawns; it paralyzes Japanese beetle grubs, effectively controlling them in your lawn, although the bacteria need a sufficient grub population and several years to become established in the soil. Milky spore disease does not work effectively on other scarab beetle grubs, nor will it kill adult beetles. Because Japanese beetles can fly as far as 5 miles, your garden might still suffer from beetle damage. To be truly effective against these insects, the disease spores must be applied throughout your community.

Effective control measures must be aimed at both beetle grubs and adults. Apply pesticides to lawns in spring and late fall. You can choose either a granular type that you apply with a lawn spreader or a liquid concentrate that you apply with a lawn sprayer.

Apply granular diazinon (Ortho Diazinon Soil & Turf Insect Control) to dry grass blades. You want the diazinon particles to bounce off the blades and sift as deeply as possible into the

Voracious Japanese beetles often feed in groups, devouring flowers, leaves, and fruit of many kinds of plants.

lawn. Water as soon as possible after spreading the granules so that the insecticide dissolves and soaks at least $\frac{1}{2}$ inch into the lawn soil.

When using a diazinon spray (Ortho Diazinon Insect Spray) or a chlorpyrifos spray (Ortho Lawn Insect Spray), apply with a nozzle that gives a coarse spray, which better permeates thick thatch. Do not apply to a dry lawn, or the insecticide will evaporate before it penetrates the soil. Irrigate the lawn the day before treating unless the container label states otherwise. Water the lawn thoroughly within one hour after application to

Rose chafers, long-legged scarab beetles, damage roses as well as many other flowers, vegetables, and fruits.

help carry insecticide to the root zone where grubs feed.

The younger the grubs, the easier they will be to eliminate. The best time to apply insecticides is just after eggs begin to hatch. (Hatching can take place over a four-week period.) Then your lawn will suffer little damage. Call your county agricultural extension agent for beetle egg-laying time in your area. Soil insecticides take some time to be effective; grubs may be active for up to 30 days.

To control adult scarab beetles on nonfood plants, spray in late spring and summer with carbaryl (Ortho Liquid Sevin®, Ortho Gypsy Moth & Japanese Beetle Killer) or acephate (Orthene® Systemic Insect Control).

On food plants, use carbaryl (Ortho Sevin® 5 Dust, Ortho Sevin® 10 Dust, Ortho Sevin® Garden Dust, Ortho Sevin® Garden Spray).

SLUGS AND SNAILS

If you are under the impression that all garden slugs are gray, one damp morning you may be in for a surprise. Of the more than 30 slug species in this country, some are white, lavender, pale yellow, purple, or nearly black with brown specks and mottlings. Size varies too, from the ½-inch-long gray field slug commonly seen on lawns to the 7-inch spotted garden slug, which feeds on almost all low-growing plants. Size does not necessarily reflect a slug's appetite, however.

In one fertile acre of land, there can be more than 300,000 slugs. You probably don't have that many slugs in your garden, but the prospect is there!

Given a choice, slugs prefer to chew on fragile seedlings and damaged plants rather than healthy ones. They first attack plant parts nearest the ground. However, if your slug supply outnumbers your supply of weak plants, slugs will eat your garden favorites too. They will also eat just about any kind of garbage, from tea leaves to bones.

Garden snails are similar to slugs, but they carry their homes on their backs. With 21,000 teeth apiece on their tongues, snails saw plants into bits before devouring them. You can find snails almost anyplace—where your baby lettuce used to be, under a patch of half-eaten strawberries, or sleeping off a meal of seedlings. Snails operate not only at ground level, they crawl up trees too. Sometimes the pickings are so good that the snails stay up there for weeks. You will see leaf holes, disappearing blossoms, and scarred fruit. If you look for well-camouflaged brown lumps on the branches and hidden by foliage, you have probably found the culprit.

Working mostly at night, slugs and snails eat large, ragged holes in leaves, leaving

Snails come out of their shells at night and on wet days to eat holes in plants.

behind a thick slime trail. They travel from one site to another over slime they produce in special glands. In the early morning, you will see sunlight glistening on silver trails that crisscross your lawn, patio, and plants. This drying slime, which can be produced in copious amounts, provides the cushion that slugs and snails need to get over rough spots.

Slime trails serve another purpose, too. Slugs and snails use them as marked pathways to find their way home. Although slime is usually clear or milky, it also can be orange or bright yellow, depending on the species. Glands under the creatures' heads secrete the slime. When slime dries, it makes a handy trail marker for the return trip. Slugs and snails have memories, and they will return many times to the current best feeding area in your garden.

Snails and slugs are mollusks, rather than insects. (Because they do so much garden damage, however, they have been included in this book.) Millions of years ago, their ancestors lived in the sea, where some relatives, such as the clam and oyster, still remain. When waters receded, some became land dwelling. Those migrating to areas without the soil calcium necessary for building shells gradually evolved smaller and smaller shells, until these almost disappeared or disappeared entirely.

A snail's shell is really an outside skeleton, growing as the snail grows. Young snails have only one shell whorl. Older snails have five whorls. Brown and yellow patterns provide camouflage. Like fingerprints, no two snail shells have exactly the same markings.

Protection for the shell-less slug comes from a folded skin area called the mantle. This is the hump on a slug's back under which it hides its head in moments of stress.

The slug controls moisture loss by staying out of the sun and wind and by secreting a special protective skin slime. A slug's body is 80 percent water, and its slime or mucus is 98 percent water. A slug can lose 19 percent of its body water supply and still do nicely. More than that kills the slug, however, so to keep from dehydrating during warm daylight hours, it hides under a clump of earth, a planter, a rock, a decaying board, a drainpipe, or anywhere else that is cool, dark, and damp.

Slugs feed during foggy weather, moist nights, and immediately after a rain or garden watering. Not only is this atmosphere more comfortable

cans looking for food. They usually hide in the same place each time, emerging at night or during cool, damp weather.

When the weather gets warm, snails retreat inside their shells. During drought periods or other unfavorable conditions, snails seal themselves inside their shells with a slime barrier that soon hardens to a leathery texture. Snails can remain dormant for up to four years.

Although there are several hundred species of snail, only a few do major garden damage. Like many carelessly imported garden pests with few native predators, these few snail species can keep you occupied trying to eradicate them. For example, the familiar and extremely destructive brown garden snail was brought here from Europe. Some entrepreneur hoped it would become a gourmet food item like its escargot relatives. This original venture did not succeed, but in the interim, a few snails escaped. Without its natural predators to keep populations down, the brown garden snail thrived and multiplied. If you do not have this snail in your state, it is due to extensive quarantine networks at state

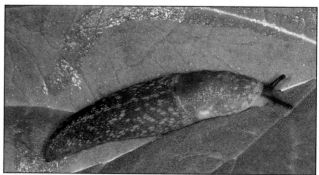
Like snails, slugs are night feeders. Because they lack protective shells, they need moister daytime hiding places.

to slugs, it provides them with necessary water, which they absorb through their skin or drink from puddles. Slugs are air breathers, however, and they can drown.

During the day, most snails hide near the earth, preferably under stones, logs, thick ground cover, or debris. Some even crawl into garbage

and national borders, where soil and plants are checked for snails and snail eggs.

Among the earliest pests to start feeding in your garden, slugs and snails arrive in spring and stay until late autumn. In warm-winter areas, some may be around all year. Slugs occur throughout the

United States but are worst in humid regions, especially the Northwest. Snails thrive in California and the South.

The Pest

Inside a snail's shell is a 1-inch-long animal made up of a head, stomach, and foot. Two pairs of tentacles that look like small horns protrude from the head. The top pair serve as eyes, but the snail doesn't see very well, so it must rely on a good sense of smell to find food. The snail's two lower tentacles serve as its nose.

Snails and slugs are hermaphroditic, that is, male and female in one, but they require another snail to fertilize the eggs that each creature carries within its body. During courtship, two snails crawl around each other in a slow dance that can last half a day. Each snail then digs a shallow hole in loose, damp soil with its foot. Forty round, transparent eggs go in the hole. Young snails—miniatures of their parents—hatch a few days later. They have a potential four-year life span.

Each hermaphroditic slug can lay 300 eggs. Peak egg-laying times are spring and fall, although if the climate is right, a slug will lay eggs any time of year. Jellylike clusters of about 25 eggs apiece are deposited in loose soil. Young slugs emerge in about a month, sooner in warm weather. Initially dull white, they gradually darken.

Control Measures

Gardeners have many home-style remedies for controlling slugs and snails. Some of them work and some of them don't. Most rely on trapping the pests and then destroying them or on dehydrating these moisture-needing creatures.

The first step in keeping slug and snail populations down is to remove all piles of decaying vegetation, boards, stones and other shelters that provide cool overnight quarters. On citrus and fruit trees, remove low-hanging branches

Slime trails on these geranium leaves are a clue that snails or slugs were feasting on them the night before.

and leaf litter from the ground to prevent snails from climbing aboard.

Homemade slug traps include overturned flowerpots, flat stones, flat boards, or anything that provides cool, dark shelter. Place these near where slugs feed or near slime trails. Each morning, turn over your trap and pick off and destroy any sleeping slugs. For added slug allure, place slices of raw potato or lettuce leaves near or within the trap.

You can create traps for snails seeking day cover out of boards or flowerpots. Make traps with boards that are 12 inches wide and 15 inches long, raised off the ground by 1-inch-high runners. Gather and destroy snails daily. Snails collected by hand must be squashed or placed in a closed container for later destruction. If you try to drown them in a bucket of water, they will just crawl out.

Repeated and careful trapping can reduce slug and snail populations, but be careful that you conscientiously remove them every day, or instead of trapping them you will be providing shelter and breeding quarters.

When the slugs and snails congregate under traps, you can sprinkle salt on them, causing immediate dehydration, but be careful—salt can injure or kill nearby plants. You can also pour boiling water on them, again keeping it away from plants that you do not want to cook.

Some gardeners recommend luring slugs and snails to their deaths with a pan of beer set in the garden. The malt in the beer attracts the snails and slugs to the pan, but many drink the beer and stagger off without falling in. If you find "drowned" slugs in traps, don't dump them on the ground afterward. Excess water can evaporate through the slug's skin, and the creature may revive and crawl away, as good as new.

Gardeners also spread all sorts of protective barriers, such as cinders or sharp sand, around tender plants to try to discourage slugs and snails from visiting—the theory being that these particles irritate a slug's foot and the slug won't travel over them. Unfortunately, these barriers must remain completely dry to be effective. If it rains or if you water, slime production enables a slug to crawl over almost any barrier. And if the food seems tasty enough, a snail will put up with some discomfort.

Snail bait is the most effective method for controlling snails. Metaldehyde (Ortho Bug-Geta® Snail & Slug Pellets) or metaldehyde-carbaryl baits (Ortho Bug-Geta Plus® Snail, Slug & Insect Granules) scattered on soil throughout the garden work in both wet and dry weather. Metaldehyde stimulates slugs and snails to produce enormous amounts of mucus. This continuous mucus loss eventually dehydrates the pests, killing them. It can be used around fruits and vegetables.

A methiocarb bait (Ortho Slug-Geta® Snail & Slug Bait) paralyzes snails so that they cannot seek shelter, causing them to dehydrate and die when the sun shines. It works better than metaldehyde baits if your area stays quite damp, but it can't be used on or near food plants.

Baits should not be scattered just anywhere, anyway. The proper technique assures success. If you have not

watered recently and it hasn't rained, sprinkle soil lightly after scattering bait pellets, because slugs and snails move about more readily in damp areas. After spreading the bait, do not water heavily—and hope it doesn't rain—for at least two days. In cool, wet weather, poisoned slugs and snails may reabsorb sufficient water to withstand the dehydration caused by the metaldehyde bait.

Spread bait granules in the evening. Slugs are most active from two hours after sunset to two hours before sunrise. Bait pellets attract slugs most effectively the first three days after application, so work for the maximal kill combination. Repeat the application two to three times at two- to three-week intervals.

Do not spread bait in open areas; put it near walls, fences, and other hiding places that

These small, transparent eggs will hatch into tiny slugs. Both slugs and snails lay eggs just below the soil surface.

slugs and snails prefer. Be certain that bait pellets are not accessible to pets or children; to make them less attractive, scatter bait lightly—do not apply in mounds or clumps. Do not allow pellets to rest on foliage.

Place bait in the same area each time you apply it because slugs and snails remember where food is and will come back. If you spread bait in a different area each time, the slugs return to the first place, scout around, find nothing, and turn to the nearby strawberry patch instead of searching for new baited areas.

SOD WEBWORMS

Also called lawn moths, sod webworms chew off grass blades close to the ground and then pull them into silken tunnels constructed near the bases of the blades. Brown, saucer-sized patches of closely clipped grass begin appearing in April or mid-May and continue through October. These patches expand irregularly, and by the time the second generation begins feeding in July and August the damage can be quite unsightly, possibly killing an entire lawn.

Sod webworms will not bother grass in heavily shaded areas. Most species prefer areas that are hot and dry during the day, even though they feed only on cloudy days and at night. Much of their damage occurs on steep slopes, banks, and other areas that are difficult to water properly.

You will often see flocks of blackbirds clustering around infested areas searching for sod webworms. You may even see probe holes left by birds searching for these caterpillars.

The Pest

These ¾-inch-long light brown, gray, or greenish caterpillars have several rows of dark spots along their bodies. Adult moths have a ¾-inch wingspread and grayish white to beige body color. While resting, sod webworm moths keep their wings folded closely about their bodies. Long sensory organs stick out in front of their heads like a snout, giving these moths the common name snout moth.

You will see these moths at dusk as they flutter over lawns, dropping eggs into the turf. If disturbed during the day, they fly erratically for a short distance and then alight again on turf. The moths do not damage lawns.

Sod webworms overwinter several inches below ground as partially grown caterpillars. During spring, the larvae complete their growth, constructing tunnels or burrowing through thatch to pupate. The caterpillars line their tunnels with webs of silklike material. They do not place any webbing on lawn surfaces. After changing into

Sod webworms specialize in severing blades of grass and dragging them down into silk-lined tunnels where they complete their meal.

adult form and mating, the females deposit eggs, which hatch in 7 to 10 days.

The young caterpillars feed for one to two weeks before pupating. Sod webworms mature from egg to adult form in about six weeks depending upon temperatures. Two or three generations may occur in a season. In southern Florida, however, sod webworm reproduction continues throughout the year.

Control Measures

To determine if sod webworms are causing your lawn to turn brown, examine the grass carefully on an overcast day or at dusk to look for feeding caterpillars or night-flying moths. Another detection method is to mix 1 tablespoon of liquid soap in 1 gallon of water. Apply this solution uniformly over 1 square yard of turf. This solution irritates sod webworms, which soon come to the surface where you can see them.

Timely insecticide treatment prevents major lawn damage. Sod webworms are killed by initial contact with the insecticide or by consuming treated foliage. Choose a spray containing chlorpyrifos (Ortho Lawn Insect Spray, Ortho-Klor® Soil Insect & Termite Killer).

Sprays have the greatest effect within the first 24 to 48 hours after application. Treat the entire lawn rather than patches, using a lawn

sprayer (Ortho Lawn Sprayer), tank-type sprayer, or lawn drop spreader (Ortho Drop Spreader). Use a coarse spray to penetrate the thick thatch and prevent drift.

Prior to treatment, mow the lawn and rake infested areas to remove dead grass and plant debris, which can absorb insecticide rather than letting it reach the plant crown where webworms feed. If you will be spraying, water the lawn the day before you treat, or spray after a rain, to prevent insecticide from evaporating. Withhold further watering for 48 hours to

Brown patches in a dry, sunny lawn may signal sod webworm damage. Birds may tell you, too, by hunting the pests.

avoid diluting the spray and reducing its effectiveness.

When you use granular products, the grass blades should be dry at application time so the particles bounce off them and sift as deeply as possible into thatch. This brings the concentrated product close to the target and also provides protection from light, which hastens insecticide breakdown.

Water your lawn lightly following treatment with granules, trying for about ¼ inch of water. Granular control begins only when the granules absorb moisture and release the insecticide. However, granules have longer protective power because they disintegrate over an extended time period.

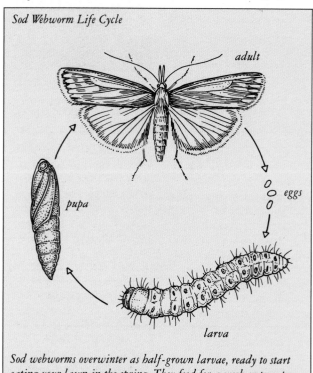

Sod Webworm Life Cycle

adult

pupa

eggs

larva

Sod webworms overwinter as half-grown larvae, ready to start eating your lawn in the spring. They feed for a week or two, pupate, and emerge as adult moths that soon lay eggs on the lawn. The cycle from egg to adult takes six weeks in warm weather.

Keep all children and pets off a treated lawn until the grass has dried or you have thoroughly watered in the insecticide.

Whether you are using sprays or granules, do not expect to see large numbers of dead insects immediately. Control can take up to two weeks, depending on the extent of insect feeding.

SOWBUGS AND PILLBUGS

Whether you call them sowbugs, pillbugs, roly-polys, slaters, wood lice, monkey peas, or bibblebugs, these gray "armor-plated" crustaceans seem to make their homes in just about everyone's garden. You might consider sowbugs a nuisance because they occasionally eat tender stems and seedling roots as part of their nightly diet. They also may nibble on lettuce and other soft fruits

More closely related to lobsters than to insects, sowbugs usually eat decaying matter but may also eat soft plant parts.

and vegetables that rest on damp soil. However, most of their meals consist of decaying leaves and overripe fruit, so sowbugs actually perform some necessary garden cleanup chores.

More often than not, snails, slugs, and insects cause damage attributed to sowbugs. Because sowbugs like to take daytime naps in holes chewed by other garden pests, you assume that they have done the damage. Only once in a while do sowbug populations get large enough to

Pillbugs, which lack the pointy tails of sowbugs, roll into balls when disturbed. They both play similar roles in the garden.

force them to make seedlings a regular part of their diet.

Sowbugs and pillbugs are not insects but animals classified as crustaceans. (They are included in this book because they are plant pests.) Their relatives include the lobster, crayfish, and shrimp. Sowbug and pillbug ancestors emerged from the sea about 345 million years ago, and they still breathe through modified gills and need damp surroundings.

Sowbugs and pillbugs cannot control water evaporation from their bodies. Without shelter, the sun's heat dries them out completely in a few hours. Thus, during the day, unless it rains, they hide under vegetation, rocks, flowerpots, or in deep soil crevices. At night, when air is moist, they come out to feed.

The Pest
The names pillbug and sowbug are often used interchangeably for the ½-inch-long garden crustaceans. Although they look and act almost exactly alike, a sowbug has a pair of small, pointy tails projecting from the rear of its body. A pillbug does not. Further, the pillbug can roll up in a tight little ball when disturbed. The best a sowbug can do is try to hunch its shell.

Depending on where you live, there can be one to three sowbug generations per year. The female carries about 24 young—smaller versions of

their parents—in a fluid-filled brood pouch created by overlapping "armor" plating under its body. This incubation period lasts almost two months. Even after hatching, the young stay with the mother until ready to survive outside the brood pouch. They can live for two years.

Control Measures
The first line of attack against sowbugs and pillbugs should be against their hiding places. Remove leaf litter, piles of grass clippings, fallen fruit, and any flower bed mulch you do not really need. Store boxes, boards, and flowerpots off the ground.

If populations increase to the point of annoyance and cultural controls do not take care of the problem, apply insecticides. You can lightly scatter propoxur bait (Ortho Earwig, Roach & Sowbug Bait) or diazinon bait (Ortho Diazinon Soil & Turf Insect Control) in a 2- to 4-foot band around nonfood plants and other areas where pillbugs or sowbugs congregate. Treat wood chips and leaf mold used as mulch. Apply bait in late afternoon or early evening, and water it lightly to carry the insecticide down into the soil. Spray food plants with diazinon (Ortho Diazinon Insect Spray).

SPITTLEBUGS

Spittlebugs, sometimes called froghoppers, build safe homes of frothy "spittle" around themselves. Children sometimes call these foamy bubbles "frog spit." You may see spittlebug froth on the stems of rosemary, alder, holly, strawberry, chrysanthemum, stock, corn, pecan, pine, willow, holly, and at least 400 other plants. The spittle itself isn't harmful—it is a combination of excreted fluid and a gluey glandular substance, the two mixed with air to form bubbles.

The adult and nymph spittlebugs suck sap from

stems and leaves. Except for a few species, however, they are harmless. The meadow spittlebug, one of the exceptions, can seriously stunt flower growth. If it attacks strawberries, fruit will be distorted and small. The twolined spittlebug feeds on holly, causing distortion of young

White froth protects feeding spittlebug nymphs from predators. Damage to infested plants is usually minor.

leaves and blotches on the undersides of mature leaves. The pine spittlebug ejects sap almost like a light rain, and the tree becomes covered with sooty mold fungus. The punctures made by the Saratoga spittlebug on ornamental trees permit fungus and pitch to enter the tree, impeding nutrient flow.

The Pest
Adult spittlebugs resemble leafhoppers—they can be brown, gray, or black and occasionally have yellow markings. Their size ranges from ⅛ to ½ inch long. They hop from place to place quite energetically. A common nickname, froghopper, is due in part to this trait and in part to their longish legs, prominent eyes, and short, wedge-shaped bodies.

Overwintering in egg form, the greenish nymph emerges in midspring and usually takes up residence at a leaf-stem junction. To create protective froth, each spittlebug nymph makes a bellows of its body. Its tail goes up and down, forcing the spittle bubbles out one by one. As each bubble forms, the nymph reaches back with its

The spittle on this fuchsia shoot tip has been blown away to reveal the spittlebug nymph inside.

legs, takes hold of the bubble, and moves it toward its head. Eventually the nymph is buried, and invisible, under a pile of white foam.

Adult female spittlebugs insert eggs in plant stems or between the stem and leaf sheath in grasses. Although most species produce one generation per year, a few have two: The first hatches in May, the second in July. Adults do not produce spittle.

Control Measures

Before you use insecticide for spittlebug control, be certain that the damage is not caused by another insect. If you don't like the frothy masses, a strong water spray from a garden hose usually removes it, although the nymphs soon rebuild elsewhere.

If spittlebugs are very abundant and appear to be weakening the plant, as the meadow spittlebug might, spray with insecticide in late summer to kill egg-laying adults, and in early spring to kill young nymphs. For spittlebugs on pine, spray in late May in the North and South and spray again in July in the South.

You will have to wash protective froth off older nymphs with a garden hose before spraying, or the insecticide will not penetrate. On food plants, use malathion (Ortho Malathion 50 Insect Spray). On nonfood plants you can use acephate (Ortho Isotox® Insect Killer, Orthene® Systemic Insect Control).

SPRINGTAILS

The wingless garden springtail is a tiny jumping pest common in seedbeds. It damages thin, fragile leaves of young plants and seedlings, often making pits in the seed leaves of sprouting seedlings. It may chew holes in any foliage that is close to the ground.

Garden springtails trouble seedlings of bean, beet, chard, cucumber, onion, spinach, and squash, among other plants. They are most prevalent where soil contains a lot of organic matter and remains constantly moist.

The Pest

Measuring $\frac{1}{16}$ to $\frac{1}{4}$ inch long, garden springtails often escape notice. Soft, round, and purple with yellow spots,

Tiny, leaping insects that damage seedlings and thin-leaved plants, garden springtails thrive in moist soil.

these pests have no wings. Instead, they jump, using a taillike appendage to spring quickly around your garden. Entomologists know very little about the life cycles of these tiny pests.

Control Measures

In vegetable beds, use diazinon granules (Ortho Diazinon Soil & Turf Insect Control). This also controls other soil-dwelling pests, such as maggots, cutworms, and wireworms. You can also spray infested plants with malathion.

Allowing the garden bed to dry out discourages springtails and reduces their numbers.

SQUASH BUGS

Squash bugs feed primarily on squash and pumpkins but also attack melons, cucumbers, cantaloupes, and gourds. Winter squashes, such as Hubbard and marrow, suffer most. Both adult and young squash bugs suck sap from leaf undersides and inject a toxic substance while they feed. This toxin causes Anasa wilt, named after the pest's scientific name, *Anasa tristis*. This condition closely resembles bacterial wilt, but unlike bacterial wilt, it can be controlled if you quickly eradicate the squash bugs.

Initial symptoms of squash bug invasion and Anasa wilt include grayish areas on leaves. Next, vines rapidly wilt, curl, turn black, and become very dry. Small vines may die; larger ones lose several runners. The greatest damage comes in mid- to late summer, when nymphs are most numerous. You may also see both nymphs and adults clustered on unripe squashes; with heavy infestations, you may not see any fruit at all.

To distinguish Anasa wilt from bacterial wilt, slit open a wilted squash stem near the base. Touch the knife to the sap and draw it out, looking for a milky ooze that strings out into a fine thread as you withdraw the knife. If you see this, then the plant suffers from bacterial wilt. This disease is carried by striped cucumber beetles (see page 50) and occurs most frequently on cucumbers and melons rather than pumpkins and squash.

The Pest

The $\frac{5}{8}$-inch-long adult squash bugs are flat backed, hard shelled, and dark brown above and mottled yellow below. They give off an unpleasant odor when crushed and may incorrectly be called stink bugs.

Squash bugs overwinter under garden litter, especially dead squash vines left in the garden, boards, or buildings. They emerge during June, at about the time squash vines start running. Mating takes place soon afterward.

Females lay clusters of 15 to 50 shiny brown eggs on leaf undersides in the angle between the veins. They each lay a total of 100 to 300 eggs. Nymphs hatch in 7 to 14 days. The young ones are fat, green creatures with pink antennae and legs. Older nymphs are grayish white and coated with a white, powdery substance. The young from a single egg cluster stay together and feed, and hundreds can infest a single vine. They reach adult size in six weeks and feed until fall. There is one generation per year, but squash bugs at all stages of development occur during the growing season.

Control Measures

Squash bugs can be quite difficult to control, even with a combination of cultural methods and insecticides. Begin treatment as soon as you see the first pests on your vines to ward off wilt.

Be very careful when choosing an insecticide for

Act quickly to control squash bugs when you see them on squash-family plants. Rapid action can prevent wilting and death of the vines.

use on squash, because some varieties get leaf burn. Read the container label carefully to see that your squash is listed. You can safely treat

Shiny, brown squash bug eggs can be found on the undersides of leaves or on flower buds. Crush them as part of your control efforts.

listed plants and soil around the plants with carbaryl (Ortho Sevin® Garden Dust) or a captan-methoxychlor-rotenone compound (Ortho Tomato Vegetable Dust). Repeat the treatment every seven days until squash bugs and nymphs disappear.

You can reduce populations by collecting and destroying egg clusters on leaf undersides. You can also trap squash bugs by placing boards between host plant rows. The bugs seek night shelter under these, and you can turn the boards over and destroy the sleeping insects early in the morning, before they return to the vines. Because adults require garden litter or similar protection from frost, you can reduce future infestations by gathering up and destroying all harvest refuse. Without insecticide controls, however, these cultural methods probably will not eliminate enough pests to prevent some wilt symptoms.

If you have continual squash bug problems, try planting resistant squash varieties. Among these are 'Butternut', 'Royal Acorn', and 'Sweet Cheese'.

SQUASH VINE BORERS

When your squash vine leaves start to wilt, they are not always suffering from lack of water or noonday heat. Inside each stem can be one or more larvae, getting plumper by the minute. Sometimes there can be as many as 140 squash vine borers in a single vine.

These pests bore into the plant immediately after they hatch, leaving behind a souvenir of yellow or tan grainy excrement on the stem exterior. The larvae feed for about four weeks, continually pushing excrement out through the entry holes. This excrement collects on the ground under the vines and will be your first warning of squash vine borer infestation.

The feeding of the squash vine borer interrupts the plant's mechanism for conducting water and food, which is why plants eventually wilt. The stems start to rot and may break off completely beyond the point of attack. If the larvae are not controlled, one plant or all affected plants can die. Late in the season, the larvae feed on fruit in addition to stems.

Squash vine borers attack all species of summer and winter squash, with Hubbard, zucchini, yellow, and acorn leading the list. They also feed within the stems of pumpkin, cucumber, and muskmelon.

The Pest

In southern states the paper wasp–shaped adult borer moths emerge in April to May; in cooler areas this occurs from June to July. This is usually about the time vine crops come up. You will see the clearwing moths making rapid, zigzag flights over your squash beds during the day. These 1-inch-long moths are quite visible, with orange-and-black abdomens, coppery green forewings, and clear hindwings. You also may hear them; they make a slight buzzing noise while flying.

The females alight briefly and repeatedly on squash plants, depositing a single pinhead-sized, reddish brown, oval egg each time. Preferred egg-laying sites are stems, especially near plant bases, but the moths may glue eggs onto all parts of a squash plant. Each female deposits about 200 eggs during its one-month life span.

Brown-headed, white, wrinkled larvae hatch in about a week and immediately bore into the stem. They grow to about 1 inch long during their four or five weeks in the stems and then emerge and burrow about 2 inches into the ground.

The larvae spin black-hued silk cocoons underground. These are initially soft, but dirt soon adheres to them, making them almost indistinguishable from the surrounding earth. In southern states, larvae may pupate immediately, allowing a second generation of borers to continue destroying squash vines until frost. In northern areas, larvae overwinter within the cocoon, changing to brown pupae in early spring and emerging shortly afterward as adult moths.

Control Measures

You can try capturing the rapid day-flying adult moths during twilight hours when they rest, wings folded, on the upper sides of leaf bases. During their resting period, they are so sluggish they cannot escape. You can also attempt to destroy or capture females alighting in the early morning to lay eggs, because they are still moving comparatively slowly at this time.

Once larvae begin tunneling inside stems and you see frass and plant wilting, insecticides offer no control. If your infestation appears light, you might make a small, lengthwise slit in each affected stem, above where you see frass exuding, with a sharp knife or razor blade. Remove the tunneling larvae, or pierce them with the knife and place the injured plant part, including the nearest stem joint, on the ground, covering it with moist soil to encourage supplemental rooting. Keep vines well watered to encourage regrowth. This surgery works only when a few borers infest the vines.

Aside from the hand destruction of larvae and vine rerooting, once borers get into vines you have few alternatives except to hope that this pest leaves you some undamaged squash for the dinner table.

To prevent borers from laying eggs, dust squash plants with a captan-methoxychlor-rotenone contact insecticide (Ortho Tomato Vegetable Dust) when you first see the brightly colored adult moths.

Cutting open a damaged squash stem reveals the culprit—a hungry squash vine borer larva—feeding inside.

Destroy all old vines at the end of the season. Fall and winter spading exposes underground cocoons to weather and predators.

Some gardeners plant a row of the overwhelmingly preferred Hubbard squash as a trap crop for borers, then plant other squash varieties, which will only be lightly infested, for themselves.

STINK BUGS

Stink bugs give off a smelly fluid if you bother them. You will probably want to bother them anyway after you discover them sucking sap from the pods, fruits, buds, blossoms, and seeds of many fruits and vegetables. Some species of stink bug can destroy entire crops.

Stink bugs attacking young tree fruit create a form of pitting known as catfacing. The pit is a sunken, curved, corky area marring the surface

Harlequin bugs are common pests of cabbage-family plants in the South. In warm areas they may feed all winter.

of the fruit; its shape resembles a cat's grin. Sometimes a gummy substance appears on the fruit. On nuts, you will see black pitting. On vegetables and tomatoes, hard calluses surround stink bug feeding punctures, creating a distorted, dimpled appearance.

On both green and ripe tomatoes, feeding punctures begin as tiny brown or black specks; decay may develop around these. On unripe tomatoes, tissue around the punctures often turns faint yellowish green, creating a mottled effect. On ripe tomatoes, light yellow to white cloudy spots occur around the punctures. The tomatoes are edible but unappetizing.

On leaves, you will see white or yellow blotches at stink bug feeding sites. If damage becomes extensive, foliage wilts, turns brown, and dies. Young, tender growth is most susceptible to attack.

There are over 180 stink bug species. Some, such as

the rough stink bug, yellow stink bug, and spined stink bug, act as beneficial predators, feeding on caterpillars and other pests. Others, including the brown stink bug, harlequin bug, Say stink bug, green stink bug, and southern green stink bug, can be quite destructive of commercial and home crops.

The southern green stink bug, also known as the green soldier bug and pumpkin bug, feeds on many plants, including apple, cherry, box elder, corn, peach, eggplant, pea, tomato, and turnip, but has a preference for legumes.

The harlequin bug, also called calicoback and fire bug, prefers cruciferous plants, such as cabbage, Brussels sprout, cauliflower, kale, radish, and mustard. It is the most destructive pest of cabbage and related crops in the southern part of the country. This brightly hued pest also attacks many other plants, including plum, chrysanthemum, rose, squash, and sunflower.

The conspicuous stink bug feeds on berries, causing them to wither and dry up. Its feeding stints leave a disagreeable odor on the berries. The western brown cotton bug attacks tomatoes.

The Pest

All stink bugs are shield-shaped insects measuring about ½ inch long. They overwinter as adults, mate in spring, and lay egg clusters on leaf undersides. The young nymphs mature in six weeks, and there may be several generations each year, so damage occurs throughout the growing season.

Harlequin bugs are ⅜-inch-long, brilliantly colored insects with red, orange, or yellow bands, stripes, and blotches decorating a black background. Adult harlequin bugs overwinter in litter or crevices near host plants. In warm areas, however, these winged insects may continue feeding throughout the year,

All stink bugs are similar in their shieldlike shape, although they vary in color.

hiding during cold spells and reappearing on warm days.

In spring, females lay double rows of 12 or more barrel-shaped white eggs with obvious black circle markings on the leaf undersides of early garden crops. Shiny black nymphs with conspicuous white, yellow, and orange markings emerge in 4 to 10 days. The nymphs immediately begin sucking sap from fruit, vegetables, and ornamental plants. Three generations can occur per year in southern states, only one in northern states.

The ½-inch-long southern green stink bug is normally bright green with narrow yellow, orange, or reddish edges. During hibernation, however, it may be dark olive-green or pinkish. The female lays egg clusters on the leaf undersides of host plants beginning in March and April. Rounded, wingless nymphs, bluish with red markings, emerge in approximately one week. The young feed together in colonies for some time after hatching. At two months, after several molts, they assume adult form.

Adults live for several weeks to several months, with as many as five generations possible in a year. Some adults overwinter under logs, in garden litter, and in other sheltered places. Others, although in lesser numbers, remain on plants and feed throughout the winter. You may still see these hardy bugs in December.

The Say stink bug is bright to dark green, ½ inch long,

and has white speckles on its back. The nymph is pale to dark green with orange markings. The conspicuous stink bug is a little smaller than the Say stink bug and is pale brown with small black specks on top, yellow underneath, and has red antennae.

The western brown cotton bug measures ½ inch long and is light brown above with yellow undersides.

Control Measures

Certain cultural control measures can keep stink bug populations within acceptable levels. You can try to trap stink bugs away from your vegetables by placing old cabbage or turnip leaves in your garden. Destroy the leaves and the collected bugs daily. Clean out garden litter regularly, and at season's end remove and destroy the remainder of the crops. Examine leaf undersides weekly, and pick off and destroy egg masses when you see them. Tachinid flies act as very efficient parasites.

If stink bugs have been a problem in the past, begin insecticide control as soon as you see stink bugs or their damage. Treat infested food plants with a spray containing pyrethrins (Ortho Tomato & Vegetable Insect Killer) or a longer-acting carbaryl dust (Ortho Sevin® 5 Dust, Ortho Sevin® 10 Dust, Ortho Sevin® Garden Dust). Repeat the treatment at intervals of 7 to 10 days if the plants become reinfested. Make sure that your infested plant is listed on the product label.

TENT CATERPILLARS

Tent caterpillars spin conspicuous, white silk webs in the limb forks of deciduous trees. These thick, irregular webs begin in branch forks and expand out from there, becoming fairly large. Both eastern tent caterpillars, sometimes called American or appletree tent caterpillars, and western tent caterpillars feed on foliage of diverse trees, especially when mature. However, eastern tent caterpillars prefer wild cherry, apple, crabapple, pear, and hawthorn, whereas western tent caterpillars feed almost exclusively on oak.

Several other species may invade your garden, including the Sonoran, forest, and Pacific tent caterpillars. Their habits are similar to those of the eastern and western tent caterpillars, except that the web of the Sonoran tent caterpillar is much smaller, and the forest tent caterpillar builds no tent. Instead, it makes a communal silken mat on a tree branch. The forest tent caterpillar prefers ash, birch, gum, maple, oak, apple, aspen, and poplar.

Tent caterpillars begin making their tentlike nests within a few days of hatching, which happens when wild cherry buds begin to open. These webs enlarge by layers as the caterpillars grow. Between each layer there is a space, enabling the caterpillars to crawl around within the nest. Old molted skins and excrement collect in the tent.

Tent caterpillars remain in their webs during nights and rainy weather. On pleasant early spring to early summer days, these gregarious caterpillars crawl out from their protective tent in groups to feed on new leaves. Silk trails mark their progress along tree branches. You will see defoliation for quite a distance from the webs, in contrast to the

damage caused by fall webworms (see page 54), which defoliate trees within their ever-expanding web in spring and fall.

Those silk trails not only mark their way to and from the nest but also relay information to other caterpillars concerning the best feeding sites.

Although tent caterpillar defoliation usually does not kill trees, because the damage occurs so early in the season, it can slow growth and reduce a tree's strength and productivity. Most gardeners object to tent caterpillars because of the leaf loss and because the large excrement-filled nests are revolting.

If tent caterpillars completely defoliate a tree, they move on to another. These pests can migrate by the millions. Massive numbers of tent caterpillars appear at about 10-year intervals.

The Pest
All tent caterpillars are moderately hairy. When full grown, they can be 2 to 3 inches long. Eastern tent caterpillars are black with a solid white back stripe and brown and yellow lines accompanied by a row of oval blue spots along the sides. Western tent caterpillars have a variety of markings and colors but always have a series of white dashes down their backs. Forest tent caterpillars are pale blue to black with distinctive white, diamond-shaped markings down their backs and bluish heads.

Tent caterpillars emerge from overwintering eggs at about the time that their host plants start leafing out. They feed until early summer and then descend to the ground on silk strands or merely fall off twigs. Once they find a protected spot, they spin silken cocoons. They attach these yellowish white cocoons to trees, buildings, the undersides of outdoor furniture, loose bark, and other nearby structures. Tent caterpillars

also spin cocoons within garden litter, in their webs, and inside rolled leaves.

Adult moths emerge three weeks later. Their color varies from yellow to reddish brown, with two diagonal markings on the front wings. Their wingspan is about 1 inch. The moths live only a few days, during which they mate and lay eggs. They can be quite abundant, however, and you will often see them clustered around porch lights.

Female moths deposit eggs in a cementing substance that forms a $\frac{1}{2}$-inch-wide and $\frac{3}{4}$-inch-long collar around small twigs. These collars have a brown, varnished appearance, and each contains from 150 to 300 eggs. There may be 20 egg masses on a tree.

Control Measures
You can prune out webs when they are still small in the spring. Use a long pole spiked with nails or a brush-ended

Tent caterpillar nests begin in branch crotches. The larvae feed most actively on sunny days. For a close-up of the insect, see page 32.

pole to destroy the caterpillar-filled web at dusk. Kill stray caterpillars by crushing them, but beware: Handling tent caterpillars or cocoons with bare hands can cause skin inflammation. Wear gloves when dealing with tent caterpillars.

Time insecticide sprays to coincide with the emergence of the tiny caterpillars, because the young pests are easiest to control, and any feeding damage can be unsightly all season long. Once tent caterpillars have reached full size, it is useless to apply

insecticide because the caterpillars stop feeding and form tough cocoons.

You can use a BT spray, which contains pathogenic bacteria, to control young caterpillars. Add spreader-sticker for best results, and repeat according to label directions, especially if it rains. Spray emerging foliage on the entire tree because this is where caterpillars feed, and they must ingest the bacteria for the control to be effective.

Malathion (Ortho Malathion 50 Insect Spray) and carbaryl (Ortho Sevin® Garden Spray, Ortho Liquid Sevin®) also control tent caterpillars on fruit trees and ornamentals. You can also use a multipurpose orchard spray containing a captan-malathion-methoxychlor compound (Ortho Home Orchard Spray).

One carefully applied pesticide treatment, properly timed, should give you adequate control. (But repeat as necessary, according to label directions, if caterpillars migrate from other areas.) Spray emerging foliage where the tiny caterpillars are feeding.

With tent caterpillars that are more mature, you can spray foliage, but you can also often achieve good results with spot treatments. Target sprays at webs, where more tent caterpillars congregate. Because these caterpillars tend to be away from the web during the day, spray webs in the morning or at dusk.

THRIPS

You will see damage from feeding thrips long before you notice these tiny insects, which are barely visible to the naked eye. Often feeding in large numbers, thrips use their unique rasping-sucking mouth parts to file away at leaf, stem, and flower surfaces and then suck up sap flowing into the wound. Emptied of chlorophyll, younger leaves

Flower thrips can ruin a pretty flower. They have left unsightly brown spots on this pansy blossom.

become distorted, and older leaves acquire silver streaks or brown blotches. Injured blossoms develop brown streaks and wither prematurely. Fruits may have scars that appear as russeted or silvery areas.

With over 600 species of thrips in this country, you may find a variety of them in your garden. Some are beneficial predators, eating moth eggs and preying on mites and small insects. Others are serious garden pests, with different species attacking almost all kinds of flowers, vegetables, fruits, and ornamentals. Some of these also transmit viral and bacterial diseases while feeding.

Both adult and young onion thrips feed on vegetables and flowers. On onion the 1/25-inch-long thrips works under the close-fitting leaves and down into the onion leaf sheaths. You will see white or gray leaf spotting that eventually extends over entire leaves. Infested plants appear unhealthy and gray. This symptom is called silver top. Leaf tips also wither as leaf

color changes. Undersized and distorted onion bulbs result from the damage.

On cabbage, onion thrips do double damage. Not only do bronze patches develop on head leaves, but the insects' black excrement dots the frame leaves. The foliage of pea, cucumber, and melon plants becomes crinkled, curled, and dwarfed. Rose and carnation petals develop spots and streaks.

Flower thrips prevent flowers from opening properly. They attack the blossoms of almost every garden plant. On roses, they prefer white and yellow varieties. Infested rosebuds turn brown, forming a ball with petals stuck together, or they may partly open into distorted blossoms with brown-edged petals. Most rose damage occurs in early summer. You can see the tiny, fast-moving thrips near the petal bases inside damaged flowers.

Citrus thrips cause the tips of new leaves to turn black and die. Other leaves wither and curl. Blossoms drop before fruits set. Thrips feeding near the stems of very young fruits cause ringlike scars. You may also see smooth, brownish, sunken streaks and blotches.

On citrus, all thrips damage occurs between petal fall and the time fruits reach about 1 inch in diameter, but damage becomes more evident as surviving fruits grow. Damaged fruits are edible, despite the scarring. Thrips activity increases as the temperature becomes warmer.

The Pest
Thrips resemble black, brown, or yellow specks darting about your plants. These tiny insects measure between 1/50 and 1/8 inch long. Their habits vary according to the species. Some fly quite actively and can remain airborne for hours. Others are wingless and crawl

about. In some species the males and females mate; others reproduce without mating.

The females of some species of thrips have sawlike egg-laying organs, which the insects use to cut slits in stems to hold their eggs. Females in other species cannot make stem slits, so they deposit their eggs in tree crevices or under bark. Emerging young nymphs resemble adults, but none have wings. When changing to adults, most, but not all, thrips young go through a cocoon stage. There are usually several generations per year.

In northern states, onion thrips may overwinter in garden litter or in onion sets waiting to be planted. In southern states, onion thrips feed all year. Most onion thrips are female. These yellow adults lay tiny, bean-shaped eggs, from which pale

Thrips damage is usually more visible than the actual insect. Here, a banded greenhouse thrips has been enlarged so that you can see it.

yellow nymphs emerge in 7 to 10 days. They reach egg-laying size within three weeks and many generations occur each year.

Citrus thrips overwinter in egg form. However, if the temperature warms up in midwinter, some young may emerge. Otherwise, they wait until March to hatch. The young reach adulthood within two weeks. Each adult female deposits between 200 and 250 eggs in new leaf tissue. Some eggs may also be laid in green stems, twigs, buds, and fruit. During the warmest months, eggs hatch within a

week. The young are initially colorless with bright red eyes, but become yellow-green as they feed on citrus tissue. There can be 12 generations per year in warmer states.

Flower thrips look like slivers of straw. They spend part of their lives on tree and grass flowers, so even if you eliminate one horde from your flower bed, new ones continually arrive from other plants. It takes two weeks from hatching to egg laying.

Control Measures
Although it is difficult to eliminate the rapidly multiplying, actively mobile, and often well-protected thrips, you can reduce damage considerably with insecticides. If you are in doubt as to when controls should start, inspect plants carefully twice a week, beginning in late spring, for signs of damage.

To prevent fruit scarring, you must spray trees when flower petals fall and fruits begin forming. A second spray during the summer might be necessary to protect new foliage.

On vegetable plants and fruit trees, use carbaryl (Ortho Sevin® Garden Spray), malathion (Ortho Malathion 50 Insect Control), or diazinon (Ortho Fruit & Vegetable Insect Control) at 7- to 10-day intervals over a two- to three-week period. On nonfood plants, spray with acephate (Orthene® Systemic Insect Control, Ortho Isotox® Insect Killer). Be certain that your plant is listed on the product label. Repeat the sprays if reinfestation occurs.

Pick off and destroy old infested leaves and flowers, and eliminate weeds to keep thrips populations down. Keeping plants well watered helps them withstand thrips attack. Try planting early-maturing crops and flowers that develop before thrips become numerous enough to cause severe damage when warm weather arrives.

TREEHOPPERS

Weirdly shaped and occasionally quite brilliantly colored, treehoppers often have strange-looking horns and knobs near their heads. These pests are not as fierce as they look, and they are troublemakers only when abundant.

The nymphs suck sap from grass, corn, bean, and tomato foliage as well as from the leaves of flowers such as aster. The adults injure tree bark.

Female treehoppers use their knifelike egg-laying organs to cut slits in twig bark. Scar tissue later forms in the shape of a double crescent. Infested trees look scaly, rough, or cracked, and they fail to thrive. The tips of injured twigs may die.

Treehoppers are common on fruit trees such as apple, peach, pear, cherry, and quince. They also trouble rose, elm, locust, willow, hickory, redbud viburnum, and grape, among others.

Sometimes canker and other disease-causing fungi gain entrance to trees through treehopper wounds. Canker takes many forms, one of which is oval or irregularly shaped dead patches on trunks, stems, or branches. These can be bumpy or sunken sap-oozing areas 1 inch to 1 foot long.

The Pest
There are many different treehopper species. Both adults and young hop readily, and the adults can also fly.

The buffalo treehopper, one of the most common treehoppers in orchards and on field crops, overwinters in egg form. A pale green, very spiny nymph hatches in late spring. It drops from trees to the ground, feeding on sap of clover, aster, weeds, grass, and other foliage until it matures in mid-July and August.

When mature, the buffalo treehopper moves to twigs on elm and apple trees, among others. The triangular, 1/4-inch-long adult is bright green

Treehoppers injure tree branches by laying eggs in them, but unless you have a serious outbreak, the damage is likely to be minimal.

above and yellowish below, with two hornlike projections at each side. These resemble buffalo horns, accounting for the pest's common name. In August, the female starts slitting twig bark, depositing eggs in the resulting wounds. Egg laying continues through October; only one generation occurs each year.

If you have locust trees, hoptrees, or butternut trees on your property, you may see the froth that covers the egg clusters of the twospotted treehopper on branch tips. Look around a bit more and you will see what look like tiny black thorns, about 1/4 inch high. These are the adult treehoppers.

The females make slits in bark and lay eggs in August and September, covering them with a white, sticky froth. This froth is particularly evident in winter, after leaves fall, and it remains even after the white powdery-appearing young emerge in May.

Twospotted treehopper nymphs prefer to suck the sap of new leaf growth and generally stay near their hatching site. By late June and July, they become very active adults, flying between host trees and ground plants such as daisies. Adults also suck foliage sap.

Control Measures
If treehoppers become quite numerous, you may want to consider control measures. Otherwise, their sap sucking generally does not cause significant plant damage, and infested trees can tolerate some egg-laying punctures.

The easiest method of handling treehoppers is to use a dormant oil spray (Ortho Volck® Oil Spray) in late fall and winter, when tree leaves have fallen. This gives the smothering spray full access to overwintering eggs.

In spring, you can spray the nymphs with malathion (Ortho Malathion 50 Insect Spray) or carbaryl (Ortho Sevin® Garden Spray).

TUSSOCK MOTHS

Brightly colored tussock moth caterpillars skeletonize the leaves of deciduous fruit and ornamental trees and evergreen trees, beginning at the tops and working downward. Younger caterpillars generally eat all of the leaves except the main veins, while older ones eat the entire leaf. Some species also scar fruit.

Among the trees attacked are apple, apricot, beech, birch, pear, maple, plum, poplar, Douglas fir, fir, larch,

Bright markings and hairy tufts characterize tussock moth larvae, which have periodic population booms.

pine, and spruce. Raspberry and rose plants can also be attacked.

Tussock moth species include western, rusty (antique), pale, whitemarked, brown-tailed, Douglas-fir, and pine tussock moths and gypsy moths. (See page 60 for details about gypsy moths.) In some years the pests appear in large numbers; other years they are almost nonexistent. Populations seem to fluctuate on 7- to 10-year cycles.

The Pest
Although caterpillar colors vary and some species have one generation per year and others have two, the habits of these insects do not differ markedly from one species to the next. Adult male moths have feathery antennae, which helps distinguish tussock moths from related moths.

Black, white, and orange hairs cover rusty tussock moth caterpillars. Four white brushes decorate their backs, and five tufts of bluish black hairs project from their sides. Mature caterpillars are 1 1/8 inches long.

The female white-marked tussock moth caterpillar has a red head, a pale brown body with yellow and black stripes, long black plumes at the front and tail ends, and four thick white tufts on its back. Some say it looks like a toothbrush.

Control Measures
BT sprays, which contain pathogenic bacteria, work on young caterpillars. On non-food plants, choose acephate (Orthene® Systemic Insect Control). Apply when you first notice caterpillar damage or caterpillars in May or early June. Repeat the spray two weeks later, following label directions. Some carbaryl insecticides can be used on fruit trees infested with tussock moths.

WEEVILS, ROOT

When you see ¼-inch-long square-cornered or crescent-shaped notches marring leaf edges, look closer and you will often find adult weevils with their sharp biting jaws hiding someplace nearby; most weevils feed at night. Later in the season, these same plants may be wilting

Root weevil larvae feed on roots, while adults chew jagged bites from the margins of leaves, as on this lilac.

and dying. If you pull them up or uncover the roots, you may find that all of the tiny white feeder roots have been eaten away. The culprit: weevil larvae.

With more than 2,500 species of root weevil in North America, you may find a variety feeding on many of your garden plants. Some long-snouted weevils feeding on fruit and nut plants are called curculios. Included in this group are the apple curculio, black walnut curculio, and plum curculio. (See page 51 for details on these destructive fruit pests.)

The strawberry root weevil feeds on strawberry, hemlock, Japanese yew, arborvitae, raspberry, and many other plants. On strawberries, you will see small fruits surrounded by darkened, bunched-together leaves. Roots and crowns can be partly or completely eaten.

Black vine weevils, also known as taxus weevils, feed on the leaves and roots of over 90 different plants, including yew, rhododendron, hemlock, and azalea. Newly

transplanted yews are particularly vulnerable to damage. Although the leaf notches look unsightly, they are not overly damaging; it is the root feeding that can fatally injure trees and shrubs.

These are the only weevils that feed on yew, so the notches are diagnostic. Look for them first at the center of the plant, near main stems.

On rhododendron, laurel, and azalea, black vine weevils cut large, crescent-shaped holes in the leaf margins. During the day they hide in garden litter or the stems of very dense-foliaged plants. The larvae eat the fragile roots of these shallow-rooted plants, causing foliage to yellow and wilt. Plants can become stunted. Branches attached to affected roots die first, and eventually the entire plant may die.

Pepper weevils feed inside peppers, causing the buds and most of the pods to drop off. Vegetable weevils attack carrot, spinach, and tomato, among other plants. They feed first at the crown and then defoliate whole plants, leaving only the stem and midribs. These weevils also attack dichondra.

The Pest

Although appearance, habits, and life cycles vary with each species of weevil, some have marked similarities. Root weevils are wingless, hard-shelled insects with black or brown bodies; they vary in size from ⅕ to ⅓ inch long. Rows of depressions dot their backs. Black vine weevils usually have a few yellow or orange blotches on their backs. Their heads have sharp cutting mouthparts, and many have long, sometimes curved, beaks. When disturbed, weevils fall to the ground, pretending to be dead.

Root weevils usually overwinter in soil as larvae, feeding heavily on plant roots in spring. They are small, C-shaped, legless grubs with white bodies and brown

Fuller rose beetles feed on leaves at night. These short-snouted beetles chew on a wide array of ornamentals and fruit trees in addition to roses.

heads. In late spring they pupate, and adult weevils emerge in May and June. Females begin depositing eggs when four to six weeks old, laying up to 500 eggs on soil, leaves, or plant crowns. Emerging larvae burrow 1 to 15 inches down into the soil and feed lightly for the rest of the summer. There is usually only one generation per year.

Control Measures

Root weevil larvae are extremely difficult to control with pesticides. They are protected by soil and sometimes feed quite far below the surface. You may have some success controlling root-feeding larvae on ornamental plants by applying acephate (Orthene® Systemic Insect Control) soon after eggs hatch, when the larvae are very young. Treatments should begin in mid-July and continue through the fall.

Insecticides used to eliminate the adult weevils before they lay eggs work best. Correct timing is the key to success. Inspect your garden every week, beginning in June, for leaf notching. If you see notching, or if plants wilt without explanation, go out at night with a flashlight and look for weevils at work. Many weevil species feed until late fall, and their presence usually indicates larvae on the roots below.

It helps to know which kind of weevil is causing the problem, because not all insecticides control all species. To get a precise identification, bring a weevil sample to your county agricultural extension service. Spread sheets of paper beneath the plant in the evening. Come back after dark, and strike the branches firmly. Then shine your flashlight onto the paper. Any weevils should have fallen off onto the paper, where you might be able to catch them as they play dead.

As soon as you see leaf notches, apply insecticide to the foliage and the ground beneath. Weevils feed for about two weeks before they mate and lay eggs. If you control adults, you will prevent them from laying eggs, thus keeping the root-feeding larvae from appearing. Repeat the spray, according to label directions, until no new leaf notches appear.

Spray nonfood plants with an acephate insecticide (Orthene® Systemic Insect Control, Ortho Isotox® Insect Killer). For root weevils on food plants, use carbaryl (Ortho Sevin® Garden Spray, Ortho Sevin® Garden Dust) or malathion (Ortho Malathion 50 Insect Spray). On vegetables, you can also use rotenone (Ortho Rotenone Dust or Spray). On tree fruits and strawberries, you can use a multipurpose spray containing a captan-malathion-methoxychlor compound (Ortho Home Orchard Spray). Repeat applications at three-week intervals.

In addition to sprays, removing leaf litter, overgrown hedges, weeds, and other overwintering spots reduces weevil populations. It sometimes helps to destroy fallen fruit and infested strawberry plants. Do not compost weevil-damaged plants.

WHITEFLIES

Whether you are pruning fuchsias or picking tomatoes, if you stir up puffs of white insects when you disturb the foliage, then you've got whiteflies in the garden. Just a few of these pests do no major harm, but they reproduce rapidly, and soon numerous white specks cover leaf undersides. Heavy infestations threaten plant health.

The whitefly lives on leaf undersides and usually stays there, inconspicuously sucking sap, unless disturbed. Several species live outdoors infesting plants all year in the South and during the summer in the North.

Besides fuchsias and tomatoes, whiteflies feed on bean, poinsettia, melon, squash, sweet potato, begonia, blackberry, lantana, hibiscus, pepper, gardenia, cineraria, geranium, and grape, among others. Citrus whiteflies do major harm to citrus trees.

Whitefly infestations reach a peak in midsummer and fall, but on favored plants these insects can become a problem beginning in spring. Leaf yellowing or mottling should alert you to a possible infestation.

Both nymphs and adults insert their strawlike beaks into the undersides of leaves, feeding on sap. The nymphs are more injurious than the adults. Leaves may dry, shrivel, and eventually drop, and fruit may be undersized. Because neither nymphs nor adults fully digest sap, the pests excrete sticky honeydew. Sooty mold fungus lives on honeydew.

The Pest

Whiteflies begin life as $1/100$-inch-long, pale yellow to gray, oval eggs attached by short stalks to leaf undersides. About 20 eggs form a circular grouping on a leaf. Four to ten days after the eggs are laid, flat, pale green nymphs, called crawlers, emerge. They may crawl around for several hours or up to two days. Once they have chosen a settling spot and begun sucking sap, they do not move. With first molt, the crawlers lose their legs and antennae and begin developing a waxy covering. This gives immature

While tiny whitefly adults flutter about, their scalelike maturing nymphs feed on leaf undersides, seriously damaging plants.

whiteflies a scalelike appearance. They continue sucking plant juices until they pupate.

The adults emerge in about a week and measure about $1/16$ inch long at maturity. When seen under a magnifying glass, adult whiteflies somewhat resemble white moths. They soon mate, and females begin depositing eggs. Each female deposits approximately 300 eggs during its 30-day life span. An entire life cycle from egg to egg may be completed in about a month, particularly in warm weather. Because there can be multiple overlapping generations within a season, eggs, nymphs, pupae, and adults are usually present.

Control Measures

Insecticides easily eliminate whitefly adults and nymphs still in the crawling phase. Eggs, feeding nymphs, and pupae defy insecticides, however, so one spraying will not give you adequate control. You must spray four times at four- to six-day intervals to control nymphs as they hatch. Because whiteflies multiply most rapidly during warm, humid weather, pay particular attention to your spray schedule during the summer. Be sure to spray leaf undersides, where whiteflies congregate.

On vegetables, spray with diazinon (Ortho Fruit & Vegetable Insect Control, Ortho Diazinon Insect Spray), malathion (Ortho Malathion 50 Insect Spray), or a pyrethrins–piperonyl butoxide com-

pound (Ortho Tomato & Vegetable Insect Killer). On fruit trees, spray with an ethion–petroleum oil compound (Ortho Citrus Insect Spray) or malathion (Ortho Malathion 50 Insect Spray). On ornamentals, use acephate (Ortho Isotox® Insect Killer, Orthene® Systemic Insect Control), or an acephate-resmethrin-triforine compound (Ortho Systemic Rose & Flower Spray).

Newly available sticky traps (Ortho Whitefly Sticky Traps) can effectively control whiteflies (see page 29).

Cultural controls include winter pruning and the elimination of vegetation attacked by whiteflies the previous year. If this is not feasible, remove older infested leaves to slow whitefly buildup. Eliminating or closely mowing whitefly-infested weeds also helps control them.

WIREWORMS

Wireworms, the larvae of click beetles, attack almost every garden crop, working underground and devouring seeds, roots, stems, and tubers. Adult beetles feed on flowers and foliage but do no significant damage.

Wireworms chew their way through carrots, corn, potatoes, beets, peas, beans, lettuce, onions, lawn grass, asters, gladioli, and dahlias, among other plants. Their underground feeding kills seedlings and stunts larger

No crop is immune to wireworms, which damage roots and tubers. They are larvae of the click beetle.

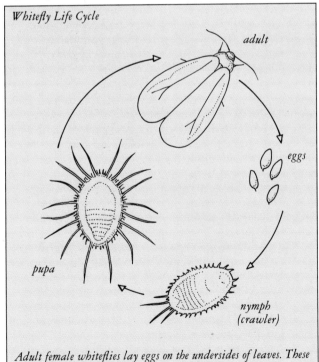

Whitefly Life Cycle

adult

eggs

pupa

nymph
(crawler)

Adult female whiteflies lay eggs on the undersides of leaves. These hatch into nymphs, which crawl briefly and then settle down, scalelike, to suck plant juices. After a short pupal stage, adults emerge to feed and mate. Several generations occur each season.

plants. Infestations are most common in vegetable plots that were once lawn.

These pests make winding tunnels through the roots of potatoes, carrots, and beets—not a particularly appetizing sight, especially if the worm is still there when you are preparing a meal.

The Pest

Many species of wireworm infest gardens in North America. The larvae vary from 1/3 inch to 1 1/2 inches long. They are worm shaped with shiny, shell-like, yellow, gray, or reddish brown skin. Otherwise, they resemble earthworms.

Adult click beetles are about 1/2 inch long and can be brown, gray, or black. When these tapered beetles are turned over on their backs, they make an audible clicking sound as they try to right themselves. After overwintering in the soil, adults emerge in April and May. The females deposit eggs 1 to 6 inches deep in damp soil, preferring grassy or weedy areas. After hatching, the young disperse through the soil. Some larvae pupate and reach full growth in a year; others may not mature for as long as six years. Because generations overlap, wireworms of all sizes and ages exist at the same time.

Control Measures

Use diazinon, (Ortho Diazinon Soil & Turf Insect Control, Ortho Vegetable Guard Soil Insect Killer, Ortho Diazinon Soil & Foliage Dust) for thorough control of wireworms. It is best to treat the soil one week before planting to prevent damage to seeds and seedlings. Work the insecticide into the top 6 to 8 inches of soil.

Click beetles lay eggs in damp soil, and emerging larvae thrive in wet soil, so providing proper soil drainage helps control wireworm populations. Deep cultivation from midsummer until the ground freezes, will destroy many larvae and pupae.

WOOLLYBEAR CATERPILLARS

In folklore, the narrower the reddish brown band around the middle of the banded woollybear caterpillar's body, the colder the winter will be. If you disturb this caterpillar, it rolls into a tight ball, accounting for its alternate name, hedgehog caterpillar.

Although the banded woollybear feeds primarily on weeds, finding its cousins the yellow woollybear and saltmarsh caterpillars in your garden foretells a lot of garden damage. Both feed on vegetables, flowers, and fruits, occasionally marching in groups from one feeding spot to another.

These extremely hairy and particularly hungry caterpillars chew on the leaves of canna,

Banded woollybears, the larvae of tiger moths, usually feed on weeds, but may damage a variety of garden plants.

carrot, morning glory, lettuce, dahlia, sweet potato, rose, melon, cherry, apple, sunflower, violet, grape, fuchsia, asparagus, petunia, and many other vegetables and flowers. Woollybear caterpillars become especially numerous during July and August.

Young caterpillars feed together on leaf undersides. Larger caterpillars feed on all leaf surfaces and on flower and fruit buds. They can defoliate an entire plant and often destroy your whole crop if they are not controlled.

Saltmarsh caterpillars, named after their habit of feeding on salt marsh grass in addition to other foods,

Beware of midsummer outbreaks of saltmarsh caterpillars. These woollybears may move in masses, defoliating a garden as they travel through it.

migrate in hordes like armyworms. They are a particular danger in home gardens located next to cotton fields. Traveling in masses, they almost seem to mow garden foliage down.

The Pest

If you see many very hairy caterpillars crawling rapidly across a garden path in September and October, chances are you have discovered woollybear caterpillars seeking a protected overwintering spot. They overwinter in caterpillar form or in hairy cocoons under boards, tree bark, or ground litter.

Adult moths appear in late spring and early summer. Banded woollybear tiger moths are dull yellow-orange with a few dusky spots on the wings and have black abdominal spots. Yellow woollybear moths are snow-white with a tiny black dot on each forewing. Saltmarsh moths have white wings with black spots and an orange, black-spotted abdomen. All measure between 1 1/2 and 2 inches wide. Male antennae can be distinctively narrow and feathery in some species.

The female moth lays clusters of eggs on host plant leaves. The saltmarsh caterpillar breeds most prolifically of the group; each female is capable of depositing over 1,000 eggs. Five days later caterpillars emerge, initially feeding together in groups. Later they feed singly.

Within four weeks of emergence, the caterpillars can grow to 2 inches long. Banded woollybears are black at both ends with bright, cinnamon-red bands around their middles. Yellow woollybear caterpillars are yellow or straw colored and so densely haired that they look like they're wearing fur coats. Saltmarsh caterpillars, occasionally called woolly worms, are initially gray and then gradually become black with broken yellow lines on their bodies and long, cinnamon red hairs on their sides.

At maturity, woollybear caterpillars seek protected places to pupate. Banded woollybears and saltmarsh woollybears produce one generation per year; yellow woollybears have two generations.

Control Measures

Because numerous woollybear cocoons can hide under the same shelter, keep garden litter removed and all lumber off the ground. You can pick up and destroy individual cocoons in the fall. Trichogramma wasps prey on some species.

Although some gardeners don't mind a few woollybears crawling about, if you see more than a few, and hand-picking does not keep numbers down, insecticide control may be necessary. BT sprays, which contain pathogenic bacteria, control young caterpillars most effectively. Or use carbaryl as directed on the product container.

INDEX

Note: Page numbers in boldface type refer to detailed descriptions and control measures; page numbers in italic type refer to photographs and illustrations.

U.S. Measure and Metric Measure Conversion Chart

	Symbol	When you know:	Multiply by:	To find:	Rounded Measures for Quick Reference		
Mass (Weight)	oz	ounces	28.35	grams	1 oz		= 30 g
	lb	pounds	0.45	kilograms	4 oz		= 115 g
	g	grams	0.035	ounces	8 oz		= 225 g
	kg	kilograms	2.2	pounds	16 oz	= 1 lb	= 450 kg
					32 oz	= 2 lb	= 900 kg
					36 oz	= 2¼ lb	= 1000g (1 kg)
Volume	tsp	teaspoons	5.0	milliliters	¼ tsp	= 1/24 oz	= 1 ml
	tbsp	tablespoons	15.0	milliliters	½ tsp	= 1/12 oz	= 2 ml
	fl oz	fluid ounces	29.57	milliliters	1 tsp	= 1/6 oz	= 5 ml
	c	cups	0.24	liters	1 tbsp	= ½ oz	= 15 ml
	pt	pints	0.47	liters	1 c	= 8 oz	= 250 ml
	qt	quarts	0.95	liters	2 c (1 pt)	= 16 oz	= 500 ml
	gal	gallons	3.785	liters	4 c (1 qt)	= 32 oz	= 1 liter
	ml	milliliters	0.034	fluid ounces	4 qt (1 gal)	= 128 oz	= 3¾ liter
Length	in.	inches	2.54	centimeters	⅜ in.	= 1 cm	
	ft	feet	30.48	centimeters	1 in.	= 2.5 cm	
	yd	yards	0.9144	meters	2 in.	= 5 cm	
	mi	miles	1.609	kilometers	2½ in.	= 6.5 cm	
	km	kilometers	0.621	miles	12 in. (1 ft)	= 30 cm	
	m	meters	1.094	yards	1 yd	= 90 cm	
	cm	centimeters	0.39	inches	100 ft	= 30 m	
					1 mi	= 1.6 km	
Temperature	°F	Fahrenheit	5/9 (after subtracting 32)	Celsius	32°F	= 0°C	
					68°F	= 20°C	
	°C	Celsius	9/5 (then add 32)	Fahrenheit	212°F	= 100°C	
Area	$in.^2$	square inches	6.452	square centimeters	1 $in.^2$	= 6.5 cm^2	
	ft^2	square feet	929.0	square centimeters	1 ft^2	= 930 cm^2	
	yd^2	square yards	8361.0	square centimeters	1 yd^2	= 8360 cm^2	
	a.	acres	0.4047	hectares	1 a.	= 4050 m^2	

Proof-of-Purchase
0-89721-097-2